VIKING

IN PURSUIT OF PEACE

Peshawar-born Satinder Kumar Lambah served the Government of India for over five decades, including two tenures in Pakistan as Deputy Chief of Mission and High Commissioner; Ambassador to Hungary, Germany and Russia; Chairman of National Security Advisory Board; Special Representative for Afghanistan under Prime Minister Atal Bihari Vajpayee and later as Special Envoy for back-channel talks with Pakistan during Prime Minister Manmohan Singh's tenure for a decade. After leaving the government, he continued to lead Track II dialogues with several key countries and was Chairman of Ananta Aspen Centre for two terms.

Celebrating 35 Years of
Penguin Random House India

ADVANCE PRAISE FOR THE BOOK

'The book provides a ringside view of a seasoned diplomat who, in his long career, spent many years dealing with Pakistan and its inexplicable perfidy. It provides a new perspective to many known and some not so well known events and circumstances that shaped vexed Indo–Pak relations. His authentic and objective narration will substantially contribute to serious historical study of bilateral relations between the two countries and also provide a rare insight for common readers. Brilliantly articulated, the book contains gripping accounts of his personal interactions with many people who shaped bilateral relations in both countries. The book also holds many lessons for the future diplomats and policy makers who will have to deal with a difficult neighbour for a long time and will have a bearing on our national security'

—Ajit Doval,
National Security Advisor of India

'A book of deep insights, drawing on Ambassador Lambah's unparalleled experience and knowledge of Pakistan, of its troubled relationship with India, and of Afghanistan. Indispensable for all those interested in the subcontinent and Asia, it is a valuable and reliable guide through the thickets of India–Pakistan relations. Ambassador Lambah was one of the select few who both understood and shaped critical relationships for India. His masterly account intersperses personal reminiscences of participating in epochal events in the pursuit of peace between India and Pakistan and in Afghanistan with comprehensive and acute analysis. He has also laid down markers for the future in his back-channel negotiations on Kashmir that later generations will be grateful for. His objectivity and humanity illuminate this treasure trove of a book. A must-read'

—Shivshankar Menon,
former National Security Advisor of India

'A brilliant epiphany combining hope and mature realism with pathbreaking insights drawn from the author's lifetime of experience, on how only unremitting diplomacy, guided by bold, visionary political leadership, can ensure a reimagining of the landscape of India–Pakistan relations'

—Nirupama Rao,
former Foreign Secretary of India

'S. K. Lambah unveils a unique perspective on the India–Pakistan diplomatic interface with his reminiscences. This brilliantly evocative memoir illustrates the enormous potential of innovative diplomacy to bridge dangerous fault lines'

—T.C.A. Raghavan,
former Indian High Commissioner to Pakistan

'Ambassador Sati Lambah has written a fascinating book, unprecedented and without a parallel, put together in the last several months of his life of high quality public service. He provides amazing insights, as one who was deeply involved, on the exchanges between India and Pakistan under the radar, in which he played a major role. This book is a great legacy of a diplomat of high standing'

—Tarun Das,
former Director General and chief
mentor of Confederation of Indian Industry

IN PURSUIT OF PEACE

INDIA–PAKISTAN RELATIONS UNDER SIX PRIME MINISTERS

SATINDER KUMAR LAMBAH

PENGUIN
VIKING
An imprint of Penguin Random House

VIKING

USA | Canada | UK | Ireland | Australia
New Zealand | India | South Africa | China

Viking is part of the Penguin Random House group of companies
whose addresses can be found at global.penguinrandomhouse.com

Published by Penguin Random House India Pvt. Ltd
4th Floor, Capital Tower 1, MG Road,
Gurugram 122 002, Haryana, India

First published in Viking by Penguin Random House India 2023

ISBN 9780143463283

Typeset in Adobe Garamond Pro by Manipal Technologies Limited, Manipal

www.penguin.co.in

Contents

Foreword

This is an important book on an important subject. Shri S.K. Lambah is a distinguished diplomat with a deep understanding of Asian geopolitics, especially India–Pakistan relations. He comes from Peshawar, as do I, and his family had very close links with the Northwest Frontier Province. This personal connection is reflected in his discussion of that region and in his commitment to peace and reconciliation between India and Pakistan.

Over the years, Shri Lambah acquired a wealth of experience in interacting closely with Pakistan. His personal account of how six Indian Prime Ministers dealt with Pakistan during the period 1980 to 2014 illuminates the complexities of the India–Pakistan relationship and the choices made at critical points.

The book reflects on the lessons of history and on the way forward for a resolution of the issues between the two neighbouring countries, which is essential for the creation of a climate of enduring peace and cooperation within South Asia.

I believe that this book will provide valuable insights to all those interested in understanding the past and the future of the relations between India and Pakistan.

Manmohan Singh

1

Pakistan: Evolution of a Military State

Pakistan Self-Destructs

Scepticism at the Creation of Pakistan

The partition of the Indian subcontinent in 1947 on religious lines led to the creation of the Hindu-dominated India and Muslim-dominated Pakistan. In the process, two wings of Pakistan, one on the western side and the other in the east, flanked India, separated by a distance of 2000 kilometres. West Pakistan's population consisted of Pathans, Baluchis, Sindhis and the predominant Punjabis; while that of East Pakistan consisted of Bengalis, which numerically outnumbered the west, and were also racially and ethnically different. Thus, the problem manifested itself from day one of its creation, which ultimately led to the war of liberation in 1971.

There was scepticism as early as April 1946 on the concept of Pakistan, even before it was created, in regard to the survival of the two wings as a nation. The British Cabinet Mission was holding its proceedings in Delhi and Simla when Maulana Abul

Kalam Azad, the then president of the Congress, in an interview to Shorish Kashmiri for a Lahore-based Urdu magazine, *Chattan* said: (published in Kashmiri's book) 'It will not be possible for East Pakistan to stay with West Pakistan for any considerable period of time. There is nothing common between the two regions except that they call themselves Muslims. But the fact of being Muslim has never created durable political unity anywhere in the world.'[1]

He added, 'After the separation, West Pakistan will become the battleground of regional contradictions and disputes. The assertion of sub-national identities of Punjab, Sindh, Frontier and Balochistan will open doors for outside interference.'[2]

Lord Mountbatten, the last British viceroy of India, who played an instrumental role in the creation of Pakistan, echoed similar sentiments regarding the birth of Pakistan, 'Administratively it was the difference between putting up a permanent building, a Nissen hut or a tent. As far as Pakistan is concerned, we are putting up a tent. We can do no more.'[3] Commenting on this statement, Ayesha Jalal, a Pakistani American historian and author, in her well-researched book writes, 'Instead of being replaced by a permanent building the proverbial tent has been metaphorically transformed into a sprawling military barrack.'[4]

It took only two years for President Field Marshal Ayub Khan's prophetic words of 26 March 1969 to come true, 'I doubt if in our political life we will have a good man for a long time. Thank God we have an army. If nothing else I have held this country together for ten years. It was like keeping a number of frogs in one basket. What sort of Pakistan will emerge is anybody's guess. There will be either force or mob rule. I hope we can find some answer between the two. There is no future in two Pakistans. The East (Pakistan) will last for a few years and the West will drag on.'[5]

In short, Maulana Azad in April 1946, Lord Mountbatten in 1947 and subsequently Field Marshal Ayub Khan in March

1969—all arrived at a similar assessment regarding the inevitable breakup of the two wings of Pakistan.

Rejection of Verdict of First General Election of 1970

Pakistanis believe India was responsible for the dissolution of their country in 1971, but in reality, the problem lay within their own country. Some basic facts and circumstances are ignored. As the population of Pakistan's eastern province outnumbered those of the four western provinces, to counterbalance its effect, direct elections at the national level were put off for twenty-three years on some pretext or another. Instead, several novel measures were conceived and introduced. One such being the controversial One Unit Scheme of 1955, under which the four western provinces formed a single political entity called West Pakistan, with the intent of offsetting the eastern province's (renamed East Pakistan) numerical advantage. The scheme was a disaster from the start—it angered the three western provincial groups, the Pathans, Balochis and Sindhis, who experienced at firsthand the dominance of the Punjabis. Additionally, a signal was sent to the Bengalis that political power was not theirs. Eventually, the scheme was dismantled in 1970, prior to the announcement of the national assembly elections. The asymmetric population distribution within Pakistan had two effects. First, it became a major cause to deny the establishment of democratic roots in Pakistan. Second, as a direct consequence of denial of democracy, conditions were simultaneously created for the induction of the army as a partner in the governance of Pakistan. Later, Ziaul Haq redefined the raison d'être for the partnership's continued sustenance.

With the result of the very first general election to Pakistan's National Assembly in December 1970 that employed the principle of *one man one vote*, one of the tenets of democracy, Pakistan opted to press the self-destruct button. Pakistan had adopted this principle in its early constitutions but could not uphold it. East Pakistan, with a population of 65 million against the 58 million of West Pakistan, clearly held the majority. In the 313-member assembly, 300 members were directly elected through a process of universal adult franchise with the remaining thirteen being women members, who were elected indirectly. Whereas the Bengali-speaking eastern wing leader Sheikh Mujibur Rahman's Awami League garnered 39.2 per cent of the total votes polled with 160 seats (plus seven women seats) thereby obtaining a clear majority, Zulfikar Ali Bhutto's Pakistan People's Party (PPP) in the western wing could get, in comparison, only 18.6 per cent of the total votes with eighty-one seats (plus five women seats).

The verdict of the election was ignored by the then president, General Agha Muhammad Yahya Khan, who neither summoned the assembly, nor invited the leader of the majority party to form the government. He probably realized that a Bengali leadership would not be acceptable to West Pakistan.

Some political leaders, including Sirdar Shaukat Hyat Khan, from West Pakistan arrived in Dacca just prior to 25 March 1971 to arrange a last-minute meeting between Mujibur Rahman and President Yahya Khan, who was already there a few days earlier. They met Yahya at midnight on 23 March. 'The President was sitting wearing his slippers, a vest and a towel as a scarf, holding a drink.'[6] Little did they realize then that Yahya was being farcical and was not interested in meeting Mujib because he had already made up his mind, as became evident from the account of his meeting with General Tikka Khan on 18 March, 'the bastard (Mujib) is not behaving. You get ready.'[7] Gen. Tikka Khan was the military commander of East Pakistan, who after the onslaught on East Pakistan came to be known as the 'Butcher of Bengal'.[8]

Pakistan Armed Forces Deployed against Its Eastern Wing

The imperatives of the Cold War might have perhaps lulled the Pakistani establishment into believing that the international community would not question its actions, a belief possibly reinforced by the fact that Pakistan was at that time, in July 1971, playing a pivotal role in arranging the secret visit of Nixon's National Security Adviser Henry Kissinger to Beijing. As it turned out, the resentment in the eastern wing had been grossly underestimated and the ability of the armed forces to contain it, highly overestimated.

Although the verdict of the people was clear, it was muzzled through sheer brute force, by West Pakistan launching an attack on East Pakistan, which necessarily compounded matters. Shaukat Hyat recounts further in his book, *The Nation that Lost Its Soul,* 'Pakistani was pitched against Pakistani in a dance to death. Both sides were equally brutal but the Army, armed with modern weapons, egged on by their superiors and fed on horror stories, naturally had an edge. About half a million had to flee for their lives to India.'[9] In his foreword to the book, Pakistani Professor Akbar Ahmed writes, 'We have one of the most penetrating accounts of the dramatic days in early 1971 when the fate of Pakistan was being decided. The bungling, the intrigue, the indecisiveness of the Pakistani leadership is clearly brought out. The situation changes from moment to moment and it spins out of control leading to the division of Pakistan and the creation of Bangladesh'[10]

Revelations by West Pakistani senior army officers occupying key posts at the army General Headquarters (GHQ) in Rawalpindi and the Eastern Command in Dacca at that time, provide corroborative evidence of the role of West Pakistan and its army in the debacle. Siddiq Salik, Public Relations Officer (PRO) of the West Pakistan Army during the 1971 war, with daily access to Lieutenant General Niazi, commander of the Pakistan forces in Dacca, who was present at the surrender of East Pakistan and subsequently accompanied Niazi as a prisoner of war in an Indian Air Force plane to Calcutta, observed on arrival in Dacca in 1970 that 'the poor of Bengal are poorer than the poorest of West Pakistan. I started finding a meaning in the allegations of economic exploitation of East Pakistan. I felt guilty.'[11] He referred to the accusation that 'West Pakistan was developed with the money earned by East Pakistan.'[12] He cites instances of fake operations conducted by the Pakistan Army. Salik had met an officer who had conducted an attack on the civilian population. The same evening, the officer confided, 'There were no rebels, and no weapons, only poor country folk, mostly women and old men got roasted in the barrage of fire. It is a pity that the operation was launched without proper intelligence. I will carry the burden on my conscience for the rest of my life.'[13] Salik devotes an entire chapter to the mockery of martial law and gives a firsthand account of Pakistani generals sobbing and crying rather than fighting.

The horrific massacre of innocent people in East Pakistan led 10 million refugees to flee to India. Appeals to world leaders to curtail West Pakistan had no effect. The presence of the overwhelming number of refugees, the Pakistan army shelling India's border areas and their air force violating its airspace, resulted in a heavy economic, social, political and administrative burden for India. On 3 December 1971, Pakistan launched a full-scale war on India attacking airfields in Amritsar, Pathankot. Srinagar, Avantipur, Uttarlai, Ambala, Agra and Jodhpur. This left India with no choice but to declare war the same day.

On 16 December 1971, Indira Gandhi announced in Parliament that West Pakistan forces had unconditionally surrendered. The instrument of surrender was signed in Dacca by Lt Gen. A.A.K. Niazi on behalf of the Eastern Command of Pakistan army. Lt Gen Jagjit Singh Arora, General Officer Commander-in-Chief (GOC-in-C) of the Indian side, accepted the surrender.

Contemporary Views on Pakistan's Role in East Pakistan from Command HQ in Dacca

The memoirs of Lt Gen. Gul Hassan Khan, commander in chief (C. in C.) of the Pakistan Army after the 1971 war, record scathing observations in respect of the happenings in the army GHQ in Rawalpindi. He had been chief of general staff during 1971, which 'ranks as the most important amongst his other colleagues in GHQ'.[14] He noted, 'the impotence of GHQ was felt by our formations'.[15] 'I do not think GHQ had ever been so ineffective as it was in the months prior to the outbreak of the war with India in 1971. Events buffeted us mercilessly owing to absence of direction and a sense of cohesion in the nerve centre of the army.' His self-explanatory description of Pakistan after the 1971 war reads, 'Pakistan, which, in next to no time, became a playground for enduring gangsters, inveterate opportunists, and chronic free booters. And of these species there appeared to be no dearth in our country.'[16]

In the foreword to Shaukat Hyat's book, Professor Akbar Ahmed wrote, 'India's shrewd handling of the Bangladesh crisis and Pakistan's inept handling of it are underlined. Pakistan's tragic failure to understand and manipulate the world media is once again highlighted.'[17] Siddiq Salik quotes Lt Gen. Niazi, who after the surrender blamed the GHQ in Rawalpindi, 'Don't they know whether three Infantry Divisions are enough to defend East Pakistan against the internal as well as external dangers . . . Rawalpindi is to blame. They promised me eight

Infantry Divisions in mid-November, but sent me only five. The remaining three had yet to arrive when the West Pakistan front was open—without any prior notice to me.'[18] Niazi defended the decision to surrender, 'I will take 90,000 prisoners of war to West Pakistan rather than face 90,000 widows and half a million orphans there. The sacrifice was not worth it.'[19]

The Role of the Pakistan Army

A Combination of Non-Democratic Principles and Power Play Creates Space for the Army in Governance

The first step towards army control in Pakistan was taken in 1954 when, with the help of General Ayub Khan, Iskander Mirza became President after forcing Ghulam Muhammed to resign. While holding the position of C. in C. of the Pakistan Army, Gen. Ayub Khan was concurrently appointed defence minister. The dual arrangement not only helped the military to gain financial autonomy but also to usurp power in the first army coup in Pakistan, in 1958. A few days earlier, Gen. Ayub Khan had been proclaimed martial law administrator, a position that would continue to be held by Gen. Yahya Khan up to the time of the creation of Bangladesh. Gen. Yahya Khan too strengthened army control. Both Generals' Ziaul Haq and Pervez Musharraf carried out subsequent coups. Although democracy was restored after Ziaul Haq's death, restrictions were imposed on Benazir Bhutto. She was coerced into accepting Sahibzada Yaqub Ali Khan as foreign minister. This trend continued. Two decades later, when her husband Asif Ali Zardari was President and Yousaf Raza Gilani Prime Minister, they faced similar coercion. Even after President Pervez Musharraf's resignation, the army continued to have a decisive say during civilian rule in major security and political developments.

Historical developments too have helped the army maintain its stranglehold on Pakistan, preventing democracy from taking root. Consequently, the army has emerged as the single most important and influential group with the power of last resort, capable of doing no wrong. Between 1947–58, there were seven prime ministers, during which period army rule came to be formally imposed. Between Ziaul Haq's death in 1988 and Pervez Musharraf's army coup in 1999, no civilian prime minister was able to complete a term. During that decade, there were four caretaker army-dominated governments. There was liberal use of Article 58 2(b) when then President Ghulam Ishaq Khan dismissed Benazir Bhutto on 6 August 1990 and Nawaz Sharif in 1993. Later, then President Farooq Ahmed Leghari dismissed Benazir Bhutto in 1996. Earlier, the army had arranged simultaneous dismissals of the civilian President Ghulam Ishaq Khan and Prime Minister Nawaz Sharif. No civilian government has completed its term to date, with the solitary exception of the PPP-led government between 2008 and 2013.

Increase of Stranglehold of Army in Governance from Ziaul Haq Onwards

Coinciding with the ripple effects of changes in Afghanistan and of the Islamic revolution in Iran in early 1979, the army under Ziaul Haq initiated a relentless campaign to project itself as the parent–guardian of Pakistan, which alone was capable of protecting its sovereignty and territorial integrity. Having already been propelled into a position of a frontline state to take on the Soviets in Afghanistan, Ziaul Haq unleashed a pro Sunni orientation of the armed forces. This led to the creation of non-state armed radical and jihadi groups to fight the Soviets. The religious Right was encouraged and nurtured which fractured Pakistan's society, arrested the modernization process and introduced a dangerous variable into a tense relationship with India. The role of the *Tanzeems* (strong conservative force in Pakistan) has been negative, both for Pakistan and Indo-Pak relations. As a part of the Islamization measures, 'one of the first changes made by Zia, after his appointment as Chief of the Army Staff, was to upgrade the Maulvis, improve their status, and require them to go into battle with the troops'.[20] In his foreword to Brigadier S.K. Malik's book *The Quranic Concept of War,* General Zia wrote, 'The professional soldier in a Muslim army, pursuing the goals of a Muslim state, cannot become "professional" if in all his activities he does not take on "the colour of Allah".'[21] Islamic teachings were also introduced in the Pakistan Military Academy and were made a 'part of the curriculum of the Command and Staff College with strong encouragement of Zia ul-Haq'.[22]

Farzana Shaikh, a Pakistani author and expert on Pakistan and South Asian Islam, has noted that the Pakistan Army's engagement with Islamic groups has been a part of their upbringing.[23] She says that it began in 1947 when the army used the religious zeal of the Pathan tribesmen to stage armed incursions into Kashmir. In 1971, the army worked closely with the armed wings of pro-Islamic parties, notably the Jamaat-e-Islami, to secure religious sanctions for its 'brutal campaign against the enemies of Islam, amongst Bengalis in East Pakistan'.[24] During the Afghan civil war, involvement of militant Islamic groups with senior military leadership is well-documented. There has also been Tablighi Jamaat's appeal to army officers, starting from Ziaul Haq's time. One senior Tablighi-led missionary, General Jawed Nassar, became head of Inter Services Intelligence (ISI) in 1993. The Soviet withdrawal from Afghanistan in 1989, promotion of the doctrines of strategic depth in Afghanistan and a thousand cuts in Kashmir have led to a low-cost proxy war on behalf of the army by jihadi and terrorist outfits. In the post-nuclear period, there has been an attempt to exploit the nuclear card.

Business Interests of the Army and its Growing Influence on Economic Matters

With power came influence, which led to the army playing a predominant role in Pakistani polity. Since the army is the only organized, functioning institution in Pakistan, it has been in a position to successfully align the national priorities with its own interests. Over the years, the army has greatly expanded its influence to cover the economy, as brought out by Ayesha Siddiqua, a Pakistani political commentator and author, in her book, *Military Inc: Inside Pakistan's Military Economy*. The author has coined the term 'Milbus' to describe 'military capital used for the personal benefit of the military fraternity, especially the officer cadre, which is not recorded as part of the defence budget or does not follow the normal accountability procedures of the state . . . It is either controlled by the military or under its implicit or explicit patronage.'[25] Milbus activities include: transfer of land from the state to military personnel, perks and privileges for retired armed forces personnel, diversion of business opportunities to armed forces personnel or the military organizations by flouting the norms of a free market economy, money lost on training personnel who seek early retirement, join the private sector and are rehired at higher wages. Milbus is designed to benefit the military fraternity individually and collectively. The corps commanders, their divisions and other units run various cooperatives. Army personnel are beneficiaries of state handouts whenever they run into financial troubles.

The extent of the Pakistani military's economic muscle can be gauged from the fact it owns 11.58 million acres, accounting for

12 per cent of the state land. The military personnel individually benefit from this as each officer of the rank of major general and above is entitled to 240 acres, lieutenants and majors 100 acres, Junior Commissioned Officers (JCOs) 64 acres and Non-Commissioned Officers (NCOs) 32 acres. In addition, the military runs four welfare foundations, namely, the Fauji Foundation, the Army Welfare Trust, the Shaheen Foundation and the Baharia Foundation that, among them, run scores of commercial projects and employ thousands of people. The Fauji Foundation has been accused of clandestine activities. 'It was rumored in 1982, that the foundation was one channel for the clandestine import of equipment used in the Nuclear weapon programme.'[26]

During Zia's tenure, there were reports of encouragement of drug trafficking by the Pakistan military, the purpose being to fund the war in Afghanistan and support the ongoing covert operations in Kashmir and Indian Punjab. The U.S. Drug Enforcement Agency estimated 'the country's earnings from the sale of heroin to be more than the total export earnings'.[27] A Karachi journal, News Line, carried an extensive twenty-two-page report on the extent to which the drug mafia 'had penetrated the government and economic institutions. Drug trafficking fetched US$ 8 billion a year to Pakistan, and its net was widened to include military men, politicians, businessmen and bureaucrats.'[28] The collateral damage of drug trafficking is that the heroin-addict population has risen from close to zero in 1979 to 5000 in 1981 and beyond 3 million in 2000.[29] The role of the Pakistan Army has been well captured by Peter Lyon in the epilogue he has written for Sir Morrice James' book on Pakistan in which he has maintained, 'Pakistan's military seems never to have accepted, or perhaps even understood, that their principle function is to defend the country and to accept the orders of the incumbent government of the day, not to dictate to it or to depose it.'[30]

Army Chiefs

Pakistan is probably among the very few countries where the military reigns supreme, whether directly or indirectly. This makes the chief of the army staff the most significant person in the country. The head of army from 1947–72 had been designated commander in chief. The last incumbent, Lt Gen. Gul Hassan Khan, who held the post for the shortest period of less than three months, was the only one to have served in that post in the rank of Lt Gen. In all, to date, there have been six commanders in chief and ten chiefs of army staff after redesignation of the post in 1972. Of these sixteen, two were British. Of the remaining fourteen, four have been Pushtoons—Gen. Ayub Khan, Gen. Yahya Khan, Gen. Abdul Waheed Kakar and Lt Gen. Gul Hassan Khan. Three had migrated from India in 1947—Gen. Muhammad Ziaul Haq from Jullundur, Gen. Mirza Aslam Beg from Azamgarh and Gen. Pervez Musharraf from Delhi—and settled in Punjab. One was from Balochistan—Gen. Muhammad Musa Khan. After declaring military rule, four became Presidents—Ayub Khan (promoted himself to field marshal), Yahya Khan, Ziaul Haq and Pervez Musharraf. All had long tenures. Those who did not become President but had more than one term were Musa, Ashfaq Pervez Kayani and Qamar Javed Bajwa. Three did not complete their term—Gul Hassan, Jehangir Karamat (forced to retire) and Asif Nawaz Janjua (died in office). I have met all three and found each to be refined and pleasant individuals. No one from Sindh has ever become army chief. Likewise, no one from East Pakistan could aspire to become army chief. Pakistanis attributed this to their lack of martial background. During the same period in India, General Jayanto Nath Choudhary, an illustrious son of Bengal, was army chief between 1962 and 1966, when the Indo-Pak war of 1965 was fought. Interestingly, only two of the fourteen have been Shias—Yahya Khan and Musa Khan, both appointed by Ayub Khan. It is noteworthy that after the Islamization of Zia, all army chiefs have been Sunni Muslims from Punjab. Dominated by the Punjabis, 75 per cent of army recruits had come from the three districts of Punjab—Rawalpindi, Campbellpur and Jhelum. Later, Ayub Khan enlarged the catchment area to include the two districts of North West Frontier Province (NWFP)–Kohat and Mardan. The Military Staff College course on geopolitics instils the thinking that Punjab is Pakistan's 'heartland', and the other provinces are described as mere 'gateways'.[31]

There appear to be no established criteria for the selection of the army chief. The appointment of Ayub Khan as the first Pakistani commander in chief of the army was 'a disappointment to most of his Pakistani colleagues. He was neither the senior most nor was he very popular.'[32] Zulfikar Ali Bhutto appointed his favourite, Tikka Khan, and later Ziaul Haq, who, once again, was not the senior most but had managed to convey the impression of being pliable. When Asif Nawaz Janjua suddenly died in November 1992, he was 'replaced by the least visible of serving co-commanders, Lt General Abdul Waheed (Kakar)'.[33] Nawaz Sharif picked Pervez Musharraf over Ali Kuli Khattak, the senior-most candidate. Both Ziaul Haq and Pervez Musharraf led military coups against those who had appointed them. Absence of established selection criteria and a fixed term (Kayani got a three-year extension over and above his regular three-year term) have become a part of Pakistani Army culture. General Raheel Sharif too, who was appointed on 29 November 2013 as army chief, was not the senior most. Selection to the posts of naval and air chiefs is done in a similar fashion. During Bhutto's final political campaign against the Pakistan National Alliance (PNA), he wanted 'the service chiefs to declare their loyalty to the government by issuing a press release which was done on 27th

April, 1977. This was an unhealthy precedent.'[34] Other than those of the army chief, promotions are by and large made on established principles. However, there have been deviations there too, when Zia, immediately after taking over, made several promotions that were not in accordance with the established procedure. Brig. Latif, in charge of Bhutto's prison cell, 'received his promotion as a Major General without the recommendation of the GHQ . . . Akhtar Abdur Rahman became a four-star general even without commanding a corps. The strangest case is that of General Arif, Zia's shadow and "man Friday, who became a four-star general without commanding a division or a corps".'[35]

I and my wife were fortunate to have direct contacts with the Pakistan army chiefs and their families during my two postings in Pakistan. I found them to be well-informed, incisive and articulate. We recall our visit to the strategically located home of Ayub Khan in Margalla Hills, which has since been converted into a virtual museum by the family, displaying his uniforms, books and other possessions. We knew both his sons and have been their guests in Abbottabad and Peshawar, and of his daughter and son-in-law, Mian Gul Aurangzeb, in Swat. Yahya Khan's son, who is the spitting image of his father, has attended our receptions. A meeting with Gul Hassan in a Rawalpindi hotel where he stayed is etched in my memory. His book is an eyeopener on the role of the Pakistan Army in the 1971 war. I had several meetings with Aslam Beg and established contact with his think tank, FRIENDS, which was far from friendly towards India. At the wedding of his son, he graciously put us on the main table with Nusrat and Benazir Bhutto, with whom by this time he had settled differences. He was a guest at our house and was a man of few words.

The army chief of Pakistan with whom I have spent the maximum amount of time of over a hundred hours, in different capacities including minutes taken, was General Ziaul Haq.

Post retirement, I met Gen. Karamat on several occasions. First, in Stanford where we were invited for discussions on nuclear issues, thereafter in Washington for Track II meetings (non-governmental, informal and unofficial contacts and activities between private citizens or groups of individuals) and later in Delhi and Vienna. I had some serious discussions with him on the back channel on Kashmir too. I had the impression he was initially encouraging but later displayed some hesitancy to talk. When I visited Lahore for a day in May 2014 to congratulate then prime minister designate, Nawaz Sharif, on behalf of Prime Minister Dr Manmohan Singh, I received a message from Gen. Karamat asking me to meet him, which unfortunately I could read only after crossing the border en route to Amritsar. We did not meet since.

Incidentally, my recollection of Gen. Frank Walter Messervy, the British first army chief of Pakistan, emanates from a letter written by the C. in C. Field Marshall Auchinleck to him seeking assistance for my mother and aunt to safely cross the border from Peshawar (which immediately became part of newly created Pakistan following the announcement of the partition of India) to present day India. I had accompanied my maternal grandparents to Solan during the summer of 1947, when the unexpected decision of the division of India into two nations, India and Pakistan was announced. This came as a devastating blow as it was realized that returning to our home in Peshawar was no longer a possibility. To be ejected abruptly from their birthplace where they had expected to spend the rest of their life, and with an uncertain future facing them, must have been agonizing for my grandparents. Added to it was the anxiety concerning the fate of my mother and her sister still in Peshawar during the turbulent time of partition. My grandfather, R.B. Dina Nath Kakar, contacted Gen. Auchinleck, whom he had known from the days when Auchinleck was a brigade commander in Peshawar and a neighbour on Islamia Road.[36] A copy of the letter was handed over to me by my grandfather, probably to reassure a six-year-old that his mother would soon join them. The family was soon reunited, but the partition resulted sadly in the blood shed of millions.

Inter-Services Intelligence

In 1947, two intelligence agencies were created, namely, the Intelligence Bureau (IB) and the Military Intelligence (MI). The weak performance of MI in sharing intelligence among different wings of the armed forces came to the fore during the Indo-Pak war in 1947–48, which led to the establishment of the directorate of Inter-Services Intelligence (ISI) in 1948. Its first head was Colonel Syed Shahid Hamid (1948–50) who was succeeded by the Australian-born British army officer, Major General Cawthorne (1950–59), the longest serving head of ISI to date. The former Pakistan army chief, General Kayani, had been Director General (DG), ISI from October 2004 to October 2007. An article written in 2002, when Musharraf was in power, confirmed that ISI is a part of the Pakistan Army. It stated,

> In any case, the ISI's independence has often been overstated. Pakistan's military remains deeply disciplined and the ISI falls directly within its chain of command. Almost all ISI officers are regular military personnel, who are rotated in and out for no more than three years. Few military officials interviewed in Pakistan would even suggest that ISI would operate out of the direct chain of command that traces back to the Chief of Staff of the Army. According to Musharraf's Communication Minister and a former Director General of ISI, Lt. General Javed Ashraf Qazi, the ISI is composed of elements inducted into the agency

for a fixed tenure from all over the armed forces, and then
returned to their units. Indeed, while the ISI does include some
non-military officials, they are usually not senior. Most often,
any separation is designed to allow the government plausible
deniability, more than anything else.[37]

The ISI is claimed to be the largest intelligence agency in the world
in terms of number of personnel on its rolls. While figures have never
been made public, estimates place these at around 10,000 officers
and staff members, which do not include informants and assets.

The dubious nature and functioning of the ISI became
evident from the way the Pakistan government/army was
embarrassed when the role played by different director generals
of ISI was made public. Four heads of ISI who held office during
the 1990s were dismissed or compulsorily retired. Lt Gen. Asad
Durrani, DG, ISI (August 1990–March 1992) was dismissed
from the army on the advice of the Chief of Army Staff (COAS)
Abdul Wahid for allegedlly giving unsolicited political advice to
Benazir Bhutto during the April 1993 political crisis, while he
was serving as commandant of the National Defence College. He
was also accused of involvement in the elections of 1990.[38] It is
another matter that Benazir Bhutto later made him ambassador
to Germany and decorated him after his disgrace. His successor
Lt General Javed Nasir (March 1992) was summarily retired from
service in May 1993. It is interesting to note he was a member of
the Tablighi Jamaat. In 2013, Pakistan had refused to hand him
over to the International Tribunal in The Hague for his alleged
role in Bosnia against the Serbian Army, despite an embargo by
the UN. The plea taken by Pakistan was that Nasir had lost his
memory following a recent road accident. Lt General Ziauddin
Butt (October 1998–October 1999) was dismissed from service
after the army coup led by Musharraf. His successor, Lt General

Mahmud Ahmed (October 1999–October 2001), hand-picked by Musharraf, was removed from service immediately after 9/11. It is well known that as corps commander (X Corps) based in Rawalpindi, he had played a key role to help Musharraf in the coup. When it was learnt he had facilitated Saeed Sheikh to transfer US$ 1,00,000 to Mohammed Atta, involved in the 9/11 hijacking, he had to be dismissed.[39] Further, the U.S. subsequently found out that Lt General Mahmud, who had gone as DG, ISI, with a delegation of mullahs to Kabul, ostensibly to pressurize Mullah Omar to hand over Bin Laden to the U.S., was present when the delegates congratulated Mullah Omar for resisting U.S. pressure and encouraged him to continue to do so. There are several other instances of the dubious conduct of senior ISI officials, but these four dismissals of former DGs, ISI, from the army (after they had completed their tenure at ISI) in a ten-year span is illustrative of the duplicitous nature of activities of ISI.

ISI has played an important role since the onset of the civil war in Afghanistan in gathering, collating and analysing intelligence, and in assisting the army and civil establishments in formulating policy. These roles apart, it remains the main agency for conducting covert operations for and on behalf of Pakistan. The policy formulation role, along with its close nexus with the army, bestows on it a role quite different from the one usually associated with premier intelligence agencies operating in other countries, where checks and balances are in place. ISI's deep involvement in the domestic politics of Pakistan has led to accusations of rigging elections, massive corruption scandals like the Mehran Bank which surfaced in April 1994, insurgency operations in Balochistan and infiltration in Jammu and Kashmir (J & K). According to Ahmed Rashid, a Pakistani journalist and bestselling foreign policy author, the 'ISI collects intelligence, decides which operations should be carried out, and then carries them out unsupervised. From the late 1950s onwards, after Ayub Khan's ascendancy as President, ISI and MI have been employed to gather intelligence on opposition politicians, primarily to strengthen and sustain military rule. This free style of an intelligence agency functioning without a provision for adequate oversight has resulted in the exercise of excessive and arbitrary power by it. The ISI's vast intelligence-gathering role has extended into areas such as influencing the media and promoting political campaigns; monitoring diplomats, politicians, and journalists; acting as the foreign affairs arm of the Army; and most significantly, having covert operation responsibilities relating to at least Afghanistan and India.'[40] The ISI wanted to take advantage of the vacuum created by Nehru's death, the direct result of which was the Indo-Pak war of 1965, 'The Inter-Services Intelligence Agency, headed by Brigadier Riaz Hussain, had convinced itself that the moment for decisive intervention had arrived.'[41] Its inimical and adversarial attitude towards India has remained intact.

The active involvement of Pakistan in the Afghan civil war since 1979 facilitated the rise of a wide array of religious parties and groups. During this period, a close nexus developed and took root between the Pakistan Army and the ISI. The army-intelligence combine has encouraged the setting up of madrassas, which have become recruiting centres for jihadi elements. Numerous surrogate radical groups advocating jihad had been created and sheltered to fight in Afghanistan and Kashmir. Zia introduced the Hudood Ordinances and strengthened the blasphemy law that had existed since the British rule. The new Article 295C of the Pakistan Constitution stipulates the death penalty for any 'implication, insinuation or innuendo' against the prophet. Its introduction has had the effect of radicalizing Pakistan society, fortifying the Sunni Muslims and linking the Kashmir issue to Pakistan. During the 1980s, large amount of funds were made available to religious fundamentalist groups by ISI to recruit jihadi elements to fight in J & K.[42] The Lal Masjid incident of 2007 brought the issue of the blasphemy law, as an instrument of oppression of minorities, to the forefront. Withdrawal of charges against Asia Bibi, a Christian woman, was demanded. Mumtaz Kadri, the killer of the Punjab Governor, Salman Taseer, acquired an iconic status after the assassination, and his death in 2016 gave rise to the Tehreek-e-Labbaik Pakistan under a Barelvi cleric, Khadin Hussain Rizvi. This group achieved some success in the Sindh and Punjab elections. After the cleric's death in 2020, his son, Saad Rizvi, succeeded him. The Barelvi, which had all along been considered a part of the Sufi tradition, appears to have changed its worldview. With no known links in J & K, it remains to be seen whether the Barelvi would be deployed against Indian interests. The Pakistan Army may be reluctant to use them as that could perhaps lead to a greater role for the Barelvi in Pakistan itself. So far, Islamic State of Iraq and Syria (ISIS) has not made any significant dent in Pakistan or J & K. Bruce Riedel, a former Central Intelligence Agency (CIA) analyst with knowledge of Pakistan, has been quoted in a conversation with Bob Woodward in which Pakistan is described as the most dangerous country in the world today, where every nightmare of the twenty-first century converges—terrorism, government instability, corruption and nuclear weapons.[43] By design or otherwise, Riedel conveniently left out radicalization from his list of issues beguiling Pakistan.

The Rise of Radicalism in Pakistan

Pakistan's paramount dilemma, more than army rule, has been the rise of radicalism. Domestic violence and sectarian tensions emanating out of radicalism have been the biggest internal problem. In the last three decades, jihad has become a part of

Pakistani society, fueled by increasing unemployment and low levels of education and income. While Bhutto had encouraged Islamization, Zia ushered in radicalization. There are hardly any politicians who have not fallen to the lure of Islam. Benazir received support from Jamat Ulema-e-Islam (JUI), and the Taliban came into existence during her tenure. Thereafter, her successors, including Imran Khan, have relied on jihadi forces. Leading political parties have lost ground to extremists, resulting in a shift to Talibanization. Unfortunately, combating Islamic radicalism does not appear to be a priority of the government. Pakistan has remained in the 'grey list' of the Financial Action Task Force since 2018. In 1947, Pakistan's non-Muslim population was 23 per cent, which dwindled to 3 per cent by 2013.[44] Threat to the Pakistan establishment from the Taliban and other Wahabi/Deobandi radical elements requires little underscoring. Having made inroads into Pakistan society, these groups have created problems for sectarian minorities as well.

Treatment of Shias

The nearly 40 million Shias who constitute around 20 per cent of Pakistan's population are in a majority in Gilgit-Baltistan, the Kurram Agency, and are in significant numbers in Lahore, Karachi, Peshawar and Quetta. Their persecution commenced under Zia when the army created an anti-Shia group, the Anjuman Sipah-e-Saheba, which later added an armed wing—the Lashkar-e-Jhanghvi (LeJ). Since then, several thousand Shias (believed to be around 12,000) have been killed across Pakistan. Hazaras, who are Shias, have become the target of Sunni extremist groups like LeJ and the Taliban. The headquarters of LeJ is in Jhang in southern Punjab. The problem gets compounded as Sunni extremists enjoy the patronage of not only the security forces but also the political parties. Apart from the Shia–Sunni conflict, the intra-Sunni Deobandi-Barelvi conflicts have increasingly surfaced during the last decade. There are, in addition, heavily armed outfits maintaining private armies with sufficient coercive power to establish their writ at the local level, in isolated pockets of Pakistan. The rising incidents of suicide terrorism against the Pakistani security establishment signal a dangerous trend. It reveals the determination of radical forces, groomed by Pakistan itself, to take on the might of the state, which in contrast has proved less determined to take on these forces.

Cross-border Terrorism

The UN-sponsored mediator on Kashmir, Owen Dixon, recorded in his report of 9 September 1950, 'I was prepared to adopt the view that when the frontiers of the state of J&K was crossed as I believe on 20th October, 1947 by hostile elements, it was contrary to international law, and that when in May, 1948 as I believe units of regular Pakistan forces moved in to the territory of the state that too was inconsistent with international law.' The trend of deploying irregular forces/cross-border terrorism continues. In the 1950s, armed training was imparted to the Indian Naga rebels in the Chittagong hill tracks of Pakistan's eastern wing; in 1960, the Mizo rebels were armed; around 1965 contacts with Sikh groups, like those of Dr Jagjit Singh Chauhan, seeking home rule were established, apart from giving early help to Jammu and Kashmir Liberation Front (JKLF). After 1993, ISI infiltration of a large number of jihadi groups took place, such as the Harkat-ul-Ansar, renamed Harkat-ul-Mujahideen after the U.S. declared it a terrorist organization in 1993, and the Lashkar-e-Taiba. The Jaish-e-Mohammed (JeM) formed by Maulana Masood Azhar after his release in 1999 was also used. Pakistan's link with major terrorist attacks around the world before and since 9/11 is well known. The 1993 World Trade Center attack,[45] the 1996 Khobar Towers bombing in Saudi Arabia, the 2000 attack on *USS Cole* in Yemen,[46] the bombings in Bali[47] and London,[48] the failed attempt in Times Square,[49] the 26/11 Mumbai attack and violent acts against Indian, U.S. and Afghan interests in Afghanistan are but a few which received attention. Many other such incidents have passed by unrecorded, especially in conflict zones.

Effect on Neighbourhood

There is a need to ponder on reasons for the unabated increase in radicalization during the past four decades. To begin with, at its core is the ethos of religious intolerance manifesting itself in several ways, including antagonism towards non-believers, moderate Muslims, Sufis and Shias. The increase in the number of madrassas and their role in promoting terrorism speaks for itself. From a modest beginning of 189 madrassas in 1947, their number has risen in 2002 to an astonishing level of 10–13,000, with an enrolment estimated between 1.7–1.9 million students. By 2008, number of madrassas had skyrocketed to 40,000.[50] Whereas the original purpose of the madrassa was to produce scholars of Islamic jurisprudence, they instead started producing zealots motivated by jihad.[51] New elements were introduced for inspiring a jihadi spirit in children enrolled in madrassas. Now *jeem* stood for *jehad, tay* for *tope*, i.e., canon, *kaaf* for *Kalashnikov,* and *khayi* for *khoon*, i.e., blood.[52] To accentuate matters, mosques took the madrassas under their wing and started collecting funds for their upkeep. This is being complemented by active support lent to fundamentalist forces by the ISI, which has in the process created safe havens, secured bases and sanctuaries for the Taliban, Al Qaeda and their supporters.[53] What has been witnessed is that the curve of sectarian terrorism and violence has moved upwards, with a deteriorating situation in regard to conflicts between the Sunnis and Shias on the one hand, and the Deobandi and Barelvi groups on the other. It has been suggested that Talibanization of Pakistan is progressing unchecked, with civil society either unable or unwilling to play a moderating role. Naturally, the army could not have been expected to remain impervious to these societal changes. What is worrying is the continued role of the army in forging alliances among militant groups for achieving strategic ends.[54] It is not clear at this juncture what is the extent of collateral damage that could have accrued out of such cat-and-mouse games and the extent to which such damage would be acceptable to Pakistan, its neighbourhood and the global community. At times, radical forces that might have turned rogue, have demonstrated the will and determination to take on the Pakistani state which is evident from attacks on strategic targets within and outside Pakistan. Resurrection of the Taliban with Pakistan's aid and abetment has led to the rise of the Pakistani Taliban, which has changed the security dynamics of the tribal areas. So far, Pakistan has demonstrated a total disinclination to bring the tribal areas under control. As Pakistan seeks strategic depth in Afghanistan, that country in particular has faced the brunt of such attacks on its soil.

Consequently, Pakistan has become a problem for the region. Its use of terrorism as an instrument of state policy to destabilize the region goes on unabated. In Kashmir it has raised terrorist outfits like the Lashkar-e-Taiba, Harkat-ul-Mujahideen, Harkar-ul-Ansar and Jaish-e-Mohammed. Radical elements groomed in Pakistani madrassas are threatening peace and stability through the growth of Islamist organizations like the Harkat-ul-Jihad al-Islami (HUJI), Jagrata Muslim Janata Bangladesh (JMJB) and Jamaatul Mujahideen Bangladesh (JMB) with known linkages to radical outfits like the Al Qaeda. HUJI has been responsible

for many terrorist attacks in India. Islamist radicalism in some
of the Central Asian and Southeast Asian countries is traced to
madrassas and terrorist outfits based in Pakistan. The rolling out
of an intensively sectarian agenda has the potential of going out
of control of the army–ISI combine. Hurriyat and Taliban were
created under different circumstances but with a gap of a few years.
The ISI was successful in managing both to their advantage.[55]

Exacerbation of Fault Lines

Wali Khan, a renowned politician, head of Awami National Party,
once remarked, he was 'a Pashtun for 4,000 years, a Muslim for
1400 years and a Pakistani for 40 years.'[56] But this is not how
the concept of nationhood has been understood and practised in
Pakistan. Whereas Pakistan continues to derive the rationale for
its existence on Islam, it has been able to sustain itself all these
years through the creation of a bogey in the form of an Indian
threat. There have been different attempts at defining Pakistan
nationhood. President Ziaul Haq injected a religious fervour to
Muhammad Ali Jinnah's original idea of limited doubtful secular
content. Subsequently, President Pervez Musharraf attempted to
somehow combine the two. The obstacles to nation-building and
the reasons for failure of democracy are on account of Pakistan's
fault lines. First, as had been erroneously believed at its creation,
Islam was not in a position to bind the society of the two wings
together. Second, differences among different Muslim sectarian
groups such as Sunni, Shia and Ahmedia continue to fester.
Third, the so-called Mohajirs, that is, the Muslims who had
worked for the creation of Pakistan and migrated from India,
have not been accepted in the mainstream despite the passage
of time. Fourth, religious minorities remain the target of attack.
Lawrence Ziring, writing in 2005, observed this, and since then

there has been further deterioration, 'Long the targets of majority community abuse, Ahmediyya and Christians were prominent victims of the self-appointed purifiers of Islamic spirituality.'[57] Fifth, demographics permit Pakistani politics to be dominated by its largest province, Punjab.[58] Sixth, regular dismissals of elected governments by the army paved the way for it to remain in power around two-thirds of the time. Seventh, very little distinction between temporal matters and religious ones has led to the involvement of the Pakistani state in championing radicalization, which has only helped to exacerbate the fault lines.

Adverse Impact on the Economy

Pakistan's low per capita Gross Domestic Product (GDP) has tended to increase vulnerability along its fault lines that begin to come into play at regular and frequent intervals. Kick-starting the economy to a higher growth trajectory might not prove to be that easy a task because of the weak macroeconomic fundamentals, which remain a cause of concern. The ratio of gross external debt to GDP is considered excessive and unsustainable. Despite a steady flow of (worker) remittances, the exchange rate value of the Pakistan rupee has shown a steady decline, primarily on account of widening trade gaps that in turn put pressure on current account deficits. The consequent high inflation has been playing hide-and-seek with stagflation, that is, low growth combined with high inflation. In comparison, the performance of Pakistan's economy in the earlier decades appears somewhat complementary. GDP growth rates averaged 6.8 per cent in the 1960s, 4.8 per cent in the 1970s, and 6.5 per cent in the 1980s. It is only the high doses of economic and military assistance received during the 1980s from the U.S. and other allies, coinciding with Pakistan's role as a frontline state, that made it possible to stave off the economic deceleration process by a decade. Pakistan's economy started faltering with the societal changes brought about consequent to Zia's radicalization process. Pakistan might have realized by now that religious radicalization and economic growth usually do not go hand in hand.

Adverse Impact on Demography

Pakistan's controversial 2017 census figures that were released in May 2021 recorded the country's total population as 207 million. The census revealed the population of Pakistan had tripled since 1981, whereas during the corresponding period India's population doubled. Bangladesh, which had been described as a 'basket case', performed better than both. Interestingly, only 9 per cent of the population of Pakistan declared Urdu as their first language, preferring Punjabi and Saraiki in Punjab. The attempt to impose Urdu as the national language on the Bengalis in 1951–52 had contributed to the Bangladesh crisis. The Hindus, who comprised 20.5 per cent of the population of Pakistan at Partition, saw their numbers drop to less than 2 per cent, a tenfold decline over a seventy-year period.[59] The increasing population could become a cause of worry for Pakistan in the future. The annual growth rate of GDP had dropped to 2.4 per cent from a higher level of 2.69 per cent at the time of the 1998 census.

Pakistan's Strategic Culture

Pakistan's strategic culture could be summed up as essentially comprising the following elements:

- India-focused, India-centric and Kashmir-oriented
- Hostility intensified disproportionately after liberation of Bangladesh

- Does not shirk from employing military solutions to settle disputes or tackle fissiparous tendencies
- Relies heavily on covert action, beginning with Kashmir in 1947
- Employs non-democratic methods of governance, with the army being at the helm of affairs since 1956
- Islamic disposition and stance right from the start. Radicalization of state and society with Zia
- Deliberate misuse of religion as a tool to reinforce strategic culture
- Creation and support of radical groups
- Close nexus between Pakistan Army and radical groups impacts strategic thinking
- Seeks military parity with India despite its smaller geographical extent, population and economy
- Reliance on external military assistance—USA's South East Asian Treaty Organisation (SEATO)/Baghdad Pact, Central Treaty Organisation(CENTO). From 1960s-China and Iran. Subsequently, Saudi Arabia.
- Permits use of its territory. U-2 base (aircraft flown by the United States for intelligence gathering, surveillance and reconnaissance), Gwadar purchase (Gwader port purchased from Oman in 1958 by Pakistan and now run by state-run China firm), ceded territory to China in 1963.
- Disproportionate military spending at the expense of the economy.
- Seeks strategic depth in Afghanistan—played an important role in the formulation of Afghan policy
- Nuclear blackmail

Of all Pakistan's foreign engagements, none has been as central to its identity as its relations with India. A desire to play a role not supported by its key national parameters has been at the core of how Pakistan would like India and some others to perceive it. An attempt to seek parity with India has resulted in military alliances with the U.S. and its Cold War partners since the early 1950s. A special relationship with China emerged with the deterioration of Sino-Indian relations. The Islamic card too has been played from time to time. A repeated raising of Kashmir in various fora reconfirms this issue has remained the cornerstone of its foreign policy. While the public outcries might have helped generate some short-lived publicity, they are definitely not demonstrative of Pakistan's intent to move forward towards a dialogue to work out a settlement, which is fair and honourable to both sides. Pakistan does not miss any opportunity to use an engagement on terrorism to project a false narrative that it too is a victim of terrorism, when it is simultaneously aiding and abetting non-state actors to carry out terrorist attacks. In so doing, Pakistan is in a position to readily accept the damage borne by its citizens emerging out of the covert action conducted by its army–intelligence combine within its frontiers and outside, which is to be treated as collateral damage. Such damage is to be tolerated as a part of a process expected to lead to attainment of larger national interests. It is not surprising that Pakistan has cleverly tried to pass off such collateral damage as genuine damage, suffered as a result of terrorist activity with which it has no relationship.

In 1979, the CIA outsourced a substantial part of the covert operation in Afghanistan, enabling Pakistan to enhance its war-making capability and in the process make substantial gains—both tangible and intangible. Gen. Zia's support to fundamentalist elements and radical groups greatly augmented covert operation capability, which was used to exploit the situation in Afghanistan. Interestingly, Musharraf, as President, in his speech on 19 September 2001 mentioned, 'What I will like to know is how do we save Afghanistan and the Taliban. And how do they suffer minimum loss.' This statement, coming as it is from the topmost person, reveals the extent to which Pakistan's foreign policy, though shaped by national security interests, has played a compensatory role in filling the gap in that country's lack of a clearly defined sense of nationhood. Pakistan seeks control of states it perceives as subordinate powers, like Afghanistan, that could be relied upon to enhance its regional profile.[60]

Ever since the 1971 war, Pakistan has repeatedly given the impression that its attitude, policy and actions towards India are determined with a view to take revenge. General Ziaul Haq had remarked, 'Once bitten twice shy. In 1971, as a result of the Indo-Soviet collusion, Pakistan was dismembered. So, this tiny little country, in comparison to India, is now a little scared about what is left of it.'[61] This line of thinking is reflected in the subsequent support for Khalistan and the radical and jihadi elements in J & K. Apart from ushering in all-round radicalization, Zia formalized covert operations as an instrument of foreign policy. It is not as if covert operations had not been employed earlier, as in 1947–48. Ahmed Rashid writes, 'In 1962 following the Sino-Indian conflict Ayub Khan secretly sent several thousand soldiers disguised as guerrillas to stir up rebellion among the population in Kashmir in what has come to be known as Operation Gibraltar, which proved to be a failure and led to the second war between the two countries.'[62] Of late, Pakistani concerns regarding India have been: I) worry about India getting permanent membership of the United Nations Security Council (UNSC), II) the Indo-U.S. strategic cooperation including Nuclear Supplier Group (NSG) waiver and III) Indian role in Afghanistan.

Who Formulates Foreign Policy in India and Pakistan

Usually, it is the civilian government that formulates government policy on important national issues. This is my perception of countries I have been posted to. On reaching Hungary, I observed no Indian ambassador had met Janos Kadar, the then Communist Party chief, for over a decade. A meeting paved the way for several economic decisions beneficial to both countries. In Germany, the chancellor's office played a pivotal role; in Russia, the Kremlin and the President's office were the keystone of Indo-Soviet/Russia relations; in the USA, it was the White House which determined foreign policy. For instance, had it not been for President George Bush, the Indo-U.S. nuclear deal would not have been signed. In Pakistan, it is not the prime minister but the army that determines policy, particularly in relation to India.

An unusual resolution of the Pakistan cabinet of 30 December 1947 that set the tone read, '. . . that no question of policy or principle would be decided except at a Cabinet meeting presided by the Quaid-e-Azam and in the event of any difference of opinion between him and the Cabinet, the decision of the Quaid will be final and binding.'[63] Jinnah informed Lord Mountbatten, 'I will be Governor General, and the Prime Minister will do what I tell him.'[64] This resolution naturally undermined the position of the prime minister as the writ of the governor general (Quaid-e-Azam) became paramount.[65] Jinnah's writ ought to be considered significant enough, for it set the ball rolling for the manner in which Pakistani politics would subsequently play out. Within less than seven years of its creation, Pakistan came under army control in 1954, which coincided with the receipt of military assistance from the United States. Jinnah's resolution would always haunt Pakistan. When an attempt was made by the constituent assembly in 1954 to change it, the then governor general Gulam Mohammed dissolved the assembly. Whereas the first two constitutions of 1956 and 1962 chose to ignore the issue, the constitution of 1973 attempted to rectify the position, but General Ziaul Haq subsequently introduced the 8th Amendment, making dismissal of successive civilian governments feasible. This amendment was used to dismiss the governments of Zia's protégé Junejo, Benazir Bhutto and Nawaz Sharif. Although Nawaz Sharif succeeded in scrapping the 8th Amendment, Musharraf restored its provisions. After the death of Jinnah and Liaquat Ali, civil servants and military officers assisted in the formulation of Pakistan's foreign policy. Bhutto played the China and Islamic cards to his advantage, and it was he who introduced the Islamic holiday of Friday in Pakistan. In later years, the army and ISI started to play a decisive role in its formulation and execution.

Further, the manner in which dismissals have been carried out is reflective of the situation prevailing at the ground level. The dissolution orders of the Presidents of Pakistan, whether military or civil, such as Gen. Zia, Ghulam Ishaq Khan and Farooq Ahmed Leghari described the prime ministers as virtual criminals and held them responsible for various alleged acts of commission and omission. Ghulam Ishaq Khan accused Nawaz Sharif of the murder of the army chief, General Asif Nawaz; President Leghari held Benazir Bhutto responsible for the death of her brother, interference in the independence of the judiciary, corruption, nepotism, mal-administration, misuse of the civil service, illegal use of banks and illegal phone tapping; and Musharraf charged Nawaz Sharif with hijacking, an offence carrying the death penalty.[66] The peculiar system of exile has been employed often, with its first victim being Iskander Mirza who, after having been discredited, was whisked away to London; other victims of exile have included Benazir Bhutto, Asif Zardari, Nawaz Sharif and

Musharraf himself. Zulfikar Bhutto was hanged to death at the instance of Ziaul Haq, who himself died in a plane crash, suspected to be an act of sabotage. Benazir and Liaquat Ali were killed at almost the same spot in Rawalpindi, the headquarters of the Pakistan Army, and their killers have never been identified. The memory of none of Pakistan's leaders has been perpetuated. At the funeral of Yahya Khan, the cabinet secretary alone represented the government. Although, at Ayub Khan's funeral a large number of people from his area were present, there was no official representation. Former leaders are forgotten; their birth or death anniversaries are also forgotten.[67] Worse, it is taboo to talk about past leaders.[68] The position of the prime minister in Pakistan has become more and more weak, mainly because of the provision of the 8th Amendment.

It is widely accepted that the army has complete control over foreign policy. 'The military resists civilian guidance . . . even when Pakistan has an elected government. The Pakistani military dictates policy towards all major powers. The Indian and Afghan policy have been considered as reserve subjects, while foreign policy objectives in general are meant to underwrite Pakistan security.'[69] Taking advantage of Pakistan's unresolved border issues with India and Afghanistan, the army created an enhanced role for itself at the beginning. Stephen Cohen, an American expert on India, Pakistan and South Asian security, notes that it started as a 'benevolent baby sitter' and later transformed that role to the 'all-encompassing role of *maa–baap* (mother–father)'.[70] Pakistan and foreign analysts both shared the view of army control on policy towards India. 'Foreign policy and strategic interests are defined, articulated and in most cases implemented by GHQ.'[71] And, 'Pakistan foreign policy has indeed become the foreign policy of an army.'[72] Cohen categorizes world armies into three different categories: armies that guard the nation's borders, armies that are concerned about protecting their own position in society, and armies that defend a cause or an idea. As per Cohen, the Pakistan Army does all three.[73]

Often the army overruled elected civilian prime ministers. For instance, two decisions of Gilani were publicly overturned at the instance of the army, clearly indicating who the boss was. After the 26/11 Mumbai attack in 2011, Gilani proposed to send the ISI chief to India for investigations, which the army prevented. Earlier, on 26 July 2008, the Press Information Department issued a notification placing the ISI under the control of the ministry of interior. Within twenty-four hours, the government was compelled to rescind the notification. The Inter Services Public Relations (ISPR) Army statement stated the top leadership of the army had not been consulted before the issue of the notification.[74] And, again, on 2 May 2011, on the killing of Osama bin Laden in a U.S. operation in Pakistan, the telephone call by the then U.S. Chairman of the Joint Chiefs of Staff Admiral Mike Mullen, following the operation, was made not to President Zardari or Prime Minister Gilani but to Chief of Army Staff, Kayani. A similar trend was observed during a brief visit to Pakistan after visiting Kabul in January 2011, when Joe Biden, then vice president, contrary to protocol, chose to call on Army Chief Kayani at the army GHQ (General Headquarters) in Rawalpindi![75]

In Stephen Cohen's assessment made over two decades ago, the Pakistan Army favours a foreign policy that would not lead to a direct military confrontation with India, without yielding to Indian pressure on core issues. He also suggested that while pushing for support for Kashmiri separatists, the army would not like assistance to reach a point from where confrontation with India could become a possibility. The army has favoured good relations with Islamic states with a view to broaden and deepen economic and military engagements without these appearing to be tilting towards one or another state, which has at times triggered sectarian violence within Pakistan. It would like to maintain and expand the nuclear programme without risking Pakistan's residual relationship with the United States and other anti-proliferation states. Relationship with the U.S., which some Pakistanis believe has 'let Pakistan down' many times in the past, is periodically recalibrated to avoid overdependence yet remains sufficiently close to give sufficient leverage for putting Pakistan's case across in Washington, and to balance Indian influence. The army would like Pakistan to do whatever is possible to hold together Pakistan's most important proto-alliance—that with China—by recognizing and encouraging Chinese interests in Pakistan.[76]

Who Makes Policy on Pakistan in India

As for India, having had the privilege of working with six prime ministers in different capacities over a span of thirty-four years, I can unequivocally say that India's Pakistan policy is decided by the prime minister, albeit with inputs from different organs of the government. The prime minister is the final arbiter. Let me elaborate. I was posted twice to Islamabad, first as deputy chief of mission (1978–82), during which, for eighteen months I was in different spells chargé d'affaires ad interim (temporarily acting in place for absent head of mission) and later returned as high commissioner (1992–95). This, coincidentally, could perhaps be the longest spell for any diplomat to have remained as head of mission in Pakistan. From 1982–86, I had served as head of the Pakistan/Afghanistan/Iran desk in the ministry of external affairs. During Vajpayee's tenure, I was special envoy for Afghanistan. When Dr Manmohan Singh became prime minister, I was appointed first as convener of the National Security Advisory Board, a body that provides inputs to the government on different aspects of national security. Subsequently, as special envoy of the prime minister (PM) (2005–14), I dealt exclusively with back-channel negotiations with Pakistan, and from 2010 onwards was given the rank of minister of state. This too perhaps could be considered the longest tenure anyone has had as special envoy of the PM. I have also taken part in Track II dialogues with Pakistan. The answer as to who makes policy in India in respect of relations with Pakistan is not startling! Since 1947, successive prime ministers of India have played a decisive role in formulating policy in respect of Pakistan. For the first seventeen years, Jawaharlal Nehru made policy with the assistance of senior officials of the external affairs ministry. In those days, the prime minister's office (PMO) was a small affair. Lal Bahadur Shastri played a key role in the Tashkent Conference (1966). Indira Gandhi and her successors made key decisions on Pakistan. Even short-term PMs like Chandra Shekhar and Deve Gowda, in spite of having influential foreign ministers, took a keen interest in relations with Pakistan. Although principal secretaries like P.N. Haksar and Brijesh Mishra with a foreign service background played an important role in formulating policy towards Pakistan, the ultimate decision has always been taken by the prime minister.

In June 2001, when Prime Minister Vajpayee invited General, later President, Musharraf for the Agra Summit, it took the ministry of external affairs (MEA) by surprise as it did others in the government, including the home ministry. The Americans, who since the 1998 nuclear tests and the Kargil conflict were keeping a close watch on the two recently declared nuclear powers, were also caught by surprise. This became evident from the conversation the Deputy Secretary of State, Richard Armitage had with a visiting Indian delegation to Washington DC later that month when he inquired about the background to the invitation. He explained he had known the general well as they had fought together in the trenches and wanted to know if we could trust him. I met Musharraf in Delhi when he came for the Agra Summit. I had been called to Delhi from Moscow, where I was serving as ambassador, for the pre-summit internal consultations. Prime Minister Vajpayee's 'Friendship with Pakistan' speech in Srinagar of 18 April 2003 caught his cabinet colleague, external affairs minister, Yashwant Sinha, by surprise. Sinha admits this in his book, *Relentless: An Autobiography*.[77] I later met Gen. Musharraf on different occasions.

Prime Minister Manmohan Singh made his impact on Pakistan policy. It was he who took the decision on the back channel and other important matters connected to relations with Pakistan. He called Nawaz Sharif immediately on learning that the latter was racing towards a comfortable victory in the election in May 2013, well before declaration of the final election results. The two spoke in Punjabi and English. Nawaz Sharif asked for supply of power and gas from India to which Singh agreed. I was immediately sent as special envoy to convey Manmohan Singh's greetings to Nawaz Sharif on his election victory, even before his swearing-in. Progress was being made until July, when it went cold from the Pakistan side, attributed mainly to pressure from the military-ISI establishment. When Musharraf came to participate in the India Today Summit, I called on him on behalf of PM Manmohan Singh, who was unwell. His role in the back-channel discussions is covered separately in another chapter.

The newly elected Prime Minister Narendra Modi invited all South Asian Association for Regional Cooperation (SAARC) leaders to his swearing-in on 26 May 2014. This was once again his call made after consulting his top advisers. He met PM Nawaz Sharif the following day. The two struck a chord. Modi's spontaneous decision, or at least it appeared to be so, to visit Lahore on 25 December 2015, was not foreseen or known. He had visited Moscow, and on his return leg he visited Kabul on 25 December to inaugurate the new Parliament building constructed by and with grant assistance from India. After a rousing and emotional speech in the new Parliament building in the morning, PM Modi and his delegation made their way to Chief Executive Officer (CEO) Abdullah Abdullah's office. It was a long journey to the office. As the motorcade halted, senior members of the delegation were informed that the PM would be stopping at Lahore on his way back to Delhi that afternoon. During the car journey from Parliament, PM Modi spoke to PM Sharif on phone to wish him on his birthday. Sharif said he was in Lahore to celebrate his granddaughter's wedding in his family home in Raiwind and invited PM Modi to stop by in Lahore and bless his granddaughter. PM Modi accepted the invitation as he would have been flying over Lahore on his way back to Delhi from Kabul.

Engagement with Pakistan is not a diplomatic choice; it is a political one. Given the deep weight of public opinion and sentiment attached to India–Pakistan relations in both countries, there appears to be little option but for the two countries to work towards calculated and intuitive decisions. A prime minister takes into account daily intelligence briefings, developments on the ground, international environment, views held by his cabinet colleagues and political advisers, political conditions at home, any back-channel signals from the other side and, of course, inputs that come from the foreign office. These might not be considered in the context of a specific decision to be made. Nor will they be a part of the formal process of decision-making. There is no other office in the government to receive the full array of inputs and assessments from diverse sources. This information which the prime minister gets on a regular basis is processed by him, and at times without the assistance of aides. Even a decision regarding whether the prime minister should meet the Pakistan PM on the margins of a multilateral or regional summit is usually taken at the top level. Such decisions are largely those of the PM, who sounds out his close and trusted advisers and once he has decided, everything else follows, including various dialogues.

In our relationship with Pakistan, it becomes difficult to identify and justify a particular course of action from a mere examination of the material at hand. Usually, clear-cut answers are neither there nor do they emerge. Bureaucratic and political processes have tended to favour safe options and status quo. Once a top-down decision is made, the wheels are set in motion and the choreography works itself out. The important turning points and debates on the agenda become less consequential than the choreography. It is left to the ministers, national security advisers and officials to work through details on the agenda. Some enduring agreements/Memorandum of Understanding (MoUs) have been MEA led, like nuclear notifications, the Lahore Declaration, water issues, etc.

Just as a decision on engagement at the highest political level can be sudden, the decision to withdraw from such an engagement can be equally sudden. It should not be difficult to appreciate that terrorist attacks make it difficult for a prime minister to remain oblivious to their consequences and continue with the engagement process. In the past, such attacks have been the cause of well-intentioned efforts evaporating in the aftereffects of the blast and heat generated in the process, as was evidenced in the aftermath of the Mumbai terror attack in November 2008 and the terror attack on the Pathankot Air Force base in 2016, just one week after PM Modi had touched down in Lahore. Every PMO has made the journey from expectation of a breakthrough to managing crisis relations. During the past four decades or more, India had to deal with an increasingly radicalized Pakistan, influenced by its army/ISI to seek vengeance and geopolitical rent. The response has to be tailored to an evolving strategic culture of Pakistan. Pakistan's reliance on external players, whether the West led by the U.S., China or some radicalized Islamic countries has to be factored in.

2

Bangladesh to Siachen: Military Wins and Peace Offers

Jawaharlal Nehru to First Tenure of Indira Gandhi

I started dealing with Pakistan during Indira Gandhi's second tenure as prime minister. However, I will begin with a brief summary of the summit meetings between India and Pakistan from Partition in 1947 till my posting to Pakistan in 1978.

PM Jawaharlal Nehru

Prime Minister Nehru, along with Governor General Louis Mountbatten, visited Lahore twice in 1947 (29 August and 8 December) to meet Muhammad Ali Jinnah. Prime Minister Liaquat Ali Khan visited Delhi twice the same year (18–20 September and 28 November) to discuss issues related to refugees and connected matters. Between 1950 and 1960 there were eight meetings between Nehru and the Pakistan heads of government—Liaquat Ali, Feroze Khan Noon, Mohammad Ali Bogra and Ayub Khan. Nehru travelled to Pakistan on three occasions.

Some meetings were for specific purposes. The Nehru–Liaquat Agreement on Minorities was signed in Delhi (April 1950). The Indus Water Treaty was signed during Nehru's last visit to Karachi in September 1960.

On Kashmir, a series of talks and efforts by the UN mediators, including Frank Graham, did not produce any results. These were followed by direct negotiations between the prime ministers of the two countries during 1953–56. Khwaja Nazimuddin announced there would be talks, but he was soon dismissed. His successor, Mohammed Ali, had three meetings with Nehru in London in June 1953 which were described as preliminary on Kashmir, minorities and evacuee properties. Nehru later visited Karachi in July 1953, and got a rousing reception. According to newspaper reports, the 6-mile route from the airport to the Government House was lined by 'jostling crowds standing on the road side and atop roofs of offices and buildings . . . with shouts of Nehru Zindabad'. The joint communiqué mentioned that a major part of the meeting was devoted to the Kashmir dispute, which was examined in all its aspects. During this period, Aneurin Bevan, a British politician, wrote, after a visit to both countries, that 'of this I am convinced, if there are two men who between them can bring Pakistan and India closer together, these [Nehru and Governor General Ghulam Mohammad] are the men'.[1]

Pakistan, joining the U.S.-sponsored military pacts, ended the first phase of negotiations. India's position on the talks was made clear by Prime Minister Nehru in Parliament on 1 March 1954 in which he said,

> The grant of military aid by the United States to Pakistan creates a grave situation for us in India and for Asia. It adds to our tensions . . . these problems can only be solved by the two countries themselves and not by the intervention of others . . .

Recently a new friendly atmosphere has been created between India and Pakistan, and by direct consultation between the two prime ministers, progress was being made towards the solution of this problem. That progress has now been checked and fresh difficulties have arisen . . . The military aid by United States to Pakistan is a form of intervention . . . which is likely to have more far-reaching results than previous types of intervention.[2]

Despite constant changes of government in Pakistan, talks continued. Both Governor General Ghulam Mohammad and Prime Minister Mohammed Ali visited Delhi and were given a warm reception. Governor General Ghulam Mohammad was later the chief guest at the Indian Republic Day parade in 1955, which was the first time the parade was held at Rajpath.

There was a perceptible change from 1954 onwards in respect of the Kashmir issue. While Pakistan hardened its stance, India too felt, as mentioned by Nehru in his letter to his sister on 2 February 1957, that India had been 'too accommodating to Pakistan over this issue . . . which now are put up before us as commitments which we must honour. Even from the narrowest point of view, these so-called commitments were subject to all kinds of conditions which have not been fulfilled.'[3]

Nehru's interaction with President Ayub Khan during his visit to Karachi in 1960 to sign the Indus Water Treaty was not warm. From available accounts, there was not much discussion on Kashmir, which Ayub Khan wanted.

Following the Sino–Indian conflict, Pakistan felt it was in the driver's seat. There were talks at ministerial level on Jammu and Kashmir (J & K) in 1963 (Swaran Singh–Zulfikar Ali Bhutto talks). Bhutto refused a solution based on making the then ceasefire line the international boundary.

Sheikh Abdullah, on his release from jail, went to Pakistan to discuss Kashmir. However, while he was still there, Nehru died and nothing materialized from this visit.

PM Lal Bahadur Shastri

The tenure of Prime Minister Lal Bahadur Shastri was brief. He devoted significant attention to relations with Pakistan. He made a transit halt in Karachi on 12 October 1964, on his return journey from Cairo, to meet President Ayub Khan.

A few months later, Rana Abdul Hamid, the food and agriculture minister of Pakistan, was the guest of honour for India's Republic Day celebrations. This was one of the rare occasions when the chief guest at the Republic Day parade was neither a head of state nor government.

On 30 June 1965, an intergovernmental India–Pakistan agreement was signed relating to ceasefire, restoration of status quo and the demarcation of the Gujarat–West Pakistan border in the area, on the basis of the award of the tribunal, which became effective from 1 July 1965. The last stretch relating to Sir Creek was not included, perhaps based on the understanding that it was covered in the 1914 Kutch–Sindh Agreement. This dispute still continues.

An insight into the thinking of Lal Bahadur Shastri is provided in B.K. Nehru's book, *Nice Guys Finish Second*. He asked Prime Minister Shastri if it was worthwhile going to war for a piece of sandy desert. Lal Bahadur Shastri's response was, 'It is not a question of a piece of desert; it is a question of a foreign power occupying a piece of our territory no matter how worthless. A nation which allows its territory to be nibbled away piece by piece has no right to exist.'[4]

Lal Bahadur Shastri led the country in the 1965 war with Pakistan, and everyone still remembers his famous slogan *'Jai Jawan Jai Kisan'*. After the war, he went to Tashkent to meet President Ayub Khan and signed an agreement with him. Unfortunately, a few hours later, he died.

PM Indira Gandhi

The only meeting that Indira Gandhi had with Bhutto was after the 1971 war in Shimla, where they signed the Simla Agreement on 2 July 1972. Indira Gandhi had led the country to a decisive victory in the war, and her attitude towards Pakistan was practical and realistic. In spite of Bhutto subsequently letting her down, she was in the forefront of the campaign to save his life following the judicial verdict against him in Pakistan, and was later critical of his hanging. The then prime minister Morarji Desai preferred to remain silent, calling it an internal affair of Pakistan.

P.N. Dhar, a close adviser of Indira Gandhi and her secretary, provides an interesting insight on Kashmir in his book covering the Simla Agreement, 'Bhutto agreed not only to change the ceasefire line into a line of control, for which he had earlier proposed the term "line of peace", he also agreed that the line would be gradually endowed with the "characteristics of an international border".'[5]

* * *

My initial contacts with Indira Gandhi were in the Soviet Union. These were not what I would describe as substantive meetings, but they gave me a measure of the Iron Lady of India: her strong and decisive leadership, her ability to protect and project our national interests, her intuitive insights, combined with her natural elegance, charm and graciousness.

My first meeting with Indira Gandhi was in early April 1966 in Moscow. She was on a stopover visit to the Soviet Union, after an official visit to the U.S. As a young third secretary, I had been appointed by the embassy as her liaison officer. As such, I was at the villa where she was staying, located in the picturesque Gorki Leninskiye (Lenin Hills), later renamed its original Vorobyovy Gory (Sparrow Hills) after the breakup of the Soviet Union in 1991. At night, on her return to the villa, she was delighted to see a bowl of beluga caviar placed invitingly on crushed ice in a silver bowl on the table. She inquired whether I had tried caviar during my stay in Moscow. I said I had. Seeing her reaction, I gave a signal to the liveried attendant, who emerged on cue from an adjoining room with a neatly arranged tray of finely chopped onions, hard-boiled egg yolks and whites chopped separately and freshly squeezed lemon juice. Adding some of these accompaniments to a couple of spoons of caviar, she asked me if I would like to join her. After some hesitation, I did. Before retiring for the night, she smilingly said she was glad I had enjoyed it too. Ever since then, I have boasted it was none other than the sophisticated and urbane prime minister of India who taught me how to savour caviar!

PM Indira Gandhi, on her visit to the U.S., got support for the new Green Revolution and food grain shipments which the media had described as a 'ship to mouth' operation. At her villa in Moscow, she called a meeting of the senior officials who had accompanied her to the U.S. Clearly upset at the precarious situation in the country after two successive drought years, she emphatically stated that she did not want to go on another begging mission and ordered on priority basis immediate plans for self-sufficiency in food.

Following the ouster of Nikita Khrushchev as both the Communist Party of the Soviet Union (CPSU) chief and prime minister in 1964, it was decided that party and government posts should no longer be simultaneously assumed by a Soviet leader, so as to prevent excessive concentration of power. Thereafter, the Soviet Union was run by a collective troika of CPSU General Secretary Leonid Brezhnev, President Nikolai Podgorny and Prime Minister Alexei Kosygin. Given Kosygin's apparent preeminent role, not just on economic issues but in the foreign policy domain, many in Delhi were uncertain about whose writ ran in the collective leadership in the Kremlin. After her meetings with the top leadership during her first state visit to the Soviet Union in July 1966, Indira Gandhi confidently told veteran diplomat and Soviet specialist T.N. Kaul that CPSU General Secretary Leonid Brezhnev was in control. This was remarkably prescient, since in an unobtrusive manner over the next decade, Brezhnev eased out Podgorny and assumed the post of President, and neutralized Kosygin as well.

Indira Gandhi's approach to both China and the Soviet Union was conditioned by her strong misgivings about the extraterritorial fraternal links of our leftist parties. This applied not only to the Chinese Communist Party (CCP), and the Communist Party of India (CPI) split in 1964 after the Sino–Indian conflict in 1962. She also kept a watchful eye on links with the CPSU, even after establishing a close rapport with the top Soviet leadership. The top leadership transition in the Kremlin and deterioration in Sino–Indian relations also coincided with heightening Sino–Soviet ideological and politico-strategic hostilities.

The shortest route from my apartment in Lomonosovsky Prospekt to our embassy, was through Ulitsa Dhruzba (Friendship Street), where the Chinese Embassy was located. Throughout my tenure I had no choice but to take a much longer detour, as the street had been blocked due to worsening Sino–Soviet relations. Chinese cuisine too was a casualty. On one occasion when I went to the famed Peking Restaurant to order Chinese food, I was told the menu had been discontinued and replaced by a Russian one. Thereafter, the only opportunity I got to enjoy Chinese delicacies was at the Chinese National Day reception.

While departing, after bidding goodbye to Prime Minister Kosygin and Chargé d'Affaires Rikhi Jaipal, Indira Gandhi whispered something to Rikhi Jaipal. The following morning at the officers meeting, Rikhi Jaipal told me, 'You have impressed the prime minister.' I must have looked bewildered, because he clarified that before getting on the plane, she asked him to thank the young liaison officer attached to her. She did not know my name but remembered to convey her personal appreciation.

This was a marked contrast to my later experience with some leaders on similar occasions. I had spent a few days in Venice and Rome with Dev Kanta Baruah, then minister for petroleum, later Congress president and famous for his comment 'India is Indira'. We enjoyed Italian food, recited Shakespeare and discussed Indian and Italian history, of which he was knowledgeable. In Rome, he expressed a desire to meet the Pope, stating it would promote his image with the Christians in his constituency in Assam. A meeting was arranged and photograph taken. However, he was visibly unhappy since the photograph showed me on the right and him on the left of the Pope. He was relieved at my suggestion that the photograph could simply be cropped to show him alone with the Pope. In spite of all this, while leaving the Rome airport, he shook hands with Ambassador Apa Pant and ignored my extended hand. It is such incidents that made me realize how gracious Indira Gandhi was.

She made another visit to Moscow a year later, as the only non-Communist leader of government to be invited to the fiftieth anniversary of the 1917 October Revolution in the Soviet Union. Due to a technical problem, her plane landed elsewhere. The Soviets immediately rushed another special aircraft to bring her to Moscow. Premier Kosygin was unable to receive her as the inaugural session had already commenced, but she was received by two deputy prime ministers. From the airport, she came directly to the Kremlin Hall, where she got a resounding standing ovation. This would not have happened had she arrived on time.

She was accompanied by her sons, Rajiv and Sanjay. I was told to take them on a sightseeing tour along with Usha Bhagat, her social secretary, who also happened to be my neighbour in Delhi. When Sanjay started criticizing, in Hindi, then home minister Gulzari Lal Nanda in the car, I requested him to change the topic as the Soviet interpreter knew Hindi. Usha Bhagat gave me a disapproving look, which made me feel I could face some difficulty due to this indiscretion. On getting out of the car, Rajiv Gandhi softly said that I had given the right advice. This made me feel better.

Bangladesh

Along with two colleagues, Ramesh Mulye and Girish Dhume, I was fortunate to be in the official gallery in the Lok Sabha on 16 December 1971, when Prime Minister Indira Gandhi informed the House about the surrender of the Pakistan forces. The atmosphere was electric. It can only be compared to the midnight speech of Jawaharlal Nehru at the time of Independence in Parliament on 15 August 1947, when he stated, 'Long years ago we made a tryst with destiny, and now the time comes when we shall redeem our pledge . . . At the stroke of the midnight hour, when the world sleeps, India will awake to life and freedom.' In a solemn voice, Prime Minister Indira Gandhi told the House,

I have an announcement to make. The West Pakistan forces have unconditionally surrendered in Bangladesh . . . Dacca is now the free capital of a free country. The House and the entire nation rejoice in this historic event. We hail the people of Bangladesh in their hour of triumph. We hail the brave young men and boys of the Mukti Bahini for their valour and dedication. We are proud of our own Army, Navy and Air Force and the Border Security Force, who have so magnificently demonstrated their quality and capacity. Our objectives were limited—to assist the gallant people of Bangladesh and their Mukti Bahini to liberate their country from a reign of terror and to resist aggression on our own land. We hope and trust that the Father of this new nation, Sheikh Mujibur Rahman, will take his rightful place among his own people and lead Bangladesh to peace, progress and prosperity. The time has come when they can together look forward to a meaningful future in their Sonar Bangla. They have our good wishes.[6]

According to what we were authoritatively told, the draft of the speech had been prepared by her principal secretary, P.N. Haksar. In her own hand she made two changes. First was the reference to Sheikh Mujibur Rahman, and second, she added the word Sonar Bangla.

The following day, on 17 December 1971, she made another statement in Parliament. Referring to relations with Pakistan, she said, 'I hope the people of Pakistan will seek a path which is more in keeping with their circumstances and needs . . . We want to assure them that we have no enmity towards them. There are more things in common than those which divide us. We should like to fashion our relations with the people of Pakistan on the basis of friendship and understanding.'[7] On 18 December, she spoke about the human cost, the sacrifices made by soldiers of the

Indian armed forces and various measures that had been taken for the welfare of the families of those killed in action.

She spoke of relations with Pakistan in interviews with different newspapers. Responding to a question whether she perceived any difficulty in negotiations with Pakistan, she replied, 'There is no difficulty at all. They can start as soon as Pakistan is in a mood to do so.'[8] In an interview with *Time* Magazine published the same day, she said, 'A stable Pakistan is in India's interest and we want normal, friendly and enduring relations with the new government.'[9]

At that time, I had no inkling that the current events would lead to my immediate transfer from Delhi. For the last three years I had been working on the U.S. desk in the ministry of external affairs, and it was hinted my next posting was Washington. However, suddenly in the second week of January, I was summoned to Foreign Secretary T.N. Kaul's office. Present too was chairman of the policy planning committee, D.P. Dhar, who was handling events in Bangladesh. (I had spent time with D.P. Dhar, then minister of Jammu and Kashmir, on his visit to the Soviet Union in 1968.) T.N. Kaul informed me that while the offer to Washington still stood, he would instead like me to immediately proceed to Dacca for opening the Indian Embassy in Bangladesh. I said I hardly had an option, as I was told a few minutes earlier by a colleague that my orders of transfer to the proposed new mission in Bangladesh were being cyclostyled. T.N. Kaul, with a smile on his face, said. 'How have they done this? I had told them not to take action till I had spoken to the officer.'

D.P. Dhar laughingly quipped, 'Tikki [T.N. Kaul], you don't seem to be in control of your ministry.' T.N. Kaul, turning to me, said the option was still mine.

I responded, 'Dacca', and the matter was settled. When asked when I was expected to go, he responded, within the next three to four days.

On 10 January 1972, when Sheikh Mujibur Rahman, after his release by Pakistan, transited through Delhi en route to Dacca, Prime Minister Indira Gandhi said,

> Sheikh Mujibur Rahman gave a pledge to his people that he would make them free and create an opportunity for building a new life. He has fulfilled both pledges. His body might have been imprisoned, but none could imprison his spirit. He inspired the people of Bangladesh to fight, and today he is free. We in India also gave three pledges to our people. The first was that those refugees who had come here would go back. The second was that we would give every kind of help to the people of Bangladesh and to the Mukti Bahini. The third was that we shall secure the release of Sheikh Mujib. We too have been able to fulfil these pledges.[10]

On 17 January, I accompanied J.N. Dixit (popularly known as Mani) to Dacca to open the Indian Embassy.

On arrival in Dacca, as all passengers disembarked, Mani and I were asked to stay in the aircraft for a few minutes. When the few minutes stretched longer than anticipated, we speculated about the reasons behind the request. Random thoughts flitted through our minds, including whether a coup had taken place, which was immediately dispelled since there was no military presence at the airport. Soon all doubts were laid to rest, when we saw a red carpet being rolled out for our welcome. The unusual, unprecedented delay was on account of their inability to locate the red carpet after the 1971 war.

During a professional career of almost five decades, (1964– 2014), I have witnessed several state/official visits and have been involved in organizing some, but none had been as iconic as the visit of PM Indira Gandhi to Bangladesh, when the newly liberated nation hosted its first state visit (17–19 March 1972). Etched in my memory was the formal parade of the Indian Army at the Dacca Stadium on 12 March 1972, five days before the arrival of PM Indira Gandhi. At the meeting in Calcutta between her and Sheikh Mujib, it had been agreed that the Indian forces would withdraw from Bangladesh by 25 March 1972. However, after the dates of her visit to Bangladesh were fixed, she preempted this by ensuring the troops left five days prior to her visit. The ceremony at the Dacca Stadium on 12 March, from 5 p.m. to 6.15 p.m. was a solemn one. The Indian troops participating included the 61st Cavalry, 4th Battalion 61st Rajputs, 9th Battalion Dogra Regiment and the 1st Battalion of the 3rd Gorkha Rifles. Music for the parade was provided by the Cariappa March and Sam Bahadur March. In his brief address, Sheikh Mujib told the Indian troops, 'You came as liberators and are leaving as friends.'

The Indian Embassy in Dacca at this time consisted of few officers. In preparation for the visit, I had regular meetings with the chief of protocol, Farooq Ahmed Chowdhury. When a suggestion on behalf of the Government of India was made, he jokingly commented that the chief of protocol for this visit was in reality Bangabandhu (Sheikh Mujib). An hour later I received a response to my query. A little-known fact is that the President of Bangladesh, Justice Abu Syeed Chowdhury, vacated the presidential house, Banga Bhaban, for PM Gandhi, on account of limited accommodation.

Indira Gandhi was given a tumultuous welcome. Her arrival on 17 March, happened to coincide with Mujib's birthday. It was declared a public holiday on account of her visit. She addressed a mammoth public meeting and was accorded a civic reception. Sheikh Mujib, in his banquet speech on 17 March, at Banga Bhaban, said, 'Today is a memorable day for the 75 million people of Bangladesh . . . the freedom loving people of India under the leadership of their great prime minister Mrs Indira Gandhi gave us unstinted help and support during our liberation struggle . . . the friendship between India and Bangladesh has been cemented forever by blood and common sacrifices.'

On a boat ride on 18 March, the two prime ministers decided to sign the India–Bangladesh Treaty of Friendship, Cooperation and Peace. This resulted in my spending the entire night at the printing press, along with the Bangladesh foreign minister, to get the treaty printed. On two occasions, I sought clarifications from Foreign Secretary T.N. Kaul at his hotel. The twenty-five-year validity of the India–Bangladesh Treaty of Friendship, Cooperation and Peace and the Joint Declaration at the end of PM Indira Gandhi's visit were both signed on 19 March 1972, just before her departure from Dacca.

At the Joint Declaration issued at the end of the visit of the Prime Minister of India Mrs Indira Gandhi to Bangladesh, Sheikh Mujib expressed admiration for the 'valiant armed forces of India who made supreme sacrifices in fighting shoulder to shoulder with all sections of the brave Mukti Bahini to end the tyrannical colonial rule of Pakistan in the sacred soil of Bangladesh. He mentioned with appreciation, the impeccable behavior of the Indian troops during their brief stay in Bangladesh.'[11] The visit was truly extraordinary. Begum Mujib, who did not go to the airport even to receive her husband on his return from Pakistan, both welcomed and saw off Indira Gandhi.

During the negotiations in Simla (before the signing of the Simla Agreement), the embassy in Dacca regularly briefed the Bangladesh government on some aspects of the discussions which were taking place in Simla, as the surrender had not been done by the Indian armed forces alone, but by the India–Bangladesh Joint Command. A subtle metamorphosis was observed in the attitude of Bangladesh, both in respect of the trial of Prisoners of

War (POWs) and their return to Pakistan. Bangladesh was then eyeing recognition from Islamic and other countries, and hence on account of these issues their stance was changing.

Indo–Pak Relations during Second Tenure of PM Indira Gandhi (1980–84)

Misperception of India's Views on Afghanistan

Immediately on taking over as prime minister, Indira Gandhi declared at a press conference that India did not support the Soviet action in Afghanistan, adding, 'No country is justified in entering another country.'[12] This was done after there was a perception based on a statement made in the UN General Assembly that India supported the Soviet Union. After the visit of the French President, Valery Giscard d'Estaing, it was stated that '. . . any situation arising out of the use of force in international relations and intervention or interference in the internal affairs of a sovereign state is inadmissible . . .'[13] After the visit of President Brezhnev to India, Indira Gandhi told Parliament that we have expressed our opposition to all forms of outside interference (statement in Parliament on 15 December 1980). Foreign Minister Narsimha Rao communicated India's viewpoints when he expressed that India hopes Soviet troops withdraw from Afghanistan.[14] Indira Gandhi was clearly following an independent policy on Afghanistan.

Joint Commission

India took several initiatives, after the Simla Agreement from 1972–80, to normalize and restore diplomatic communication links, ruptured during the conflicts of 1965 and 1971. Various suggestions were made for consolidation of political, economic and cultural relations. On 26 June 1982, India's draft for an Indo–Pak Joint Commission was handed over to the Pakistan chargé d'affaires in New Delhi. Pakistan's initial reaction was negative. On 1 November 1982, Gen. Ziaul Haq, transiting through New Delhi, met Prime Minister Indira Gandhi. The ministerial-level discussion was led by Indian Foreign Minister Narasimha Rao and Pakistan Finance Minister Ghulam Ishaq Khan. The Pakistan delegation, that also included the powerful chief of staff, Gen. K.M. Arif, was not agreeable to consider a proposal of a joint commission. Surprisingly, in the adjoining room, Gen. Ziaul Haq and Mrs Gandhi agreed to the proposal. A clear example of how many vital decisions have been taken by prime ministers overriding the recommendations and suggestions made to them. The joint press statement issued at the end of the visit stated that an agreement had been reached for the establishment of an India–Pakistan Joint Commission and instructions were issued for rapid conclusion of the modalities and formalities.

The Joint Commission Agreement was signed by the two foreign ministers on 10 March 1983, in the presence of Prime Minister Indira Gandhi and President Ziaul Haq during the 7th Conference of the Heads of State/Government of Non-aligned Countries in New Delhi.

The Joint Commission comprised four subcommissions and held three meetings at Islamabad (1–4 June 1983), New Delhi (2–4 July 1985) and Islamabad (18–19 July 1989). At the meetings of the Joint Commission and its various subcommissions, India repeatedly made several proposals relating to increased people-to-people contacts between the two countries, including freer trade, travel, cultural exchanges, institutional contacts, removal of visa restrictions, facilities for pilgrimages, etc. Pakistan later did not agree to further meetings of both the Joint Commission and its subcommissions.

Proposed Treaty of Peace, Friendship and Cooperation between India and Pakistan

On 15 September 1981, Ambassador Natwar Singh and I went to the foreign office where the Pakistan government gave a statement, the concluding portion of which stated that Pakistan was ready to enter into immediate consultation with India for the purpose of exchanging mutual guarantees of non-aggression and non-use of force in the spirit of the Simla Agreement. On entering the foreign office, we observed a group of correspondents discussing the same statement which was later given to us. The reason behind this was that the U.S. had agreed to give assistance to Pakistan, which was reported under blaring headlines in the *Pakistan Times* the following day on 16 September 1981, 'Positive Turn in Dialogue with U.S.'. On receiving the statement, we reported it was clearly in the context of U.S.–Pak relations that Pakistan had made the suggestion. Two months later, on 22 November 1981, the Pakistan government confirmed their offer of a No War Pact in official notes given both in Islamabad and Delhi. A month later, on 24 December 1981, the Indian ambassador in Islamabad handed over to the Pakistan foreign office a seven-point aide memoire stating the elements of an agreement on non-aggression and no use of force between India and Pakistan. Pakistan responded on 12 January 1982, with a note mentioning their eight elements. This appeared to be a public relations exercise.

Pakistan Foreign Minister Agha Shahi visited Delhi towards the end of January 1982. In a meeting with Pakistani journalists on 30 January 1982, Prime Minister Indira Gandhi suggested a friendship treaty with Pakistan. Later, when this came up during her discussions with Agha Shahi, he interestingly told the chairman of the policy planning committee, G. Parthasarthy, at a breakfast meeting at the latter's residence on 31 January 1982, that Pakistan would not agree to a peace treaty at this stage. However, the press statement issued at the end of his visit on 1 February 1982 stated that officials of the two countries would meet in Islamabad, to continue their exchange of views on the content of the proposed agreement.

Towards the end of May 1982, Natwar Singh, who had taken over as secretary in the ministry of external affairs in March, visited Islamabad. The visit was initially not publicized. He travelled under the name K.N. Singh (initials of his name) and stayed with me rather than at a hotel. At that time, I was chargé d'affaires till the arrival of the new ambassador in July. Journalist M.J. Akbar, travelling on the same flight, was told not to mention anything till a public announcement was made. Natwar Singh was carrying a letter from Prime Minister Indira Gandhi for President Ziaul Haq. Once his meeting was fixed, the visit was no longer confidential. On 31 May 1982, Natwar Singh met President Ziaul Haq and handed over the letter. Prime Minister Indira Gandhi had suggested restarting the process of negotiation. As a first step, she proposed a meeting of the Joint Commission, which would pave the way for discussions on a friendship treaty and No War Pact. During the same visit, Secretary General Shah Nawaz handed over to Secretary Natwar Singh on 1 June 1982, a draft of an 'Agreement on Non-Aggression, Renunciation of Force and Promotion of Good Neighbourly Relations'.

On 11 August 1982, Foreign Secretary Maharaj Krishna Rasgotra, on a visit to Islamabad, gave Pakistan a draft of the Treaty of Peace, Friendship and Cooperation between India and Pakistan. These drafts were discussed during transit visits of President Ziaul Haq to Delhi on 1 November 1982, Foreign Secretary Niaz Naik's visit to Delhi on 22–24 December 1982 and the visit of Foreign Minister Narasimha Rao to Islamabad on 4 June 1983.

It had been agreed that discussions on the draft treaty would take place in Pakistan, during the visit of Foreign Secretary Rasgotra in May 1984. Prior to the visit, I accompanied Rasgotra to a series of preparatory discussions with senior leaders and officials. By this time, after completing my first tenure in Islamabad, I had taken over as joint secretary in MEA looking after Pakistan, Afghanistan and Iran. We met G. Parthasarthy at his house, where Rasgotra asked for Guru Mantra. Along with some good vodka, we got some thoughtful comments. Discussions with Principal Secretary P.C. Alexander at his residence, over a glass of scotch, were useful. We also met visiting governor of Jammu and Kashmir, Jagmohan. Before meeting the PM, we met Foreign Minister Narasimha Rao at his Motilal Nehru Marg residence. He had just returned from a game of badminton. Offering us excellent south Indian coffee, he surprisingly said, 'Meet the PM. She has a sixth sense on Pakistan.' He probably had an idea of what she was going to say. (In retrospect, comparing his remark a decade later with his subsequent precise comments on Pakistan, made me realize how holding the highest office can transform a person's way of thinking.) The meeting with the prime minister in the committee room, adjoining her office in South Block, was on the eve of our departure for Pakistan. Brief, with specific instructions, she told the foreign secretary, 'Go ahead and finalize the Treaty, ensuring two aspects. One emphasizing bilateralism in Article IV and second non-grant of bases in Article V (2).' The instructions were clear-cut.

A seven-member delegation was led by Foreign Secretary Rasgotra to Pakistan from 19–23 May 1984, to discuss the Friendship Treaty/No War Pact. On the first day, 20 May, a protocol on group tourism between India and Pakistan was signed. At a reception after the signing, I introduced Arif Khan as head of the foreign secretary's office to the Pakistan interior secretary. His immediate reaction was that he was not aware that Naik Sahib (Pakistan foreign secretary) had changed his head of office. I clarified that Arif was heading Foreign Secretary Rasgotra's office in the ministry of external affairs in Delhi. Things which felt normal to us came as a surprise for them. With a smirk, Arif moved on. The next day we proceeded to Murree for the talks. Rasgotra had told me that he would separately discuss the two clauses on bilateralism and non-grant of bases with Niaz Naik, while the rest could be sorted out with the Pakistan delegation. This was done without difficulty. In the evening, after completion of our work and while the two foreign secretaries were still engaged in discussions, both delegations went for a walk in the state guest house. Abdul Sattar (later Foreign Minister of Pakistan) apparently had not been told about the two separate levels of discussions. Upset, he said, 'Do they think without us they can sort it out?' Another thing he said has always guided me. Every morning, he said there were a huge number of cipher telegrams to be seen. His criteria was to select those which were short or from important missions, or those which in the first paragraph gave an indication of the content, even if they were long. I found his advice invaluable.

Meanwhile, the two foreign secretaries, as expected, resolved the clause of bilateralism, on the basis of the Simla Agreement, but were unable to find an answer to the main clause of non-grant of bases. Bridging of perceptions and a common text of the non-core articles and the preamble was evolved on an ad hoc referendum basis. However, no agreement could be made on draft Article V (2) regarding non-grant of bases. Gen. Ziaul Haq's first reaction was that he could not bind his successor, but he tried to keep the door open. Rasgotra, in his book, has also written that he had even told Naik in the strictest confidence that if his President wanted the clause to be dropped altogether, he would try and secure his prime minister's agreement to that.[15] I was unaware of this development. However, there were two reasons for Gen. Ziaul Haq's rejections. Rasgotra had already got independent information from a friend in the U.S., which Niaz Naik confirmed, that the Americans were vehemently opposed to the clause as they did not want any future possibility of bases being blocked. Indeed, after 9/11 2001, this proved correct when Musharraf permitted them to use Pakistan territory. The other reason was as developments in Punjab were deteriorating, Ziaul Haq wanted to take advantage, by not giving an impression of agreement with India.

This was the last serious attempt to discuss the Friendship Treaty, though pro forma discussions were held during the visit of Ziaul Haq to India on 17 December 1985, and subsequently at the foreign secretary level.

Siachen Glacier

The conflict in 1984 between India and Pakistan brought the Siachen Glacier into the public domain. The glacier, 76 km long with a width varying from 2 to 8 km, is considered one of the largest glaciers in the world. Beginning from the Indira Col Pass in the west, it runs in a south-eastern direction and is the source of the Nubra River, which flows south to meet the Shyok River. The Karakoram range is to the east and the Saltoro range to the west. Sia La, Bilafond La, Gyong La and Yarma La are the important passes along the Saltoro range. Information regarding this area was discovered in the works of Vigine, who visited Skardu in 1835. The Gazetteer of Kashmir and Ladakh, compiled at the end of the nineteenth century, covers more details. The Indian troops had bravely defended the glacier in temperatures of minus 50 degrees Celsius at an altitude of 20,000 feet. Some strategic thinkers in Pakistan overestimated the inhospitable conditions and costs incurred by India, as a reason for Indian keenness for a settlement in Siachen.

There have been exaggerated accounts of the financial expenditure incurred by India. Initially, the cost of food prepared for the soldiers in those conditions was high, but thereafter the manufacturing costs declined.

Following the 1947–48 Indo–Pak war, the Ceasefire Line (CFL) separating areas under control of the two countries remained valid, even after the 1965 war, when, following the terms of the Tashkent Agreement, both countries withdrew troops to their respective positions on the CFL. The 1971 war changed the situation—the CFL was replaced by the Line of Control (LoC). Both the CFL and LoC terminated in the remote areas of the Karakoram Pass. The point is referred to in the map as NJ9842. According to the Karachi Agreement, the NJ9842 would extend thence north to the glaciers. India's position was that NJ9842 should extend to Sia Kangri, while Pakistan claimed it should join with the Karakoram Pass. The dispute is not about the point where the LoC ends, but about the interpretation beyond NJ9842.

The areas north and east of the NJ9842 have always been under India's administrative control, with our troops located at Daulat Beg Oldi, Sasoma and Zingrulma. Since 1950, Indian troops have regularly patrolled the Siachen area up to the Karakoram Pass. A shift in Pakistan's attitude was first noticed in the 1970s and 1980s, both in respect of cartographic changes and mountaineering expeditions. Pakistani maps surfaced with the unacceptable arbitrary line, from the agreed reference NJ9842, to the Karakoram Pass. They also succeeded in getting their viewpoint published in some foreign journals. The *Times Atlas of the World*, which had earlier shown the LoC going north of the NJ9842, suddenly connected it to the Karakoram Pass. The *American Alpine Journal* in 1982 reported expeditions entering this area sponsored by Pakistan. This was part of a campaign by Pakistan to build their case. An Indian Army expedition led by Colonel Narendra Kumar in 1978 observed these activities, leading to a decision to regularly patrol the area during the summer months. By 1983, India had specific information regarding Pakistan sending aerial photo missions and having snow clothes made. Pakistani attempts to send trained forces for occupation of passes west of Siachen Glacier failed. Under these circumstances, India had to ensure its military presence in its own territory.

The situation as it prevailed before Indian troops were stationed in Siachen has been aptly described by Indian and Pakistani writers. The failed Pakistani attempts at intrusion in the area are described. 'In September–October 1983, a column of Pakistani troops was detected by Indian intelligence as moving toward the Siachen ridge, presumably with the intention of occupying the passes. The Saltoro range—an offshoot of the Karakoram range—is topped by a high ridge punctuated by several passes which offer the only viable route to the Siachen Glacier from Pakistan Occupied Kashmir [POK]. Inclement weather, however, prevented the Pakistani troops from reaching their destination that season,' noted A.G. Noorani in a paper prepared for the Henry L. Stimson Centre in 1994.

Pakistani writer, Zulfikar A. Khan, describes what happened next. 'Pakistan decided to establish a permanent picket at Siachen. To preempt this move, the Indians airlifted a Kumaon battalion by helicopters.'[16] An Indian preemptive strike in Saltoro and Sia La established India's control over its own region. The decisive action was on 13 April 1984, just 3 km short of Bia Fond La. Three days later, the Indian Army established itself at Sia La.

Once the Indian troops re-established themselves in Siachen, instructions from Prime Minister Indira Gandhi were that the Indian troops, after their excellent performance, should have time to consolidate their positions—the substance being that rejoicing should not be converted to celebration immediately. Initially, being a military man, Gen. Ziaul Haq underplayed India's control, knowing it was difficult to dislodge Indian troops. It was only later, when he faced criticism, particularly when Benazir Bhutto returned to Pakistan, that Siachen became an issue.

Hijacking

Unfortunately, in a short span, there was a spate of hijacking incidents during my tenure in Pakistan and thereafter when I was posted to Delhi as head of the Pakistan desk in the MEA. On 29–30 September 1981, an Indian Airlines plane was hijacked to Lahore, followed by another, hijacked by Dal Khalsa in August 1982. On 5 July and 24 August 1984, two more Indian planes were hijacked to Pakistan.

On 29 September 1981, S.R. Datta, the manager of Indian Airlines in Lahore, informed the Indian Embassy in Islamabad at around lunchtime, that the Indian Airlines Boeing flight 423, with 117 passengers on board on the Delhi–Amritsar–Srinagar sector had been hijacked to Lahore. Ambassador Natwar Singh and I promptly met Foreign Secretary Riaz Piracha and boarded the next flight to Lahore, reaching there at 4.30 p.m. First secretaries Ajit Doval (later National Security Adviser) and Vijay Kumar followed by car to Lahore. Immediately on arrival, along with S.R. Datta, I went directly to the hijacked plane and observed passengers moving around in a leisurely way. As we climbed the ladder and entered, a senior Pakistani official who was already in the plane, blocked our further entry, on the grounds that it was not safe, and persuaded us to return. However, in that brief duration, we came away with the distinct impression that the atmosphere in the plane was relaxed and the hijackers were unarmed. This was later verified by the hostages who believed they were only carrying kirpans, though they tried to convey the impression of carrying hand grenades. Ambassador Natwar Singh and I immediately met Lt Gen. Lodhi, corps commander, Lahore, who had been nominated by the Pakistan government to take charge of the hijacking. It was later confirmed that there were five hijackers led by Gajendra Singh.

That evening, at 8.30 p.m., the leader of the hijackers was suddenly brought to the VIP (Very Important Person) room. The Press Trust of India (PTI) correspondent, Arun Kumar, was present and recorded all conversations. A Pakistani official introduced the hijacker to the ambassador. 'This is Gajendra Singh.' Ambassador Natwar Singh, not in favour of talking to the hijacker in the full glare of publicity, asked the security staff to get the room vacated and asked me to speak to the hijacker. Gajendra Singh said slowly in Punjabi,

> The hijacking which we have done is a result of the resentment caused by the arrest of our leader, Sant Jarnail Singh Bhinderwala on September 20, and the jailing of many members of our organization to crush the Khalistan Movement. Earlier we had released women and children. Now we have released all foreigners and some Sikhs who were among the passengers. We want to convey three demands to the Government of India.
> 1) The unconditional release of Sant Jarnail Singh Bhinderwala.
> 2) All members of our organization, Dal Khalsa, who are in jail on charges of treason should be released and sent to Pakistan.
> 3) And a demand of 5 lakh U.S. dollars.

They set a deadline of 10 p.m. the same evening. I asked some questions regarding their demands, their organization and the number of remaining passengers in the plane. I told them their demands would be conveyed to the Government of India. There were high-level discussions in Delhi, and Foreign Secretary Ram Sathe told Ambassador Natwar Singh that force should be used by Pakistan to bring the hijacking to an end. At midnight Ambassador Natwar Singh told Lt Gen. Lodhi to put the heat on. Gen. Lodhi informed him commandos had already been flown in. Early the next morning on 30 September, when breakfast was being served, three hijackers came down to talk to the Pakistan officials and were captured. In the confusion, some passengers also came out of the plane. This happened while Gen. Lodhi was trying to give the impression that a fierce struggle was on. Simultaneously, I entered the room and told the ambassador to congratulate the general as the hijacking was over. The nexus and bonhomie between the hijackers and the Pakistani authorities was obvious to all present. In the evening, at the Chinese National Day reception in Islamabad, Gen. Ziaul Haq informed Ambassador Natwar Singh that the hijackers would be handed over to India after interrogation, but he wanted this information to be kept confidential. In fact, the hijackers were never returned and were used instead to promote the Khalistan movement.[17] The trial carried on endlessly. Ajit Doval covered the trial for an extended period.

(Hijacker Gajendra Singh's recent photo shown standing in front of a gurdwara in Pakistan in newspapers in early September 2022 is proof he is alive and still in Pakistan.)

Hijacking of IC 421 on 24 August 1984

A scheduled Indian Airlines flight from Chandigarh to Jammu was hijacked on 24 August 1984. The commander of the aircraft was forced to land in Lahore at 9.45 a.m., and after refueling, was allowed to take off in the evening at 7.50 p.m. The plane was again refueled in Karachi and eventually landed at Dubai where the hijacking was terminated with the active help of the Government of United Arab Emirates (UAE). By then I had been transferred to Delhi as head of the Pakistan desk. Along with Foreign Secretary Rasgotra, I was present in the meetings in the cabinet secretary's room, from where I came to the foreign secretary's room, and for the next two hours, I was in touch with our ambassadors and authorities in the UAE and neighbouring countries, which could not be ruled out as possible destinations for the hijackers. During the Lahore stopover, the authorities handed over a pistol and some ammunition to the hijackers. This information was later brought to our notice through passengers that included foreign nationals. This was covered by the international media and subsequently confirmed by debriefing of the crew and passengers. Among the passengers was K. Subrahmanyam, then director of the Institute of Defence Studies, who required medication. However, his son, after consulting his mother, confirmed he had enough medication for the next few hours. A decision was taken not to mention his problem, to avoid misuse of information by the hijackers. The UAE authorities repatriated the hijackers to India.

The pistol recovered from the hijackers was handed over by the UAE authorities to the Indian ambassador, Ishrat Aziz, who personally carried it to Delhi, and interestingly, had problems with our immigration and customs authorities on arrival—however, the matter was immediately resolved. Since the pistol was manufactured in Germany, the Central Bureau of Investigation communicated its particulars to Interpol, Wiesbaden in Germany to make necessary inquiries. The following reply received from Interpol is self-explanatory:

BEGINS. REFERENCE YOUR TELEGRAM NO. 681 OF 18.10.1984 CONCERNING HIJACKING OF AN AIRCRAFT COMMITTED ON 24.8.1984 BY KAMALJIT

SINGH SANDHU AND OTHER PERSONS. PLEASE BE INFORMED THAT PISTOL MAKE WALTHER P.P. CALIBRE 7. 65 NO. 445 901 WAS PRODUCED BY THE FIRM 'WALTHER GHBH' P.O. BOX 4325 KARLSTRASSE, 33, D-7900 ULM AND DELIVERED ON 23.9.1975 TOGETHER WITH 74 OTHER PISTOLS. CONSIDER C.A.G. P.O. BOX 1040, ISLAMABAD, PAKISTAN. INTERPOL WIESBADEN. ENDS.

On receiving this information, it was felt that the matter needed to be taken up at a higher level with the consul of the International Civil Aviation Organization (ICAO). A note was sent to Prime Minister Indira Gandhi's office, but even before she could see it, she was assassinated. For a while, her office thought the note had been misplaced and asked us to prepare a duplicate. It transpired that the note was among the files in the box, taken over by the CBI, the day the former prime minister was assassinated. The box was returned much later. The file was put up for approval to the new Prime Minister Rajiv Gandhi. In December 1984, this was formally taken up with the ICAO.

It was pointed out to the ICAO that in the hijacking incident of 24 August 1984, direct and circumstantial evidence conclusively established that instead of terminating the offence at Lahore, Pakistan authorities deliberately contributed towards escalating it. They went to the extent of aiding and abetting the hijackers by providing a pistol and ammunition, which seriously jeopardized the lives of the passengers and safety of the aircraft. The arming of hijackers with an offensive weapon is an unlawful act and is unprecedented on the part of a contracting state of ICAO in the history of civil aviation.

In the 1970s and 1980s, the epicentre of big power tensions moved from Europe to Asia, covering West Asia, Southwest

Asia, South Asia and Southeast Asia. These not only affected our national security environment, but exacerbated our trade, finance and economic difficulties. The Sino–American entente aimed at the Soviet Union had a profound impact on South Asian and Asian security as a whole. The trebling of petroleum prices after the Yom Kippur war in West Asia in October 1973, and the unwillingness of Arab countries to introduce a dual pricing mechanism for friendly developing countries, had a major impact on India. Our oil import bill was twice our foreign exchange reserves, and with the resultant shortage of petroleum-based fertilizers, our food production declined precipitously, inflation soared and social unrest increased. It was also not possible to insulate India–Pakistan relations from the pulls and pressures of Sino–Soviet and Soviet–American competition and confrontations. It was in this challenging environment that Indira Gandhi brilliantly dovetailed and orchestrated our political, strategic, diplomatic, military, intelligence and public relations efforts, leading to the liberation of Bangladesh in December 1971 and the conclusion of the Simla Agreement in July 1972. This was a significant development which gave a new setting to India–Pakistan relations.

In May 1975, Indira Gandhi merged the erstwhile kingdom of Sikkim, which became the twenty-second state of India under the 36th Amendment of the Constitution of India and later the Siachen Glacier in 1984. Her contribution to India's progress will always be remembered.

Despite our reservations about the Soviet invasion of Afghanistan in December 1979, Indira Gandhi maintained close ties with the Soviet Union. At the same time, she accelerated the diversification of our arms procurement with supplies from Europe, reached out to the U.S. and responded constructively to Chinese overtures since 1981 for normalization of Sino–Indian relations. In 1982, she sought to work with Ziaul Haq, for a broader improvement in India–Pakistan relations. Her tragic assassination in October 1984 interrupted these and other initiatives.

President Ziaul Haq, accompanied by his foreign minister, Yaqub Khan, was among the several presidents, vice presidents and prime ministers who attended the funeral of Prime Minister Indira Gandhi on 4 November 1984. After a courtesy meeting with Rajiv Gandhi, Ziaul Haq remarked that he was 'looking forward to a much better, more positive, fruitful, trustful and happy relationship between India and Pakistan in the future'.[18]

3

A Fresh Start Cut Short

Except for Lal Bahadur Shastri's stopover visit in Karachi in 1964, no Indian prime minister had been to Pakistan between Nehru's 19–23 September 1960 visit to Karachi and that of his grandson, Rajiv Gandhi's 16–17 July 1989 visit to Islamabad. Interestingly, Rajiv Gandhi's trip in 1988 to China, to reset Sino–Indian relations, was also the first prime ministerial-level one since 1954. His grandfather Nehru's first and last visit to China as prime minister was in October 1954. Zhou En Lai came to Delhi in April 1960.

Rajiv Gandhi, wanting India–Pak relations to be similarly reset, made efforts both with the military and the newly elected civilian prime minister. His tenure as prime minister in respect of relations with Pakistan can thus be divided into two sections—dealings with Gen. Ziaul Haq (later President) and with Prime Minister Benazir Bhutto. He met President Ziaul Haq and Prime Minister Mohammad Khan Junejo at different venues. There were five meetings with President Zia in 1985 itself, in Moscow (March), New York (October), Muscat (November), Dhaka, (Dacca changed to Dhaka in 1982) (December for the SAARC

summit) and again in New Delhi (December). He met PM
Junejo in New York, Muscat, Dhaka, New Delhi, Bangalore and
Kathmandu. President Venkataraman attended President Zia's
funeral after his death in an air crash in August 1988.

Keen to improve bilateral relations, and with the issue of
Pakistan's support for Sikh militancy uppermost on his mind, Prime
Minister Rajiv Gandhi lost no opportunity in raising his concerns
at every discussion with President Zia and Prime Minister Junejo.

The first SAARC summit, held in Dhaka on 7 December
1985, was attended by both Rajiv Gandhi and President Ziaul
Haq. All heads of state/government were participating in an
exhibition of special postage stamps issued by each member
country. However, while the heads of state/government were
still on a boat ride, prior to the inauguration, we discovered
that Pakistan had wrongly portrayed the border of Jammu and
Kashmir on the postage stamp. I sent a wireless message to our
prime minister's foreign policy aide, Chinmaya Gharekhan, who
was with Rajiv Gandhi on the boat, requesting him to meet me
immediately on his return to Dhaka. Subsequently, the matter was
taken up with the host, President Hussain Muhammad Ershad
of Bangladesh, resulting in the cancellation of the exhibition.
President Zia, however, claimed total ignorance of the content of
the Pakistani stamp. That evening I had a twenty-minute meeting
with PM Rajiv Gandhi in the corridors of the conference venue
on Indo–Pak relations.

The SAARC Charter was signed by heads of state and
government on 8 December 1985, which is observed as SAARC
Day by member states. Article X of the charter states:

1. Decisions at all levels shall be taken on the basis of unanimity.
2. Bilateral and contentious issues shall be excluded from the
   deliberations.[1]

On the return journey to Delhi, I travelled in the prime minister's plane. The security was apprised that I was carrying a packet of giant prawns and hilsa fish, the smell of which if opened could be overwhelming. Once assured these had been purchased personally by then deputy high commissioner, Himachal Som, a food connoisseur, the package was permitted on board.

On arrival at Delhi airport, Chinmaya Gharekhan told me that Rajiv Gandhi, while in the plane, had looked into some files, including some on diplomatic assignments abroad. I had at that time, at my request, been posted to Hungary. Two days later, I was informed that while my appointment to Hungary stood, I should be moved out of Delhi only after the current India–Pakistan talks had concluded. As a result, I remained in Delhi till the latter half of 1986. The administration division in the MEA was unhappy, as Budapest remained without an ambassador for over a year.

On 17 December, President Ziaul Haq stopped by in Delhi on his way home after visiting some countries in the region. I was asked to jot down the salient points of the discussion, which later got transformed into a brief statement by Minister of External Affairs Bali Ram Bhagat in Parliament. The main points were:

(1) The finance ministers of the two countries will meet in Islamabad, from 5 to 7 January 1986 to consider agreements on expansion of trade and economic relations.

(2) The foreign secretaries of the two countries will meet in Islamabad in the third week of January 1986, to continue discussions on a comprehensive treaty and to discuss other confidence-building measures.

(3) The four subcommissions set up under the Indo–Pak Joint Commission will meet towards the end of January/ early February 1986 to finalize their work. The full Joint

Commission led by the respective foreign ministers will
meet towards the end of February 1986.

(4) The two sides have agreed to work out an agreement
whereby each will undertake not to attack the nuclear
installations of the other.

(5) A cultural agreement will be signed between the two
countries.

(6) All the above measures will culminate in the visit of the
prime minister to Pakistan during the first half of 1986.

In January 1986, I accompanied Foreign Secretary Romesh
Bhandari on a visit to Pakistan. While in Peshawar, I heard on TV
that the Pakistan Muslim League had passed a resolution stating
relations between India and Pakistan could be normalized only after
the Kashmir issue was settled on the basis of the UN Resolution.
Prime Minister Junejo was the elected chairman of the Muslim
League. This matter was taken up with President Ziaul Haq and
PM Junejo, who tried to underplay it. Junejo said we should go
ahead with the opening of the Khokhrapar–Munabao rail link on
the Sindh–Rajasthan border. Interestingly, after he left the room,
Foreign Secretary Niaz Naik told us not to follow up on his prime
minister's suggestions for the time being. It was clear that the army
and security agencies were not in favour of the proposal, which
Junejo, hailing from Sindh, wanted. There were several other
exchanges, including a meeting of the finance ministers.

Prime Minister Rajiv Gandhi held intensive interactions with
Pakistan leaders. On 16 November 1986, he met Prime Minister
Junejo during the Bangalore SAARC summit and proposed
measures by both sides to resolve problems of illicit crossing,
drug trafficking, smuggling and terrorism. In October 1987,
India initiated talks with Pakistan on resolving differences on the
Tulbul Navigation Project in Jammu and Kashmir.

On 20 January 1988, Rajiv Gandhi visited Peshawar for ninety minutes following the demise of Khan Abdul Ghaffar Khan. Sonia Gandhi, P.V. Narasimha Rao, minister of human resources development, Buta Singh, home minister, Mohsina Kidwai, minister of urban development, Saroj Khaparde, minister of state for health, P. Chidambaram, minister of state for internal security, Khurshid Alam Khan, former minister of state, Muhammad Yunus, chairman Trade Fair Authority of India (TFAI), Mani Shankar Aiyar and Ronen Sen accompanied the prime minister.

Rajiv Gandhi's decision to visit Peshawar to pay his last respects to Badshah Khan was immediate and spontaneous. He did not seek any analysis of the pros and cons, and his approach was that when he had made up his mind, it was for the others in the team to sort out the details.

The major concern was about his personal security, in the backdrop of the threat by Khalistani groups, the near fatal attack by a Sri Lankan Army man during the farewell guard of honour ceremony the previous year, the uncertain security environment in Khyber Pakhtunkhwa (NWFP), no advance intimation to the Pakistan government for security arrangements, or even for VVIP flight clearance, etc. Secretary (security) T.N. Seshan made impassioned pleas and a strong last-minute attempt at the airfield to stop the visit, but he was brushed aside.

There was a special Air India 747 aircraft readied for the PM's visit to Stockholm for the Six Nation Nuclear Disarmament Conference. Most delegation members were kept waiting at the technical area of the Delhi airport while Rajiv Gandhi took off for Peshawar in a smaller Indian Air Force special aircraft. It was only after the takeoff that the flight clearance was sought at the last moment from Pakistan. Before leaving, Rajiv Gandhi declared a five-day state mourning in India. He later thanked President Zia for the flight clearance.[2]

Immediately on landing in Peshawar, PM Rajiv Gandhi and party were taken straight to where Bacha Khan's body lay. He offered the Janazah prayer (*Salat al–Janazah*) next to the coffin. He offered condolences to the bereaved family, after which they went on to another venue for tea with senior local government officials. On returning to Delhi airport, Rajiv Gandhi immediately enplaned for Stockholm. This was the only visit of an Indian prime minister to Peshawar. PM Jawaharlal Nehru visited Peshawar in the 1940s and PM Manmohan Singh had attended school there. This visit at short notice without pre-security precautions can only be compared to the sudden visit of Prime Minister Modi to Lahore to meet Nawaz Sharif, twenty-seven years later in 2015.

SAARC Summit

During Prime Minister Rajiv Gandhi's visit to Pakistan for the fourth SAARC summit (29–31 December 1988), India and Pakistan signed the agreement on prohibition on attack on nuclear installations and facilities (this had been proposed by Rajiv Gandhi to President Zia in December 1985, later ratified in January 1991 and came into force in January 1992). In addition, two agreements on cultural cooperation and avoidance of double taxation of income derived from international air transport were signed.

The discussions between 1985 and 1989 covered, inter alia, Pakistan's covert nuclear weapons programme, its support to militants/separatists in Punjab and Jammu and Kashmir, Siachen, border security and military confidence building measures (CBMs), the promotion of bilateral trade, transportation, communications and cultural links.

Rajiv Gandhi was not happy with the response from Pakistan, which is clear from his statement in the Lok Sabha on 20 April 1988,

We proposed a treaty of peace and friendship. We proposed an agreement on non-attack on nuclear facilities. We have proposed discussions on new ground rules on the border. We have proposed an MOU on hijacking. We proposed MOU on air space violations by military aircraft. We proposed expansion of private trade. We have proposed a move to non-discriminatory regime and MFN treatment. Indo–Pakistan joint ventures have been proposed [including an] exchange of writers, of intellectuals, troupes, films, drama, music, dances. We have proposed the exchange of books, periodicals and newspapers. We have proposed many other confidence-building and risk-reduction measures as mutually agreed. On the other hand, Pakistan forestalls people to people programmes. They pursue what is very obviously a nuclear weapons programme. They assume hostile postures in areas such as Siachen and they allow their territory to be used for the support, maintenance and sanctuary of terrorists and separatists.[3]

Rajiv Gandhi was effusive in his greeting to Benazir Bhutto on 2 December 1988 when she assumed the office of prime minister. 'You and I are both children of the same era . . . I would wish to work closely with you for removing the irritants which have needlessly vitiated relations between our countries in the past.' Striking a personal bond, he said, 'The Simla Agreement signed by your father and my mother, provides the basis of our building together a relationship of mutual trust and friendship, which promotes peace and co-operation between our countries in our time and in generations to come.'[4] However, at her press conference the following day, PM Benazir Bhutto debunked the talks with India about the no war pact and accused the military regime of treating India as an elder brother instead of maintaining the relations on an equal basis. There was a marked difference in the public statements of Rajiv Gandhi and Benazir Bhutto.

Back-Channel Talks with Pakistan during the Tenure of Rajiv Gandhi with President Zia and PM Benazir Bhutto

Back-channel R&AW–ISI Talks on Line of Control (LoC)/Siachen

Rajiv Gandhi had close personal relations with King Hussein of Jordan. Both shared interests in flying and driving. His brother, then Crown Prince Hassan, considered a one-man think tank in Jordan, was widely respected. During one of their informal freewheeling talks, the king mentioned two factors which he felt could be used to bring India and Pakistan together—Prince Hassan's friendship with General Ziaul Haq, during the latter's posting in Jordan in the 1970s (before the army coup in Pakistan) and Hassan's wife, Sarvath's family ties with Pakistan and India. Rajiv Gandhi welcomed the idea.

After President Ziaul Haq, adroitly sidelined India from playing a major role in Afghanistan and the signing of the April 1988 Geneva Accords that continued U.S. arm supplies, President Zia took the initiative to request Crown Prince Hassan to facilitate and host back-channel talks between Director General ISI Lt Gen. Hamid Gul and Secretary R&AW, A.K. Verma in Amman.

Rajiv Gandhi agreed and entrusted the initial task of working out the details (assumed names and dates, etc.) to his aide, Ronen Sen, in consultation with Crown Prince Hassan. There was a subsequent meeting in Geneva. Just before his death, A.K. Verma summed up the outcome of the Amman and Geneva discussions and Hamid Gul by writing, 'The final agreement between the two Intelligence Chiefs envisaged: a) withdrawal of the Pakistani forces to the west to the ground level of the Saltoro Mountains b) giving up of Pakistani claims to territory from NJ9842 to the Karakoram Pass c) the Line of Control to run North from NJ9842 along the western ground level of Saltoro exactly North till the Chinese border and d) reduction of Pakistani troops strength by two divisions with some corresponding adjustments on the Indian side.'[5]

The agreed line was delineated on a Pakistan GHQ map and handed over by Hamid Gul to A.K. Verma with President Zia's approval. The Indian ministry of defence was asked to look into this in detail, so as to enable its processing at the operational/official level by both sides and subsequently at the political level. However, just when delegations led by defence secretaries were to meet, the process was brought to an abrupt end with President Zia's death in an air crash in August 1988. If the line agreed to had been ratified at the intergovernmental level, it would have been a major politico-strategic step forward, which would have been relevant not only for peace and tranquility along the India–Pakistan LoC in Jammu and Kashmir but also in a crucial sector of India–China border areas. This was not to be, since there was real or feigned ignorance at all levels in Pakistan about the existence of such an agreement. As a result, the subsequent discussions between Rajiv Gandhi and Benazir Bhutto were bereft of strategic content, with the focus narrowed to just a Siachen settlement on the basis of mutual force withdrawal from recorded actual ground position locations (AGPLs) and establishment of a jointly monitored demilitarized zone (DMZ). During these discussions, Yaqub Khan appeared to be less ambivalent and more pragmatic than Benazir Bhutto.

There were confidential exchanges at other levels. Rajiv
Gandhi agreed to Benazir Bhutto's proposal for continued
interaction between Ronen Sen and her designated representative,
her cabinet-level national security and foreign affairs adviser, Iqbal
Akhund, and her businessman friend, Daryus Happy Minwala
whom she had appointed as ambassador-at-large. Her friend and
personal lobbyist in the U.S., Peter Galbraith, was also allowed
access to Rajiv Gandhi. On our side, for a while, diplomat Aftab
Seth kept in informal touch with her.

Ronen Sen had a one-to-one meeting with Benazir Bhutto in
Karachi in December 1988 at short notice when he travelled on
a border security force (BSF) aircraft. At the outset, she signalled
that the meeting room was likely to be bugged and that sensitive
issues would be communicated by handwritten exchanges on a
notepad passed back and forth while discussions for the record
could continue simultaneously. At the end of the meeting, she
asked him not to record or circulate her personal remarks meant for
Rajiv Gandhi. It was conveyed to her that our agencies had major
concerns about the security threat to Rajiv Gandhi in Pakistan
and our need for ironclad guarantees in this regard. If something
untoward happened, an Indo–Pak conflict could not be ruled out.
Rajiv Gandhi's desire to make a new beginning with Pakistan after
the restoration of democracy was also conveyed. Both sides should
have a forward-looking agenda while resolving differences on the
basis of the Simla Agreement. Benazir was in complete agreement
on the surface, but pointed out the objections she faced from the
military and intelligence set-up in Pakistan. India's concerns about
Pakistan's accelerated programme on development of nuclear
warheads and delivery system were conveyed. Benazir claimed that
the military establishment, which was in control of this programme,
had kept her out of the loop. She said an agreement on non-attack
on nuclear installations was going to be helpful. Another concern

was about terrorism emanating from Pakistan. Benazir said that an agreement in the SAARC framework may be easier than in the bilateral context. It was also conveyed to her that despite India being on the receiving end of infiltration and terrorism, Rajiv Gandhi would be amenable to liberal India–Pakistan travel arrangements, to encourage people-to-people ties, thereby broadening the base of stakeholders in peace in civil society, media, cultural, trade and economic spheres in both countries. Benazir Bhutto agreed but said that to begin with, only some categories should be considered and that too within the SAARC framework. She was told that we would let them decide on the scope and pace they felt comfortable with.

Detailed talks took place in the margins of the fourth SAARC summit in Islamabad in December 1998, between Prime Ministers Benazir Bhutto and Rajiv Gandhi. To review the progress in implementation of decisions taken at Islamabad and in preparation for Rajiv Gandhi's visit to Pakistan, Ronen Sen visited Islamabad as special envoy again to meet Prime Minister Bhutto. High Commissioner Dixit was present at this meeting at her official residence in Islamabad. In a brief, private aside at that time, she confided that she continued to face strong resistance from President Ghulam Ishaq Khan and Army Chief Aslam Beg with respect to her India and Afghanistan policies.

Rajiv Gandhi's landmark bilateral visit to Islamabad, from 16–17 July 1989, was rich in symbolism, and the talks with Prime Minister Bhutto and President Ghulam Ishaq Khan were cordial and constructive. However, the prospect of a Siachen settlement, on the basis of the earlier back-channel understanding on extending the LoC in Jammu and Kashmir beyond NJ9842, appeared remote. Yet there was incremental progress in normalization of our bilateral relations in the diplomatic, defence, economic, cultural, agricultural and other areas. The meetings of the joint commissions were resumed after a gap of five years.

People-to-people exchanges were facilitated by a significant easing of visa restrictions. India cleared the way for Pakistan to rejoin the Commonwealth, which it did on 1 October 1989. There were exchanges of visits by India's External Affairs Minister P.V. Narasimha Rao and his Pakistani counterpart Yaqub Khan.

The impression given by those involved in these talks was that Prime Minister Benazir Bhutto took a stronger stand on some important issues than President Zia and her ex-military foreign minister, Yaqub Khan. This assessment was confirmed during her subsequent tenure, when she put the India–Pakistan dialogue on hold and stayed away from the New Delhi SAARC summit in 1995. This attitude of Yaqub Khan is at variance with his discussions with I.K. Gujral. Perhaps Yaqub Khan was reflecting the views of the army.

The next meeting between Prime Ministers Rajiv Gandhi and Bhutto was during the seventh nonaligned summit in Belgrade in September 1989. There was, as expected, no headway made in the meeting at that time between Akhund and Sen, who later conveyed to Akhund that the dialogue on Siachen and the extension of the LoC beyond NJ9842 could be resumed only after the general elections in India.

Ronen Sen, who accompanied Foreign Minister P.V. Narasimha Rao for the Commonwealth Heads of Government Meeting (CHOGM) meeting in Malaysia in December 1989, had a long one-to-one meeting with Benazir Bhutto at the retreat for delegation leaders in Langkawi. She regretted the 'pause in progress' in India–Pakistan relations due to Rajiv Gandhi's electoral preoccupation, as her room to manoeuvre was being increasingly restricted, due to hostility and a 'conspiracy being hatched' against her. She confided she had made a mistake in taking on the military and drug mafia simultaneously and added (very presciently) that she may even be ousted by the autumn of next year.

Following the defeat of Rajiv Gandhi in the election, V.P. Singh became prime minister. He had no time for foreign affairs due to his preoccupation with domestic political developments. His was a continuation of Rajiv Gandhi's policy. Chandra Shekhar too did not pay much attention to foreign affairs and was constrained by remote control from 10, Janpath. However, Prime Minister Chandra Shekhar had a useful one-to-one meeting with Nawaz Sharif during the November 1990 SAARC summit in Malé. He arranged to send a copy of the Indian Constitution updated with latest amendments to Nawaz Sharif, whose specific interest lay in the powers of the President, through confidential channels in the Gulf. When I met Nawaz Sharif, after taking over as high commissioner to Pakistan in January 1992, he described his meeting with Chandra Shekhar as one of the best.

My last interaction with Rajiv Gandhi was when he came to Budapest on an official visit where I was posted as ambassador. While I was escorting him to one of the meetings, he said, 'I have not been able to discuss Pakistan with you—there have been several developments.'

Rajiv Gandhi's untimely death took place while I was posted as consul general to San Francisco. In addition to the normal condolence book in the consulate, a candlelit march was held a few days later, attended by a large number of Indians and Americans. He held no office at the time of his death.

I distinctly recall a conversation I had with an elderly lady who came to condole. She said she was sorry at the passing away of young Rajiv Gandhi and inquired why dignitaries such as the U.S. vice president and Prince Charles were attending his funeral in Delhi, considering he was no longer the prime minister.

I responded it was out of respect for Rajiv Gandhi. She said a prayer and left flowers beside Rajiv Gandhi's photograph.

4

Deft Handling Amidst Surging Challenges

After Rajiv Gandhi's untimely demise, the choice for the new leader of the Congress party fell on Pamulaparti Venkata Narasimha Rao. On 29 May 1991, the Working Committee of the then 105-year-old party elected him unanimously as its president. The following days witnessed lobbying for the office of the prime minister. Rao was sworn in as prime minister on 21 June. On 22 June, in his first address to the nation, he spoke about problems facing the country—Punjab, Kashmir, Assam, communal violence and the acute economic situation. Stating, 'there is no time to lose',[1] he started working in earnest to resolve the issues. With the priority to save the economy, he appointed Dr Manmohan Singh as finance minister.

Narasimha Rao wanted Pakistan to stop support to both the Khalistan movement in Punjab and Kashmir militancy. Despite the fall of the Babri Masjid, the Mumbai blast and constant changes of government in Pakistan, he maintained the policy of engagement, suggesting new ideas. He met Nawaz Sharif on six different occasions—Harare (October 1991), Colombo (SAARC meeting December 1991), Davos (February 1992), Rio (Earth summit, June 1992), Jakarta (10th NAM meeting, September 1992) and Dhaka (April 1993, SAARC summit), where he raised the issue of the Memon family.

With his experience of dealing with Pakistan, Prime Minister Narasimha Rao told the Indian Parliament on 18 September 1991, 'Every time there was a change of government either in Pakistan or India there is a sense of euphoria created and some new hopes are aroused.'[2] He did not expect much, as India had not been successful in persuading Pakistan to improve relations up to then.

Convinced of the need for a direct back channel, Narasimha Rao wanted a messenger, a receptor of messages—not someone who had the background, seniority or experience to respond to or initiate messages on their own. Pakistan Foreign Secretary Shahryar Khan met Narasimha Rao, one-on-one when he visited Delhi as special envoy of his prime minister, in August 1991. After the meeting, Narasimha Rao informed his private secretary, Ramu Damodaran, that he had been designated to be the point of contact. Shahryar Khan, however, made contact with A.N. Verma, principal secretary, some weeks later, having confused principal with private. In any case, this did not materialize. The advantage that Narasimha Rao had was that when he took over as prime minister, he was fully aware of what had happened in the past and knew that Rajiv Gandhi had made good use of his adviser, Ronen Sen, as the back-channel negotiator. Eventually at the insistence of Nawaz Sharif to have back-channel talks, unknown to others, he appointed R.L. Bhatia as the Indian interlocutor. He told his private secretary that he wanted the next high commissioner of his choice to also act as the back-channel negotiator.

In his Independence Day address at Red Fort on 15 August 1994, Narasimha Rao, in respect of Pakistan, said, 'With you, without you, in spite of you, Kashmir will remain an integral part of India.'

Taking a deep interest in issues related to J & K, he worked hard to ensure that elections were held, which eventually took place just after he demitted office. He wanted the newly created separatist group to be kept under control, by trying to involve them in mainstream politics. His speech from Burkina Faso, promising autonomy and his famous words, 'Sky's the limit' won many hearts in Kashmir. At the same time, he was firm. During his tenure, the Parliament resolution of 1994 was passed, which reiterated the Indian stand on Pakistan Occupied Kashmir (POK), urging Pakistan to vacate areas under its illegal control.

My first contact with Narasimha Rao was in June 1981. On my first posting to Pakistan as deputy chief of mission, he visited Islamabad as minister of external affairs, and I had several occasions to interact with him. The visit resulted in a diffusion of tension. In Karachi, addressing the Pakistan Institute of International Affairs, he said, 'It is not unusual to find next door neighbours not being on talking terms for a while but neighbourness prevails in the end. This is the experience.' He addressed a select group in Rawalpindi in Urdu, over which he had an excellent command. Though the audience was impressed, Narasimha Rao was not. After leaving the meeting, he told me he was under the impression that the deliberations would be in Urdu, but found more use of 'Punjabi'. Four Indian prime ministers spoke better Urdu than their counterparts—Narasimha Rao, I.K. Gujral, Atal Bihari Vajpayee and Manmohan Singh. In fact, it is now being lamented in Pakistan that 'Urdu is becoming a dying language'. Fakir Syed Aijazuddin, Pakistani historian and commentator, wrote, 'In 1947, our founding fathers had hoped that Urdu would be the adhesive that would bind our provincial disparities together. The separation of East Pakistan in 1971 put paid to that. Since then, regional languages such as Punjabi, Pashto, Sindhi, Balochi or dialects like Saraiki, Hindko and Brahui, to name a few have struggled for air.'[3]

A reception hosted by External Affairs Minister Rao in Lahore introduced him to various sections of Punjab society. Among his guests was Nawaz Sharif, then finance minister of Punjab. A few weeks later, Nawaz Sharif thanked me for the khadi silk material presented to him, saying he had had it stitched as a salwar kameez. I corrected him saying it was a gift from the foreign minister. When he laughingly said that the foreign minister could hardly remember all guests present at such a large reception, I responded that he never forgot his special guests. None could have predicted at that time that both would be counterpart prime ministers a decade later.

Narasimha Rao visited Pakistan on four other occasions as minister of external affairs—in June 1984 for the Indo–Pak Joint Commission meeting, in December 1988, he accompanied Rajiv Gandhi on his visit to Islamabad for the SAARC summit and later a bilateral visit to Islamabad in July 1989, when he stayed on for a foreign minister-level visit for the third meeting of the Joint Commission. He accompanied Rajiv Gandhi on his ninety-minute visit to Peshawar (January 1988) to condole the death of the 'Frontier Gandhi', Khan Abdul Ghaffar Khan, and later with President Venkataraman to Islamabad in August 1988, to attend the funeral of President Zia, this being the only visit of a President of India to Pakistan. During these visits, he travelled to all provincial capitals (Lahore, Karachi and Peshawar) except Quetta. He did not visit Pakistan as prime minister.

Narasimha Rao was foreign minister when I was joint secretary in charge of the division dealing with Pakistan, Afghanistan and

Iran in the MEA on my return to India. As such, I worked closely with him. There was proximate interaction also when I was deputy secretary general of the nonaligned summit and later coordinator of the Common Wealth Heads of Government (CHOGM), both held in 1983. On meeting him before my departure in August 1986 for Budapest as ambassador to Hungary, he was warm and laughingly said I was a one-country man. In the same spirit, I responded, 'Sir, don't say this loudly as it will ruin my professional career.' He added, 'Loudly I will always say you are good for everywhere.'

From Hungary I was posted to San Francisco as consul general, and while on home leave to India in August 1991, I received an invite for a lunch hosted by PM Narasimha Rao, who had recently taken over the office. The lunch was in honour of Karimov, President of the Soviet Republic of Uzbekistan. Some senior officials advised Narasimha Rao not to host a lunch for the head of a Soviet republic. Anticipating the disintegration of the Soviet Union, Narasimha Rao decided to go ahead with the lunch, the only exception being there were no formal speeches. After lunch, the PM asked me to see him before I left Delhi.

At the meeting his queries were on Pakistan and U.S.–Pakistan relations. I said that being on the West Coast, I was not fully conversant with the latest developments but shared my views with him. I informed him that the foreign secretary had agreed to my request for an extension of my tenure in San Francisco to enable my children to complete their schooling. When asked why he had agreed, I said that it was in appreciation for spearheading the establishment of two chairs of Indian Studies at the University of California at Berkeley, financed by the Indian community. Surprisingly, he had been apprised of this by some Indian academicians in the U.S. He was quiet for some time, then wished me success. After the meeting his private secretary,

Ramu Damodaran, inquired whether any other discussion had taken place. When I said no, he appeared surprised. This was in August 1991.

On 1 October 1991, I received a call in San Francisco from Ramu Damodaran. In hushed tones Ramu said that the PM had decided to post me as high commissioner to Pakistan and wanted my response within the next twenty-four hours. Ramu was the prime minister's trusted aide, having earlier been his private secretary when Narasimha Rao was minister of external affairs, home, defence and human resources development, and was treated like a member of the family.

At that time veteran journalist Inder Malhotra and his wife were our houseguests. Ambassador Abid Hussain arrived from Washington the same day to attend the inauguration of the chair of Indian Studies at Berkeley. The following evening, I hosted a dinner for Ambassador Hussain, the only other guests being Shankar Bajpai (former envoy to Pakistan and the United States and at that time teaching at Berkeley), his wife Meera, and our houseguests. It proved to be interesting. Discussions ranged from U.S. history, literature, Indo–U.S. relations to U.S.–Mexico relations. At the end a toast was raised by both Abid Hussain and Shankar Bajpai. Inder Malhotra added that following my handling of Pakistan for several years, he hoped Islamabad would be my next destination. My wife and I exchanged glances, concerned about whether he had overheard the conversation with Ramu. Later we realized that this was not possible as our bedrooms were far apart and the conversation had taken place in muted tones.

Though I was happy to get the offer, there was some disappointment within the family as my tenure was being cut short. Normally, children joined a neighbourhood school. Our daughter had been selected to join Lowell High School, where admission was on merit. Graduates from Lowell were ensured admission in good universities in America, and according to regulations at that time, fees for children of diplomats posted in California were considerably less. Once the family agreed to the Pakistan posting, I conveyed my acceptance. As compensation, I took the family for an enjoyable holiday to Hawaii.

As I was told to keep this information to myself, I did not share it with Ambassador Abid Hussain. When he was told later, he understood. While we were in Hawaii, the Indian papers carried a report on my posting to Pakistan, which came as a total surprise even to our family in India. This was the first diplomatic head of mission appointment made by the new prime minister.

On Christmas Day 1991, we left San Francisco for India with a brief stay in New York followed by a halt in Switzerland to attend my cousin Yogini's wedding. In Delhi, there were extensive briefings on Pakistan with government and non-government organizations and individuals. Prime Minister Narasimha Rao made it clear that his immediate priorities were stabilizing the Indian economy and bringing normality to relations with Pakistan.

While every ambassador carries credentials from the President formally appointing him as his envoy, I was, in addition, carrying a personal letter from Prime Minister Narasimha Rao for Prime Minister Nawaz Sharif which read, 'This note is just to tell you that Sati Lambah whom I am sending as our High Commissioner to Pakistan enjoys my personal confidence.' This message indicated that discussions in the back channel could be shared with me.

The appointment of an ambassador or high commissioner is by diplomatic concurrence conveyed to the country of assignment for the request of an agreement. Deputy high commissioner, M.K. Bhadrakumar, was at Islamabad airport awaiting the arrival of the Czech prime minister. It was the practice at that time for all heads of mission to be present when a foreign head of government visited. When Nawaz Sharif saw the acting high commissioner, he asked when India was sending its next high commissioner. Bhadrakumar apprised him that an agreement was awaited for S.K. Lambah. Nawaz Sharif inquired, 'You mean Satinder Lambah?' When affirmed, he said it would be given by the evening. That same evening, Foreign Secretary Shahryar Khan informed Bhadrakumar he should consider the formal agreement as having been given today, though it would take two days to convey it in writing. This was a sign of a warm welcome in Pakistan.

I arrived in Islamabad in mid-January 1992. Soon thereafter, the date of presentation of credentials was fixed. I got a call from the prime minister's office extending an invitation for lunch after the credential ceremony, for me, my wife and children, Vikram and Diya. This was unusual. Though I had known Nawaz Sharif during my earlier posting in Islamabad before he joined active politics and had remained in touch with him, the situation had changed, as he was now prime minister.

Priorities of Narasimha Rao on Taking Over as PM

India's relations with Pakistan impinged upon every other major relationship: internal (Jammu and Kashmir), multilateral United Nations Human Rights Council (UNHRC), bilateral (U.S.) and disarmament Comprehensive Nuclear-Test-Ban Treaty (CTBT) among others. The prime minister's first major foreign policy decision—the resumption of relations with Israel—was anchored in the same premise as his attitude to Pakistan. The constant preoccupation with how the Muslim population in India would react had become less relevant.

The priorities of Narasimha Rao on India's neighbourhood included China, where he wanted consolidation of the gains made during Rajiv Gandhi's visit there. In respect of Nepal, he wanted to undo the perceived damage caused by the trade and technology blockage. In Sri Lanka, he wanted to preserve the progress achieved by the 13th Amendment as a result of the Indo–Sri Lanka Accord (ISLA) Agreement of 1987, but isolated Sri Lanka to the degree possible from the domestic and political fallout of Tamil Nadu. Iran was also among his priority considerations. In respect of Afghanistan, he did not wish to immediately do anything in view of the fluid situation. He realized improvement in relations with Pakistan would be difficult immediately after President Zia's death, in view of the civil–military differences in that country, yet progress in this field was one of his priorities. Relations with the U.S. were uppermost on his mind too. He took great interest in understanding the role of Jewish-American organizations, and was keen to establish full diplomatic relations with Israel.

A transformation in Pakistan's Kashmir policy began even before Narasimha Rao became prime minister. During the 1970s and 1980s, Pakistan was involved in issues concerning the aftermath of the disintegration of the country in 1971, followed by developments in Afghanistan. With focus primarily on assistance to Khalistan rebels in India, initially only rhetorical references to UN resolutions were made. But developments in Jammu and Kashmir in the late 1980s led to Pakistan taking advantage of the evolving circumstances. A metamorphosis of policy in the handling of Kashmir happened to coincide with civilian rule in Pakistan. Those now in power wanted to project an inflexible attitude on Kashmir to justify their existence. But the basic policy, regardless of different civilian regimes, was determined by the army. The Pakistani viewpoint, articulated by Ahmed Rashid, a Pakistani journalist and bestselling foreign policy author, was that the Pakistan government was taken by surprise at the developments in Kashmir in the late 1980s. This perspective was supported by then U.S. ambassador in Pakistan, Oakley.[4] The state of affairs provoked President Ghulam Ishaq Khan to repeat the earlier slogan of Kashmir being the 'unfinished agenda of Partition'. Benazir, as prime minister, convened a meeting of military and POK leaders, which included General Aslam Beg, to ascertain how they could take advantage of conditions in J & K. According to Robert Wirsing,[5] an American writer, they wanted to be careful so that the situation did not 'boomerang on Pakistan'. A decision to curb the Azadi forces was taken. She held a meeting with all political leaders and made the Pakistan Parliament, at a joint sitting, adopt a unanimous resolution on Kashmir on 10 February 1990. On 13 March, after addressing a meeting in POK and a joint session of the POK assembly and council, in a public speech, she referred to a 'thousand-year war'. On 24 May 1990, Benazir rejected the idea of an independent Kashmir, believing it would be dangerous for the region.[6] After her dismissal, Nawaz Sharif resumed the rhetoric and chanted the slogan, 'Kashmir banyega Pakistan' (Kashmir will become a part of Pakistan).

Narasimha Rao had to deal with several aspects of Pakistan's emerging Kashmir policy when he took over as prime minister of India. First, India had to reckon with Pakistan's assistance to Kashmiri militants through jihadi organizations with army support. These included the United Jihad Council led by Syed Salahuddin, an umbrella organization of fourteen small groups active in POK, including Al-Badar and Tehrik-e-Jihad. Organizations like Lashkar-e-Tayyab (established 1987), the so-called Army of the Pure in Urdu, and Harkat-ul Ansar (established 1993) and Hizb-ul-Mujahideen (established in 1989) were also active. Pakistan encouraged and indoctrinated jihadi groups to take advantage of the developing situation in J & K by providing them sophisticated weapons.[7] Following the collapse of the Soviet Union, the Pakistan authorities were hopeful that India would meet a similar fate. Victoria Schofield, a British author, quoting[8]

Azam Inquilabi, a senior separatist leader, in March 1994, wrote, 'We can establish military training camps there (in POK) and we have been doing it.'[9] When she visited India in 2018, she confirmed to me the presence of these training camps. Second, the new policy on Kashmir was to dilute the Simla Agreement and increase rhetorical references to UN resolutions. President Ghulam Ishaq Khan, in his address to the joint session of Parliament on 2 December 1989, referred to the UN resolution. The third element was strongly worded critical speeches and public statements on Kashmir.

Another important aspect of Pakistan's new policy was to make all-out attempts to internationalize the Kashmir issue. These included calling a conference of Pakistani envoys, raising the matter at the UN and other international conferences, the establishment of the Kashmir Committee of the National Assembly and sending delegations to different regions of the world to apprise them of the situation. This yielded some results. The European Community passed a resolution on 12 March 1992 supporting the right of self-determination in Kashmir. The Swedish Parliament expressed its 'deepest concern' on the human rights situation in Kashmir. It also attracted backing from British parliamentarians, like Lord Avebury.

There was support for Pakistan from the U.S. President Clinton, in his address to the UN General Assembly in September 1993, when he referred to Kashmir being 'a trouble spot where bloody ethnic religious war ranges'.[10] The U.S. statement on Kashmir, made by U.S. assistant secretary of state for South Asian affairs, Robin Raphel in October 1993, caused worry in India, 'We view Kashmir as a disputed territory and that means we do not recognize the instrument of accession as meaning that Kashmir is forevermore an integral part of India.'[11] Immediately thereafter she visited Pakistan. On the day of her arrival, U.S. Ambassador Monjo hosted a dinner, where I too was invited. Prior to coming to Pakistan, she had messaged Ambassador Monjo, asking to arrange a meeting with me. She told me at our meeting she had been misquoted. I said as she had made the statement publicly, the clarification should also be made in public, rather than in private. She agreed. At the dinner she appeared perturbed. After her speech she raised a toast, but much to the chagrin of those present, she said India instead of Pakistan, but hurriedly corrected herself. This slip, however, prompted the chief Pakistani guest, interior minister, Babar, to humorously comment that this was undoubtedly the doing of the Indian high commissioner, who had been observed talking to her just prior to entering the dining room.[12]

Narasimha Rao adeptly countered Pakistani actions on Kashmir in manifold ways. He handled them at both an international and regional level by depriving Pakistan of support from the USA, China and Iran, on crucial occasions. By the end of 1993, there was a U.S. tilt towards India. Robin Raphel, who had made the controversial statement challenging the instrument of accession, now denied it. To quote her, 'It is time to move forward, not to look at past prescriptions but to come up with a prescription that fits the situation on the ground.'[13] After a successful visit by Narasimha Rao to America in May 1994, the U.S. advised Pakistan 'to forget about history and see ahead'.[14] According to Farzana Shakoor, a Pakistani senior research officer at the Pakistan Institute of International Affairs, the 'Kashmir issue and U.S. global objective' has stated that the U-turn in the U.S. Kashmir policy put Pakistan in a disadvantaged position vis-à-vis India.[15]

Narasimha Rao also engaged with China at the same period. In 1993 a peace agreement was signed to reduce tensions on the Sino–Indian border. China hinted that Pakistan should consider accepting the LoC as the permanent border.[16] A leading Pakistani academic observer wrote,

Not only did the U.S. Kashmir policy undergo complete change but also Chinese Kashmir perception of Kashmir also showed a discernable shift. Chinese authorities were apprehensive about spillover effects of the uprising in Kashmir in its two border provinces, Tibet and Sinkiang. China implicitly complained of foreign interference. The dominant fundamentalist trait of the resistance movement was the main reason behind Chinese reluctance to provide all-out support to Kashmiris. This also provided plausible explanations behind the Chinese role in dissuading Pakistan to withdraw its resolution at UNHRC.[17]

During the same period, China also began working towards improved relations with India. As a result of India's efforts, Iran and China played a helpful role at the UN Human Rights Conference in Geneva.

The British attitude too underwent a change. The foreign secretary, Douglas Hurd, on a visit to Pakistan in January 1995, laid emphasis on the stated British position that contact between India and Pakistan should be bilateral. Pakistani officials were critical, 'this position is at variance with history, law and reality in Kashmir'.[18] The British High Commission hosted a lunch for Mrs Hurd where my wife was invited, together with several Pakistani ladies. At the lunch table, Mrs Hurd asked my wife what the problem in Karachi was. She responded that during Partition, those who had migrated to India were referred to as refugees for the first two years, after which they were accepted as equal citizens of the country. In Karachi, however, those that had migrated to Karachi from India were even now called Mohajirs (refugees) fifty years later. This was the basic cause of the unrest. Pin-drop silence followed.[19]

A fortnight after I took over the office of high commissioner, Prime Minister Narasimha Rao had a good meeting on 2 February 1992, with Prime Minister Nawaz Sharif in Davos on the sidelines of the World Economic Forum. Three days later, Nawaz Sharif's statement on 'Kashmir Day' in Pakistan spoilt the Davos spirit. Nawaz Sharif later explained that the 5 February statement had been approved prior to his departure for Davos and was customarily issued on that day every year, thus it should not be read as a change in attitude. I told him that the timing of the statement was read differently in different countries.

Pakistan's Victory in Cricket World Cup, March 1992

The victory of the Pakistan cricket team in the World Cup in March 1992 was welcomed in India. President Venkataraman sent a congratulatory message, within minutes of the victory, to the President of Pakistan on 25 March. I sent a handwritten note to Nawaz Sharif, which was perhaps the first congratulatory message he received. Those days there were no internet facilities available. An official of the high commission was sent to Amritsar to collect Indian newspapers and journals that commented on the victory. A few hundred booklets were made overnight with photocopies of these together with editorials and other comments which were widely distributed in Pakistan. Foreign Secretary Shahryar Khan requested an additional twenty copies which he handed over in the plane to the prime minister's delegation visiting Vienna. At the reception hosted by the President of Pakistan for the victorious cricket team, many guests including the captain, Imran Khan, spoke appreciatively of the high commission publication.

Invitation to Pakistan Army Chief and Signing of Code of Conduct, August 1992

Life for Indian officials working in Pakistan was not easy. They were subject to constant surveillance, harassment and physical assault. Pakistan complained of similar treatment. I discussed with PM Rao that as the Vienna Convention was not being followed, perhaps we could attempt to have a bilateral code of conduct.

I also suggested we invite the army chief of Pakistan, because at some level there was a feeling that India was the only key country which did not have a connection with the Pakistan Army. We realized it may be difficult for the Pakistan army chief to visit India, but the initiative would be appreciated, and silence those who thought that India was avoiding contact with the army. The invite was extended during the foreign secretary-level meeting, and the Code of Conduct signed in August 1992.

First and Only So Far Structured Meeting Between Director General ISI DGISI and Indian High Commissioner

The ISI and its director generals have occupied a special position in Pakistan. The director general has always been a nominee of the army. Nawaz Sharif made a change, and on 2 March 1992 appointed Lt Gen. Javed Nasir as director general ISI in place of Major Gen. Asad Durrani. Although a senior army officer, Javed Nasir was not the choice of the army. A man of radical views, over the years he became a puritanical religious person with a Tablichi background. Earlier, he had enjoyed a normal life like other soldiers, as confirmed by India's Lt Gen. Satish Nambiar, for both had attended the same course in Australia. Within two months of his taking over as DGISI, harsh action was taken against Consular Rajesh Mittal of the Indian High Commission. On 24 May, Rajesh Mittal was abducted outside his house as he was leaving for his office. He was released seven hours later after inhuman treatment.

Intelligence agencies have always played an important role in Pakistan. The ISI and the Military Intelligence (MI) are a part of the army, while the Intelligence Bureau (IB) is under civilian control but very often has deferred to the other two organizations. During the martial law regime of President Zia, ISI was assigned a dominant role and the IB functioned as an adjunct. Both Lt Gen. Ghulam Jilani Khan and later Lt Gen. Akhtar Abdur Rahman as ISI chiefs constantly meddled in domestic policies. The trend continued. Lt Gen. Javed Nasir encouraged Pakistan's involvement in abetting terrorism in Kashmir. After the sacking of the Nawaz Sharif government in 1993, he was dismissed and retired from the army.

In early July 1992, at a reception at the official residence of the President of Pakistan, Aiwan-e-Sadr, I met Lt Gen. Javed Nasir who told me he had asked his men to trace me. I jokingly said he should dismiss them if they failed, because they were constantly following me. We both had a big laugh and he asked if we could formally meet in his office. We met on 6 July, followed by another meeting on 23 November. Both meetings were one-to-one and lasted a few hours. Discussions were on different issues in respect of our bilateral relations. When asked as to why Counsellor Mittal was brutally treated, he responded that in Delhi a man in uniform had been insulted, referring to military attaché Brig. Zahirul Islam Abbasi, who had been declared persona non grata by India on 30 November 1988. He kept quiet when I told him that Brig. Abbasi had been promoted as Maj. Gen. immediately on his return from India, but subsequently the Pakistan Army itself had found him unsuitable. When he was force commander northern area, he launched an attack in the Siachen area, resulting in the loss of many lives. A Brigadier too was killed in a helicopter crash during the operation. (Later he was dismissed for his involvement in Operation Jackal, which was an unsuccessful attempt against the government of Benazir Bhutto. This happened long after my discussions with Javed Nasir.) Emphasizing the need for army-to-army contact, he suggested a beginning could be made with some kind of exchange between the national defence colleges. We ourselves had been giving some thought to this. On my return to the office, I spoke to Defence Secretary N.N. Vohra, and a note was sent the same day to the Pakistan foreign office, suggesting exchanges between the national defence colleges of the two countries. I sent a copy to DGISI. There was no response from the Pakistan government. Clearly, the Pakistan Army was not in favour—neither had they acknowledged the invitation to the Pakistan army chief. When I later asked Javed Nasir about the fate of the proposal (actually made at his behest), he said I had moved very fast, and the matter was pending. Several decades later it was still pending.

During our meeting, Javed Nasir went to an adjoining room to say his prayers. On his return, as he was talking very fast, I asked him to slow down so that I could make a note of the salient points. I added this may not be necessary for him as he was probably recording our entire conversation. He laughingly nodded and gave me a long lecture on the fictional book written by the son of Indian Gen. Rikhye on a war between India and Pakistan. At the end, he asked what I thought of our conversation. I responded that hearing that the DGISI was basing his views on a fictional book, I was leaving a worried man.

When I briefly reported my conversation to PM Narasimha Rao, his response, keeping the National Defense College (NDC) exchange in mind, was that even senior army officers holding important positions could not have their way without the backing of the army headquarters.

Visit of Leader of the Opposition to Karachi

Pakistan watches India closely but at times misreads it. Benazir Bhutto, as leader of the Opposition, organized in September 1992 (which so far is the only one) a meeting of opposition leaders of SAARC countries. In that context she invited V.P. Singh, former prime minister of India, to Karachi. The foreign office in Islamabad was surprised that I, as the high commissioner of India, wanted to discuss arrangements for the visit. When informed that an advance team of the Special Protection Group (SPG) would be coming to discuss security arrangements, they were astonished, as in Pakistan, former prime ministers were either dismissed or were in disgrace. I was asked if SPG was a private security agency. They were told this was an official agency for the protection of prime ministers of India, including former prime ministers. At the Conference of Opposition Leaders of the SAARC region, a statement promoting democracy was issued, which the government in Islamabad interpreted as directed against it. Their attitude, from the beginning, was lukewarm. A proposal for V.P. Singh to visit Islamabad after Karachi was never considered seriously, and eventually was not agreed to, so V.P. Singh returned to Delhi directly from Karachi. I had asked our consul general in Karachi, Rajiv Dogra, to be present at the meeting whenever possible and to extend all courtesies to the leader of the Opposition, in accordance with our established practice. Benazir Bhutto later told me that consuls general of most countries made some excuse to keep away from the conference, adding the sole exception was India. The Indian consul general was the only one to associate himself with the conference.

Indian Assistance after Floods in Pakistan, September 1992

In September, devastating floods hit Pakistan causing countrywide damage. Losses were estimated at over US$1 billion. Under instructions from Prime Minister Narasimha Rao, two Indian

Air Force (IAF) AN-32 aircrafts carried medicines for the flood-affected people. The Indian Women's Association made a cash donation to the Government of Pakistan, and the cheque was handed over by my wife to a senior Pakistan minister, Anwar Saifullah. India's contribution was appreciated.

Siachen

On the eve of the sixth round of discussions between India and Pakistan on Siachen (November 1992), I came from Islamabad to Delhi to discuss with PM Narasimha Rao the genesis of the progress made in the five rounds held till that time. Having been, at different periods, minister for external affairs and defence, Narasimha Rao was fully aware of all details, which have been briefly mentioned earlier.[20]

Negotiations between India and Pakistan on Siachen started in 1986. The atmosphere in the first round, held in Rawalpindi in January 1986, was marred as Pakistan prominently displayed a huge map joining NJ9842, the terminal point of the LoC, with the Karakoram Pass. Pakistan was clearly told that no discussion was possible on the basis of a straight line. However, despite differences, it was decided to hold the next round in Delhi. No statement was issued. The second round in Delhi (June 1986) will be best remembered for a convincing presentation by Brig. V.R. Raghavan. Quoting from historical records, he proved that Nubra area was never a part of Pakistan as had been claimed by them in the first round. It became clear that the NJ9842–Karakoram Pass line was a nonstarter. Rounds three (May 1986) and four (September 1988) witnessed further discussions without much progress. Round five, held in June 1989, was the first after President Zia's death. Expectations were high as it was held after informal contacts. The joint statement said, 'There was agreement by both sides to work towards a comprehensive settlement, based on redeployment of forces to reduce the chances of conflict, avoidance of the use of force and determination of future positions on the ground so as to conform with the Simla Agreement and to ensure durable peace in the Siachen area. The Army authorities of both sides will determine these positions.'[21] Pakistan claimed there was agreement, further strengthened by the statement of two foreign secretaries at the press conference in Rawalpindi a day later. There was in fact no final agreement. The joint statement of this round clearly mentioned at the end that an in-depth examination of the proposals will be made in the next round.

In the sixth round held in November 1992, there was a broad understanding on disengagement and deployment. It was informally agreed that there would be no occupation of vacated positions, no military mountaineering or any other activity in the zone of disengagement. There was also to be a monitoring process whereby in case of any violation of the agreement, each side was free to respond.

Clearly the ground reality was decidedly in favour of India, who was willing to accept a mutually agreed pullback, without Pakistan's insistence on the pre-1971 position and its earlier demand for being physically present in the Siachen glacier. Pakistan has yet to clarify its exact location to enable India to verify whether it's correct. Pakistan surprisingly inquired if their patrols could come to Karakoram Pass through Chinese territory. This was unacceptable and they did not raise it again. Pakistan's main concern focused on India's presence in the Siachen glacier.[22]

I had called on President Venkataraman, who was the defence minister in 1984. He said there was still blood in the snow. I reported this to Prime Minister Narasimha Rao. The opposition party also had reservations. The prime minister, who at that time was heading a minority government, had his own doubts and was not happy with the attitude of the Pakistan military officers during the talks. In the draft agreement Pakistan agreed to India's demand 'to mark the existing position'.[23] Narasimha Rao had doubts about Pakistan's intentions which 'were later confirmed by Pakistan's response to the non-paper'. He told me to tell Foreign Secretary Dixit that as Pakistan had not given a clear-cut response, there was no need to give any impression of a settlement. I informed the foreign secretary late in the evening, and he conveyed the PM's instructions to the defence ministry. J.N. Dixit later wrote that if this was the government's position, there was no need for the two sides to have detailed discussions.[24] The factual position which Narasimha Rao grasped, in addition to the other problems, was that there was no firm commitment from Pakistan about authentication of positions. Subsequently, in response to India's non-papers, Pakistan stated in writing that they did not agree to any authentication. There was some progress in the sixth round but not enough to announce a settlement.

Later, the seventh round of talks in June 1997 and eighth round (August 2004) also did not result in any progress. India's suspicion about Pakistan's attitude on Siachen was reinforced after the Kargil episode.

The participants from India and Pakistan included important military personnel. I had an opportunity to meet many, being a member of the Indian delegation in the first two rounds in my capacity as joint secretary dealing with Pakistan in the MEA, and in the sixth round as high commissioner of India in Pakistan. Among the important people who participated at different times were former governor of J & K, N.N. Vohra, former national security adviser, J.N. Dixit, and S.K. Singh. Participants on the Pakistan side were diplomats Riaz Khokhar and Aziz Ahmed Khan. As regards military personnel, the most prominent on the

Indian side was Lt Gen. V.R. Raghavan, as Brig. (deputy Director General of Military Operations (DGMO)) in the first and second rounds, as Maj. Gen. (additional DGMO) in the third and fourth rounds and as Lt Gen. (DGMO) in the fifth round. His book on Siachen is perhaps the best reading on the subject. On the Pakistan side, Maj. Gen. Jehangir Karamat (later Gen. and COAS) participated in the third, fourth and fifth rounds. Among the participants in the fifth round was Brig. Ali Kuli Khan Khattak, who later resigned as Lt Gen. when Musharraf superseded him to become army chief.

Babri Masjid, 6 December 1992

In my professional career, one of the most difficult days as high commissioner in Pakistan was 6 December 1992, on the destruction of Babri Masjid in Ayodhya. The news of developments in India spread like wildfire with the BBC reporting live the unfolding events of the demolition of the Masjid.

With the National Day reception of Finland scheduled later the same evening, I had to take the decision to attend or not, given the exceptional situation. After brief consultations with my colleagues, it was decided to stick to normal activities as far as possible. Needless to say, at the reception I was the centre of attraction. Voicing disapproval, some Pakistani guests questioned the reason for the demolition. The secretary general of the Pakistan foreign office gleefully kept directing Pakistani journalists towards me. To all my response was brief, stating that I was extremely unhappy at what had happened. In principle I was against any place of worship being a target of attack, but added, Indian democracy was strong enough to bear such shocks. Throughout the reception, I happened to be standing next to a table offering a variety of cheese, and with everyone constantly approaching me,

I was aghast to discover I had consumed a considerable amount that evening!

A statement was issued immediately by Prime Minister Nawaz Sharif expressing a 'deep sense of shock and horror'[25] at the Ayodhya developments. This was followed by reports of stone throwing at Shivaji court in Karachi, which housed some members of the high commission staff.

The next day, I was called to the foreign office by the Pakistan government where I was handed over an aide-mémoire protesting the demolition of the Babri Masjid, on the basis of the Inter-Dominion Agreement of August 1947 and the Nehru–Liaquat Pact of 1950. They were reminded that the Nehru–Liaquat Pact no longer existed, as confirmed by a statement made in the Pakistan Assembly on 25 July 1974 by the then Pakistan defence and foreign affairs minister, Aziz Ahmed. He had said, following the April/May Sadar Bazaar riots in Delhi and under the Simla Agreement, such issues would be treated as an internal matter. Simultaneously, there were other developments. The Indian Airlines office in Lahore was set on fire. Security became our priority.

The Pakistan cabinet meeting in Islamabad the same day condemned the Ayodhya incident and declared 8 December a day of protest and mourning. Several temples, gurdwaras and churches were damaged. The residence of the consul general, Rajiv Dogra, was ransacked by a mob. I was on the phone talking to Rajiv's wife, Meenakshi, during the ransacking. She had locked herself in a room together with the children and the maid, and was completely traumatized by the unexpected assault on their residence. The house was destroyed in the presence of security services. The mob was selective in arson. Looting included both valuables and, interestingly, cases of alcohol. Kris Srinivasan, secretary west in the MEA, Delhi, lodged a strong protest to Riaz Khokhar, Pakistan high commissioner in India, at the burning of the consul general's residence. Given the security concerns, families of the Indian officials in Karachi were temporarily sent back to India. A detailed aide-mémoire was handed over to the deputy high commissioner of Pakistan in Delhi by the MEA on 11 December, expressing concern at the destruction of places of worship of minorities in Pakistan.

Earlier that day, I made several attempts to contact Prime Minister Nawaz Sharif and Interior Minister Chaudry Shujaat Hussain. There was no response from either. Later, on the 8th evening, Shujaat Hussain called, saying he was calling from his car on his way back from a dinner. I said I had made one call to the honorable interior minister and four to my friend, but unfortunately no response. He said he was responding now and wanted me to meet him at his residence the next morning.

On the 9th morning, I was unaware that telephone lines at home had been cut and only realized it when Chaudhry Shujaat sent a messenger on a motorcycle to advance the meeting by half an hour. We had preliminary discussions on precautionary security measures for Indian missions in Islamabad and Karachi and the Indian Airlines offices in Lahore and Karachi. As a follow-up, Shujaat called up the secretary of the ministry of interior and told him to reconnect the telephones of the high commission which they had disconnected. The secretary, perhaps, aware I was sitting with the minister, appeared to deny charges of having done so. This was apparent from the minister's response that regardless of who was responsible, it should be ensured telephones were working again to enable him to be in touch with the high commissioner. He added that the inspector general of police in Islamabad had been instructed to meet me in my office to discuss details regarding security of the mission. Thereafter, he left for Lahore, which was the very reason, he explained, the timing of the meeting was advanced.

By the time I reached the office, the inspector general of police was waiting for me. Together with the officers in charge of the security of the mission, we had detailed discussions. His advice in a nutshell was to vacate the few residences which were far away and to make mobile phones available for the mission. Immediate action was taken on both. Prompt arrangements were made to shift families to new premises. Our request for mobile phones had been pending with the finance division in Delhi, but under these unexpected circumstances, I immediately ordered the purchase of mobile phones.

Meanwhile, some Pakistani leaders and media went on a roll. Official connivance encouraged demonstrations. To quote the *Frontier Post* editorial, 'Mr. Wyne [chief minister] lifted Section 144 from the city to let the Muslims vent their feelings.'[26] The *Friday Times*, 'In Punjab, the police stand and watch. The chief minister says this is because, "the policemen are also Pakistanis. They have their feelings and emotion as well."'[27] The *Dawn*, quoting opposition leader Sardar Farooq Ahmed Leghari in Parliament, 'the Punjab chief minister Ghulam Haider Wyne had said all the damage and arson was being done with the permission of the government', adding that Mian Shehbaz Sharif, brother of the prime minister, too talked of revenge.[28] With emotions running high, bulldozers were used to bring down temples. Later, from 11 December onwards, Fridays became days of tension as provocative speeches to congregations in the mosque enticing mobs to attack, was a possibility that could not be ruled out.

At the earliest opportunity I visited Karachi. Rajiv Dogra had moved to a hotel. I was deeply impressed by the positive attitude of the staff. As all were without families, arrangements had been made for a common kitchen. Regardless of the difficult circumstances, they carried on performing their official duties.

In Islamabad, we were in a state of isolation for the next few weeks. Our first visitors came on 18 December. Dr Zafar Niazi (Zulfikar Ali [Z.A.] Bhutto's dentist) with his wife, and Asifa Khattak, a neighbour and close friend came for a quiet lunch. We have always remembered them with warmth and affection as this decision could not have been an easy one.

Similarly, Gen. Habibullah came to meet me on 22 December, while I was visiting Karachi. He made the effort despite being unwell and said he had come especially, as he did not want me to think he was avoiding me. This was to be my last meeting with him. He died a year later. We had gone to Peshawar to attend the wedding of his grandson, where he too was expected. Unfortunately, instead his body was flown there and I attended his funeral.

A few months later, a cabinet minister told me that at the height of the Babri Masjid crisis, there was a demand for the Indian high commissioner to be declared persona non grata. This was overruled by Nawaz Sharif, claiming international implications could be negative for Pakistan. Later, it was conveyed by a friend that Nawaz Sharif had not wanted my tenure to end because of his action.

During the days of turmoil following the fall of Babri Masjid, our presence at a few select functions helped to dispel the impression created by the militant political leaders that we were social pariahs. The Indian mission in Islamabad continued to function as normal. My wife attended a ladies' function at the Chinese Embassy where both the host and Pakistani ladies present were surprised at her presence. She was able to face the expected animosity with composure.[29] On 28 December, we attended the wedding reception of Foreign Secretary Shahryar Khan's sons. Though most guests maintained a distance from us, President Ghulam Ishaq Khan made it a point to greet me warmly.

There were several calls to boycott our Republic Day reception on 26 January 1993. Because of this, we were advised by some friends to cancel the reception. The Pakistani intelligence agencies worked overtime to prevent visitors from coming, but amazingly the attendance surpassed all previous years. Papers attributed it to the high commissioner's personal friendships regardless of the fact that the invite was official and not private.

Immediately after the demolition of the Babri Masjid, we engaged in public conversations with journalists and newspaper columnists, and as far as possible, discussions with knowledgeable and influential Pakistanis. Their complaints were regarding the conditions of Muslims and treatment of minorities with jibes at Indian secularism. Highlighting the role of Muslims in secular India and the outstanding contribution of minorities in comparison with conditions in Pakistan, was our terse response. Some points made in private to a select audience proved effective. A remark made to some important Pakistanis, including erstwhile senior military personnel, emphasized that during the 1971 war, the Indian Army top brass was virtually led by people belonging to the minority community. The chief of army staff (Sam Manekshaw) was a Parsi, the army commander of the Eastern Command was a Sikh (Lt Gen. Jagjit Singh Arora) and the chief of staff of the Indian Army Eastern Command was a Jew (Lt Gen. Jacob). This, I added, was not by design but the result of the normal functioning of the Indian Army, a matter of pride for every Indian. Even at the political level, the foreign minister was a Sikh (Sardar Swaran Singh), the defence minister was a leader of the Harijan community (Jagjivan Ram) and the overall leadership was under a woman (Indira Gandhi). This appealed to thinking Pakistanis. One commented that while they were aware that Muslims had occupied top posts in the country, they were nonetheless impressed that a Muslim held the sensitive position as chief of air staff earlier from 1979–81. I responded this was a normal occurrence which did not surprise us, as it did our friends in Pakistan.

Our public and private statements focused on the encouraged attacks on temples and gurdwaras by miscreants following the Masjid demolition.[30] Public statements by senior ministers and politicians appeared to depict more happiness and gloating at India's predicament rather than any genuine sorrow.

Unfortunately, decades later, the situation in India too is undergoing a change. For instance, as Indian journalist Aakar Patel points out, India does not have a Muslim chief minister in any of its twenty-eight states, in fifteen there is no Muslim minister and in ten just one, usually in charge of minority affairs. Patel called this a deliberate exclusion of 200 million people. He also made the astonishing charge, of which I had no knowledge, that Muslims are excluded from R&AW.[31] I must confess my personal knowledge on this was limited. However, well-informed retired intelligence officers since then have revealed that even admission of minority officers like Sikhs was limited. I, however, remember with great satisfaction dealing with A.S. Siyali, an able Sikh head of R&AW, during the Narasimha Rao regime, and Asif Ibrahim, the Muslim director of the intelligence bureau during the United Progressive Alliance (UPA) period of PM Manmohan Singh, when I was special envoy in his office. There have also been some unfortunate statements by ministers of the Union government linking India's policy towards Pakistan with domestic developments and references to Muslims in India.[32]

Bombay (now Mumbai) Blasts, March 1993

On 12 March 1993, Bombay was devastated by bomb blasts killing more than 200 people. The blasts indicated ISI involvement, and by 17 March, India had definite knowledge of the Memon family having engineered these blasts and escaping to Pakistan via Dubai. A fortnight prior to the incident, I had warned our government regarding the pending disaster in Bombay, so that timely action could be taken. A news item in the *Pioneer* of 17 March 1993, 'Paying the Price', claimed the Indian High Commission in Islamabad had warned of such an eventuality.

After the attack, I was asked about the source of the information. I was surprised that instead of taking action, they only wanted to know the basis on which I had sent the warning. Thereafter, on a visit to Delhi I expressed my anguish to the prime minister. The news regarding the warning had by this time leaked in India.[33]

Prime Minister Nawaz Sharif sent a message of sympathy on 12 March, to Prime Minister Rao. The Pakistan foreign office on 15 March regretted in a statement the alleged tendency of Indian politicians to blame Pakistan for any unpleasant event in India. The Government of India supplied evidence to Pakistan about their complicity on 15 September 1993 in a note verbale. There was no response as usual on such critical issues.

On 16 May 1993, I met caretaker (acting head of Pakistan government following dissolution of the National Assembly) Prime Minister Mazari, who admitted that six members of the Memon family had arrived in Karachi on 17 March and there was no trace of them thereafter.

The culprits remain unpunished in Pakistan. Decades later, when India once again became a member of the UN Security Council (UNSC), External Affairs Minister S. Jaishankar, in his address to the UNSC open debate (12 January 2021), said that the crime syndicate responsible for the 1993 Mumbai bomb blast was 'not just given state protection but enjoying 5-star hospitality'. He was referring to the fugitive terrorist Dawood Ibrahim who lives in Pakistan.[34]

Restoration of Nawaz Sharif as Prime Minister, May 1993

On 26 May 1993, the Pakistan Supreme Court in its judgment restored Nawaz Sharif as prime minister, along with the National Assembly of Pakistan. Justice Nasim Hassan Shah, who took over as Chief Justice a few days earlier, on 29 April, was able, through this judgment, to redeem his image as he was part of the majority judgment which ordered the execution of Z.A. Bhutto. The judge had friends in India, including in the legal fraternity. Extracts of his judgment, following a request to me, were delivered to them in Delhi. PM Narasimha Rao immediately sent a message of facilitation to Nawaz Sharif and I was told to ensure its delivery before the media release at 2 p.m. in Delhi. I requested an appointment through private channels, as Nawaz Sharif had yet to formally take over. As a precautionary measure, I planned on getting the message delivered to the foreign office. However, within minutes, I got word to meet PM Nawaz Sharif immediately. On arrival, I was received at the entrance of the prime minister's secretariat by minister for petroleum, Chaudhary Nisar, who was also designated as his special assistant. Nisar, whom I knew well, told me he had been instructed to receive me by the PM. The office had been taken over by his party supporters and appeared more like a public platform. Political leaders, party members and senior officials in large numbers had engulfed the office. Sitting in an adjoining room, I observed the senior bureaucrats and political leaders vying to congratulate the prime minister on his restoration. I was ushered into the prime minister's room. He greeted me very warmly and thanked me for being in touch with his colleagues during his period of 'incarceration'. He mentioned I was the first diplomat he was meeting, though the media had been told that the Saudi ambassador was the first. I handed over the message from PM Narasimha Rao, which was the first he received from a foreign head of government. A brief discussion on Indo–Pak relations followed, and he renewed his commitment to strengthen them. The atmosphere within the building was informal. While sitting with him, his brother Shehbaz Sharif and chairman of Pakistan International Airlines (PIA), came in through another entrance. Shehbaz told him that he would like to place the special plane of the prime minister at his disposal. (He probably did not know who I was. This plane had been one of the controversial reasons for his dismissal by President Ghulam Ishaq Khan on 18 April 1993.) When they left, Nawaz Sharif asked what I thought of his suggestion. I said it was not for me to comment, but as he had asked, I felt he should not announce a decision straight away. He said that was exactly what he had in mind too. I left the room and saw dozens of people struggling to enter. The message from Narasimha Rao got wide publicity in Pakistan.

Sattar's Comments on Prime Minister Narasimha Rao, August 1993

Nawaz Sharif's tenure as a restored prime minister did not last long. Interestingly, both he and President Ghulam Ishaq Khan had to step down together under a formula brokered by army chief Gen. Abdul Waheed Kakar. General elections were called on 6 and 9 October. Meanwhile, Senate Chairman Wasim Sajjad took over as acting President, and former World Bank vice president, Moeen Qureshi, was flown in to head a new neutral interim caretaker government. Abdul Sattar became caretaker foreign minister. The significance of this development revealed the special position the army held in Pakistan. Only recently the powerful President Ghulam Ishaq Khan had appointed his fellow

Pashtun, Abdul Waheed as army chief, superseding a few generals. The same army chief simultaneously got rid of both his mentor Ghulam Ishaq Khan and Nawaz Sharif without a problem.

Pakistan reacted strongly to PM Narsimha Rao's Red Fort Independence speech that stated Pakistan was 'fueling Muslim militancy and a guerilla campaign in an integral and indispensable part of India'.[35] Sattar described the prime minister's reference to Kashmir as, 'claiming ownership of robbed goods'. This was countered by the spokesman of the MEA, if 'India claiming Kashmir was robbery, then Pakistan's occupation of one-third of the state . . . was nothing less than armed dacoity'. Narasimha Rao later told me that he did not attach importance to Sattar's statement, and personal criticism should not in any way come in the way of formulation of our policy towards Pakistan.

Message to Benazir Bhutto on Becoming Prime Minister, October 1993

Just before the elections, journalist Karan Thapar visited Pakistan. When he was leaving Islamabad for Larkana to meet Benazir Bhutto, I asked him to convey the assessment of the high commission that she would win the election. She was happy to hear this. Following her victory and before her swearing in, I asked her political secretary if I could convey Narasimha Rao's greeting to her. I was told she was with her hairdresser and would be proceeding directly for the oath ceremony. I handed the message to her then trusted colleague, Farooq Leghari, who apprised me that he would be among the two ministers taking oath and would be handling foreign affairs. I said in that case, I was giving my prime minister's letter to the right man. Shortly thereafter, he was elected president and would later dismiss his patron Benazir Bhutto.

Talks between Foreign Secretaries, January 1994

Relations started cooling with Benazir Bhutto taking a more stringent attitude on Kashmir. The seventh round of foreign secretary-level talks took place in Islamabad, between 1 and 3 January 1994. Before the talks, it had been agreed that all issues including J & K would be discussed. Benazir was in Karachi in connection with celebrations of Zulfikar Ali Bhutto's sixty-sixth birth anniversary on 5 January. The Indian delegation was flown in a special aircraft to meet her. Both sides recognized the 'basic divergence' and agreed to make 'sincere efforts to resolve the problem'. India promised to forward non-papers on contentious bilateral issues. The lists of nuclear installations were exchanged for the third time. After the Indian delegation left Islamabad, I observed Pakistani officials collecting correspondents present at the airport for a briefing. While I left for the office, I kept in touch with the media correspondents. The Pakistan briefing was there would be no further talks at foreign secretary level till there were meaningful discussions on Kashmir. Delhi was immediately informed, so that the foreign secretary on arrival kept this in mind while briefing the media in Delhi.

A few days later, the new foreign minister of Pakistan, Sardar Asif Ali, at a press conference in Tashkent on 8 January 1994, said,

> Unless the Kashmir dispute is solved peacefully on the terms of international law and United Nations resolutions there cannot be lasting peace in South Asia and there is always the danger of a fourth war in South Asia; and this time around, the concern of the world, the concern of South Asian countries and regional countries is that if a war takes place in South Asia it might become a nuclear war. It is very important for all countries in

the region to recognize the immense danger to the world of a war in South Asia which could become the first nuclear war in the history of this part of the world.[36]

Benazir Bhutto, stepping up the verbal campaign on 23 January 1994, stated, 'We do not want to give a wrong signal to the Kashmiris by holding meaningless talks with India.'[37] She was preparing the country for a victory at the Human Rights Conference in Geneva, where she was proposing to raise the Kashmir issue. She had underestimated Narasimha Rao.

Six Non-Papers, 24 January 1994

As there had been misrepresentations in Pakistan regarding the Indian position on different issues, I suggested to PM Narasimha Rao, before the scheduled foreign secretary-level talks, that we could express our views on five or six issues in writing, in the form of non-papers to clarify our stand. He approved, and on 24 January 1994, India handed over to Pakistan six non-papers with concrete proposals relating to: (a) Siachen (b) Sir Creek (c) Tulbul navigation project (d) draft agreement on maintenance of peace and tranquility along the LoC (e) confidence-building measures (CBMs) (f) revival of the India–Pakistan Joint Commission. The package of CBMs included two measures in the nuclear field: the proposal that the existing agreement on prevention of attack on nuclear installations and facilities be extended to include population centres and economic targets, and second, an agreement undertaking that neither state will be the first to use or threaten to use its nuclear capability against the other. The Indian proposals underlined that through a series of negotiations at the bilateral level, there is full scope for addressing outstanding issues between the two countries.

As expected, on 19 February 1994, Pakistan gave its comments on the Indian non-papers and added two non-papers on: 1) modalities for holding a plebiscite in J & K and 2) measures required to create a propitious climate for talks on the J & K dispute. As regards Siachen, Pakistan stated that there was no agreement or understanding in 1992 (sixth round), but there was only an agreement in 1989 (fifth round). The note also categorically stated that Pakistan did not agree to any authentication of the positions held by the two sides in Siachen. The underlying message was that discussions should focus only on J & K.

In my address to the National Defence College of Pakistan in December 1994, I got an opportunity to respond to the Pakistan non-papers. I mentioned that three of the non-papers (Siachen, Tulbul and Peace and Tranquility on LoC) have a bearing on any ultimate resolution of differences over the Kashmir problem. In response to a question, I categorically stated our views on a plebiscite in Kashmir. In October 1947, Pakistan aided and abetted a massive tribal invasion of J & K. It was India which took the question of invasion of Kashmir to the UNSC. Deliberations in the security council led to the establishment of the United Nations Commission on India and Pakistan (UNCIP). The UNCIP resolution of 13 August 1948, accepted by both India and Pakistan, provided for: (i) a ceasefire, (ii) a truce agreement which directed Pakistan to withdraw all its forces from the territory of J & K and (iii) only thereafter ascertaining the will of the people of the state in a peaceful manner. The UN resolutions were accepted by India subject to the assurance given by the UNCIP, which, inter alia, stipulated that plebiscite proposals would not be binding on India if Pakistan did not implement parts i and ii of the UNCIP resolution of 13 August 1947 (mandating ceasefire and withdrawal of Pakistani troops from POK). India had also made it clear that its acceptance was time-specific. Though the ceasefire came into effect on 1 January 1949, Pakistan failed to implement part II of the UNCIP resolution. The failure to hold a plebiscite was the result of Pakistan's default to carry out, within a reasonable time, the obligations imposed upon her by the UN resolutions as conditions required for holding a plebiscite. Meanwhile, a democratic process was put in place that adopted a constitution for J & K by an elected assembly in 1956. This process was reinforced by several elections through which the people of Kashmir exercised their democratic choice. Furthermore, in 1972, India and Pakistan signed the Simla Agreement which enjoined upon them to settle their differences through bilateral discussions. The idea of a plebiscite is clearly irrelevant under the changed circumstances.

Parliament Resolution on Kashmir in India, February 1994

On another level, PM Narasimha Rao decided to give a befitting reply to Pakistan's rhetoric on the UN resolution, dilution of the Simla Agreement and attempts at internationalizing Kashmir. For the first time, the passing of the resolution by the Indian Parliament made it clear that POK was a part of India.

PM Narasimha Rao applied his mind to India's policy in respect of POK. Conscious that China was taking a more active role in J & K because it occupied 20 per cent of the territory, including in the Shaksgam area occupied in 1962, and part of the Northern Areas ceded by Pakistan in 1963, the declaration sent a clear message to Pakistan and those in the international community helping to internationalize J & K.

There were other trends which required to be reversed. The Organisation of Islamic Cooperation (OIC) decided to send a fact-finding mission to Kashmir and sought visas for the visit on

5 February 1993. The U.S. and UK were also active. Pakistan's rhetoric had increased. Heading a minority government, Rao wanted to make clear, both to his supporters and opponents in India, the firmness with which he planned to deal with J & K. While I was on a visit from Islamabad, he discussed the draft resolution, and some suggestions I made for modifications were accepted.

K.N. Pandita, the director of the Centre of Central Asian Studies, Kashmir University, aptly remarked, 'India had to react. Astute statesman, Prime Minister Narasimha Rao played his cards with rare alacrity. At this critical juncture he got the unanimous resolution passed.'[38]

Finally, the resolution on J & K was moved in both houses of Parliament on 22 February 1994 by the presiding officers and adopted unanimously by the Lok Sabha and Rajya Sabha.[39] The Resolution on behalf of the People of India firmly declares that:

a) The state of Jammu and Kashmir has been, is and shall always be an integral part of India and any attempts to separate it from the rest of the country will be resisted by all necessary means;

b) India has the will and capacity to firmly counter all designs against its unity, sovereignty and territorial integrity;

and demands that

c) Pakistan must vacate the areas of the Indian State of Jammu and Kashmir, which they have occupied through aggression

and resolves that

d) All attempts to interfere in the internal affairs of India will be met resolutely.

The Parliament resolution responded to Pakistan's claim that since 1947, Kashmir was 'the unfinished business of partition'. India's rightful claim on POK was also clear. Narasimha Rao never bragged about this resolution because he knew the message was evident with the passing of the resolution.

Pakistan's Resolution against India in Geneva on Human Rights Violation

As discussed with the prime minister, when Pakistan protested at the resolution, I explained to them that it only reconfirmed the policy of their own government. Five days after the resolution of the Indian Parliament, Pakistan got a resolution tabled at the UN Human Rights Commission in Geneva through the OIC, condemning India for violation of human rights in J & K. This resolution provided another opportunity for Narasimha Rao to reveal his farsighted approach.

Prime Minister Narasimha Rao and the then leader of the Opposition, Atal Bihari Vajpayee, shared a special relationship. Though political opponents, they were good friends who had a common view on India's interest. During one of my visits to Delhi as high commissioner to Pakistan, the prime minister, after the briefing, surprisingly said that I should give the same briefing point by point to the leader of the Opposition, including the sensitive aspect which I had reported to him. His private secretary fixed my appointment. The following day, when I called on Shri Atal Bihari Vajpayee, his private secretary too was present. Immediately a Cola drink was offered, which smilingly Shri Vajpayee said was from the funds of the government, to which he was entitled as leader of the Opposition. I was perplexed at this remark, till a few minutes later, a glass of fresh juice was offered. He smilingly added, 'This is from my house sent by my daughter.' His adopted daughter, Namita, had stayed with us during my posting as a mid-level officer to Rome in the early 1970s. Shri Vajpayee thanked me for the briefing and said he would be speaking to the prime minister. He agreed with all proposals but added that these should be made in a manner that Pakistan did not take them as a sign of weakness on our part. These wise words always remained in my mind when dealing with other countries too.

As high commissioner to Pakistan, I always proudly brought to the attention of visitors how the Chancery building reflected India's democracy. The foundation stone was laid by Atal Bihari Vajpayee on a visit to Pakistan when he was foreign minister of the Janata government. On a later visit, it was inaugurated by Narasimha Rao, as foreign minister of the Congress government.

From Islamabad we reported that keeping in view the deteriorating ground situation in Kashmir and their domestic difficulties, Pakistan wanted to raise the Kashmir issue in Geneva, at the Human Rights Commission and in New York at the Third Committee. Pakistan considered the UN Geneva Human Rights venue a fertile ground to embarrass India. As early as February 1982, when India's relations with Pakistan were showing signs of improvement, Agha Hilaly, a senior Pakistani diplomat, raised the Kashmir issue in Geneva, forcing India to postpone the foreign secretary-level talks. I was at that time posted as deputy chief of the Indian Embassy in Islamabad. Pakistan was taken aback at Indira Gandhi's firm response. In 1993, by which time I was again in Pakistan, now as high commissioner, Pakistan escalated its offensive and tried to bring a resolution against India. PM Nawaz Sharif even addressed the UN Human Rights Commission in Geneva, but the attempt failed. In 1994, after the Parliament resolution had been passed in India and the ground situation was improving from India's point of view, Pakistan, with Benazir

Bhutto as prime minister, decided to attack India in Geneva and was confident of success. She made a fiery address at the plenary of the Human Rights Commission. The Pakistan media and officials believed that India was isolated. Dr Manmohan Singh's sober and dignified response restored some balance in the debate, but it was clear that Pakistan was not going to spare any effort to internationalize the Kashmir issue by criticizing India's human rights record. The ground situation in J & K had already been placed by our diplomats at the UN at the instance of international NGOs' and the Human Rights Commission's own mechanism. On account of the reports of rising incidents of human rights violations against India, there were calls to have visits and inspection by a fact-finding mission.

The situation posed a critical and diplomatic challenge for the governments in both India and Pakistan, who would face a domestic crisis depending on the fate of the UN resolution.

Indian Delegation

PM Narasimha Rao took a personal interest in all aspects of the Geneva meeting. His masterstroke was to ask the leader of the Opposition, Atal Bihari Vajpayee, to lead the Indian delegation. Both his request, and later, the acceptance, conveyed a message of bi-partisan consensus in India on Kashmir. The delegation included minister of state in external affairs, Salman Khurshid. A noteworthy addition was Farooq Abdullah and finance minister, Manmohan Singh, who filled the visitor slot, which only a minister could fill as Benazir Bhutto had decided to make a personal appearance, to indicate the importance she attached to the Pakistan resolution. India's leading experts in the UN, Brijesh Mishra and L.M. Singhvi, were included in addition to stalwarts like Hamid Ansari, permanent representative in New York (much later vice president of India) and Prakash Shah, ambassador in Tokyo, who was a former permanent representative to Geneva, thereby making the Indian delegation strong. Unlike in the past, the Indian NGOs were not ignored. Madhukar Gupta, head of the Kashmir desk in the home ministry, was also a member of the delegation. Our observations from Islamabad were on the basis of daily exchange of messages with our mission in Geneva, which was under the proficient management of the permanent representative to Geneva, Satish Chandra, who later replaced me as high commissioner in Islamabad. The wise and experienced leadership of Atal Bihari Vajpayee ensured regular consultations among the members of the Indian delegation and no duplication. Constant monitoring of likely votes in favour of India and damage control was undertaken whenever any slippage was detected. In Delhi, PM Narasimha Rao monitored developments.

Pakistan Delegation

Considerable debate took place in Pakistan regarding the composition of their delegation. It was decided not to send any political heavyweights. Iqbal Akhund, who knew the UN system well, was nominated leader of the Pakistan delegation, which included some of their ablest multilateralists, Munir Akram, and their outstanding permanent representative in Geneva, Ahmed Kamal. The India expert, Shafqat Kakakhel, was added to the delegation. Several ground-level experts were deployed for effective canvassing and lobbying. Neelam Sabharwal, deputy permanent representative in Geneva, told me that the Pakistan delegation had fewer generals and more foot soldiers.

Pressure from international NGOs did not help. The debating exchange in Geneva was clear before tabling of the resolution. A powerful statement was made by Salman Khurshid on behalf of

India. The right of reply was left to Ambassador Hamid Ansari, and the deputy permanent representative, Neelam Sabharwal, dealt with statements by Munir Akram and Shafqat Kakakhel.

As the debate progressed, we reported from Islamabad, which was confirmed in Geneva, that Indonesia, Libya and Syria might not support Pakistan. Subsequently, the position for Pakistan became bleaker as the tally of confirmed votes dwindled. Towards the end, the Pakistan delegation sought verbal approval from their foreign office in Islamabad to amend the resolution by dropping the demand of a fact-finding mission being sent to J & K. This was rejected, as we reliably learnt in Islamabad. By now, Pakistan had lost hope of the resolution going through, and any official dilution would later have created more trouble domestically.

Visit of Dinesh Singh to Tehran

PM Narasimha Rao, during his tenure as foreign minister, had been in close contact with Iran and shared a close bond with then Iranian foreign minister Velayati. In fact, after the fall of the Babri Masjid when as prime minister, Narasimha Rao visited Iran in 1993, he was the first non-Muslim leader to be asked to address the Iranian Majlis. President Rafsanjani hosted a private meal for him, and supreme leader Ayatollah Khamenei received him.

When PM Narasimha Rao got disturbing reports from Geneva, Islamabad and other world capitals, he called a meeting at his house on Sunday, 6 March 1994. Suggesting immediate action should be taken to ensure a positive reaction in Geneva, he floated the idea of sending a special envoy to Tehran. Foreign Minister Dinesh Singh, who was very unwell, volunteered to undertake the task. Narasimha Rao was concerned about his health, but in view of his insistence, agreed to let him go. The Indian Air Force was asked to make arrangements, and the

Iranian Embassy, though unaware of the purpose, were requested to hurriedly arrange the visit. On the plane, Dinesh Singh told his accompanying delegate that he was glad to get this opportunity to do something in respect of Kashmir, as developments on the issue were worrisome. On reaching Tehran, he was received by Foreign Minister Velayati. Himself a medical doctor, Velayati was surprised that Dinesh Singh had embarked on this journey in his condition. Immediately on arrival at the guest house, Velayati was informed about the purpose of the visit and the ongoing discussions in Geneva at the UN Human Rights Conference. Velayati apprised Dinesh Singh that the Chinese Foreign Minister Qian Qichen was currently visiting Tehran too and asked if he would like to meet him, to which the response was that he would think it over. Meanwhile, Dinesh Singh informed him that he was carrying a special letter from PM Narasimha Rao for President Rafsanjani. An hour later, Velayati confirmed a meeting with the President. At the meeting, there was no formal response to the letter, but the Iranian President assured him that they would give the matter careful consideration.

Later, Dinesh Singh agreed to meet the Chinese Foreign Minister Qian Qichen. At the meeting he stressed that Indo–Pakistan relations could best be handled on the basis of the Simla Agreement and bilateral contacts. Qian Qichen described the relations as a backlog of history, but his attitude was positive. He had already been briefed by Velayati about the purpose of Dinesh Singh's visit.

At the airport, when Dinesh Singh was departing from Tehran, Velayati held his hand and informed him that the President had instructed him to say that India's interest would be kept in mind. This had a positive impact from India's point of view on the deliberations in Geneva. The seeds of Pakistan's withdrawal of the resolution were sown during Dinesh Singh's one-day visit to

Iran, which was to be his last diplomatic initiative as he passed away a few days later.

On the final day of deliberation, 9 March 1994, when Pakistan was still hoping to get their resolution through, the Iranian permanent representative took the floor and asked for its deferral. Ambassador Prakash Shah at this stage, surprised by the unexpected move, sought procedural clarification. Very little was known to the Indian delegation as to what had transpired during Dinesh Singh's visit to Tehran. Brijesh Mishra had an inkling, and tapping Prakash Shah on the shoulder, advised him to accept the deferral proposal. The Indian delegation, meanwhile, held discussions with A.N. Verma, principal secretary to the PM in Delhi. After checking with the prime minister, Verma advised them to take any deal but ensure the resolution did not go through.

Before the resumption of the afternoon session, the Chinese ambassador approached the Indian delegation saying he had been in touch with Iranian Ambassador Naseri and was going to ask Pakistan to withdraw the resolution. At the same time at another venue, where a debate was going on about China, an Indian official cast his vote in favour of China. George Fernandes' proposed international seminar on Tibet did not take place as he was persuaded not to go ahead. The Chinese noted this. When the session reconvened, the leader of the Pakistan delegation, Iqbal Akhund, announced withdrawal of the Pakistan resolution.

An important aspect during the Geneva deliberations was that no important concession was yielded by India to the Commission or Centre for Human Rights on ground by committing to more transparency in the runup to the tabling of the resolution. Several parties tried to extract different undertakings by India. In Delhi the European Union (EU) hinted to the secretary west, MEA in Delhi, Vinod Grover, to give an undertaking for allowing a select team of rapporteurs to visit J & K as a quid pro quo for their support, which would have been no more than mere abstention. Fortunately, stout resistance from our mission in Geneva prevented this, because they rightly perceived this was another way of bringing Kashmir on the yearly agenda of the committee. It was as a compromise that it was decided to allow the EU Troika to visit instead. I had extended my support to this formula from Islamabad. This was safer as it resulted in a one-time report.

The downside in terms of Pakistan, was that it succeeded in raising though not internationalizing Kashmir in terms of the UN action. Mr Vajpayee reportedly remarked that it was humiliating for a big country like India to go around begging for votes of support from big and small countries.

The credit for the diplomatic triumph went to the team led by Shri Atal Bihari Vajpayee, but masterminded at every stage by the erudite Narasimha Rao. Vajpayee had said on different occasions that if their efforts failed, he would get the blame, and credit for the success would go to the prime minister. Years later, Manjeev Singh Puri who had worked at the UN and other international venues commented,

> In his inimitable style, Vajpayee often mentioned thereafter that the request from Prime Minister P.V. Narasimha Rao to lead the delegation left him with no choice other than accept even though he recognized that failure would mean opprobrium for him while the bouquets of success would go to the PM! He also noted that we had to learn lessons from this episode. The energizing of the then recently established National Human Rights Commission followed thereafter along with our even giving the International Committee of the Red Cross access to detainees in Kashmir.[40]

The diplomatic triumph was a result of a well-coordinated campaign backed fully by the PMO under A.N. Verma, MEA under K. Srinivasan, Ministry of Home Affairs (MHA) under N.N. Vohra, and, above all, with a high-level political and professional leadership. Pakistan has not forgotten what happened in Geneva in 1994 and continues to think of revenge for its defeat. Even decades later, there are suggestions to go back to Geneva. Dr Maleeha Lodhi, Pakistan's former envoy to the UN, told the Pakistan Senate Foreign Affairs Committee on 12 March 2020, that the Kashmir issue could lose international focus if urgent steps were not taken for convening a ministerial meeting of the Organization of Islamic Cooperation (OIC) and a special session of the UN Human Rights Council in Geneva exclusively on occupied Kashmir.[41]

Army Chief Gen. Asif Nawaz Janjua

As high commissioner in Islamabad, I was able to meet Chief of Army Staff, Asif Nawaz on social occasions. At these gatherings, I deliberately maintained a distance so as not to attract attention. But there were times when we were able to have good discussions. At a lunch sometime in 1992, we happened to arrive at the same time and shared the same golf cart to the venue. En route, I found his talk on Afghanistan most revealing. He said the Westerners, unlike 'you and me', will never understand Afghanistan. They will commit mistakes and the Afghans will do what they want to. Arrival at the venue cut short our brief talk. In July 1992, I met him on what I knew was a difficult day as he had reprimanded Abbasi for his misadventure in the Siachen area, leading to the death of several Pakistani soldiers. He did not know I was aware of these developments, but to his credit, throughout the meeting he did not give any appearance of being perturbed. He unfortunately passed away while still in office in January 1993. My wife called on his widow at Army House to offer her condolences. This surprised some, but was also appreciated. Later, when we met her by chance at Murree, she greeted us warmly. There was speculation around the controversy regarding his death. Interestingly, around the same time, the chief of staff of the Indian Army, Gen. Bipin Chandra Joshi, also died in office in November 1994. These were the only two chiefs in both India and Pakistan to have died in office. I recall comments made in Pakistan that the medical corps of the two countries did not properly evaluate the medical condition of their chiefs.

Changes in Northern Areas–Gilgit-Baltistan since 1947

During the British regime, Gilgit was divided into two parts— Gilgit Agency, which was administered by the British, and Gilgit Wazarat, which, though administered by Maharaja Hari Singh, was leased to the British in 1935. Both were part of the state of Jammu and Kashmir and were returned to the maharaja on 1 August 1947. The maharaja then deputed Ghansara Singh as the governor. However, Major Brown, commander of the Gilgit Scouts, an armed force which the British had raised in 1930, decided to intervene on behalf of Pakistan. The Muslim scouts, assisted and guided by Brown, arrested Governor Ghansara Singh on 1 November 1947 and raised the Pakistan flag. In a secret message to Pakistan, Brown asked them to take over the administration of the area. Pakistan immediately sent Sardar Muhammad Alam, previously a tahsildar in the NWFP, as governor. Brown states on record that he supported Pakistan to prevent Soviet penetration in the area. Though the British denied any role against India, it is interesting that Brown got both a Pakistani award and Order of the British Empire (OBE) simultaneously. Thus started the tragic story of Gilgit-Baltistan in 1947 which continues till now.

Two years later, by virtue of the Karachi Agreement of 1949, the POK government, on the pretext of geographical and administrative reasons, was asked to surrender administrative and legal control of Gilgit-Baltistan to the Federal Government of Pakistan. Henceforth, the political and administrative affairs of the region, Gilgit-Baltistan (G-B) were managed through the frontier tribal regulation (FTR). Accordingly, POK and Northern Areas became two distinct entities, without having any formal relationship between them. Pakistan had started describing G-B as Northern Areas. The Karachi Agreement also gave the Pakistan government the responsibility for the defence and foreign affairs of POK. It is significant that Sardar Ibrahim Khan, the then President of POK and a signatory of the agreement, claimed that he never signed the Karachi Agreement. While on a visit to London, he commented, 'Please do not blame me for this sin . . . I did not sign it . . . I want to clear my name while I am alive.'[42] This was also confirmed by Dr Shabbir Choudhry, a POK leader, in his blog. In legal terms, it makes the Karachi Agreement nonexistent.

I observed developments in the area during my two postings in Pakistan. General Ziaul Haq wanted to make the Northern Areas a part of Pakistan. In 1982, he asserted that the people of Northern Areas were not a part of the state of J & K, and extended his martial law to Northern Areas but not to POK. He was drawing a distinction between the two. In an interview to the Indian journalist, Kuldip Nayar (1 April 1982), Ziaul Haq said Gilgit, Hunza and Skardu of the Northern Areas were not a part of the disputed area.[43]

While addressing the Majlis-e-Shoora on 3 April 1982, Gen. Zia announced that three observers from Northern Areas would be appointed to the federal council or the Majlis-e-Shoora. I

was chargé d'affaires on that day in Pakistan and was present at
the Majlis-e-Shoora session, along with other foreign heads of
diplomatic missions in Islamabad. I returned to the embassy,
consulted colleagues and viewed old records which revealed that no
protest had been lodged earlier on Pakistan's penetration in G-B.
There was no time to consult Delhi. I concluded that an immediate
protest was necessary which I lodged with the additional secretary
in the Pakistan foreign office. This was perhaps the first time that
this matter had been formally taken up with Pakistan. The MEA
also took up the matter with the Pakistan Embassy. I ensured
that the minister was also briefed. Twelve days later on 15 April
1982, the Minister of External Affairs Shri P.V. Narasimha Rao
informed the Lok Sabha that Northern Areas are 'judicially and
constitutionally part of the Indian state of Jammu and Kashmir.
Our chargé d'affaires has already lodged a protest over the matter
with Pakistan Foreign Office,'[44] and the government was awaiting
the response from the Pakistan government. There was no official
reply to this but Pakistan did not appoint an observer from
Northern Areas to the Majlis-e-Shoora.

More than a decade later, the matter was again raised in
the back-channel negotiations with Pakistan, which I handled
during the tenure of PM Dr Manmohan Singh. The then
Pakistan foreign minister, Khurshid Mahmud Kasuri, wrote that
during the early period of back-channel discussions on Kashmir,
Pakistan accepted Gilgit and Baltistan as a part of Jammu and
Kashmir. He added,

> Before Independence, the Northern Areas including inter alia
> Gilgit and Baltistan, were part of the princely state of Jammu
> and Kashmir . . . During the back-channel negotiations also,
> the Indians made it abundantly clear that they could only
> accept an agreement regarding Jammu and Kashmir if the

Northern Areas were also included in the entire scheme. We confronted a dilemma . . . We therefore reached an agreement after many arguments and negotiations that there would be two units for the purposes of the agreement . . . comprising the areas respectively controlled by India and Pakistan.[45]

During my tenure as high commissioner to Pakistan, there was another interesting development. Right from the beginning, Pakistan separated G-B from POK so as to maintain greater control over it. This had throughout caused great concern to people of the area. A writ petition challenging the position of Pakistan on the status of Northern Areas was filled in the High Court of POK in the 1990s in what came to be known as the Muskeen case. The High Court of POK decided that the Northern Areas were a part of POK, and its administrative control should be with the Government of Azad Kashmir and not the Government of Pakistan. Pakistan did not implement that decision and had it vacated by its Supreme Court, which maintained that the high court had no jurisdiction to issue any such order in the matter. It described the matter as political, rather than a legal issue.

The location of G-B is unique, as in addition to India and Pakistan, it shares borders with Afghanistan and China. It was apparent Pakistan showed greater concern for the territory of Jammu and Kashmir it occupied than for the people living there. The economic and political interests of the people of the area have throughout been neglected. India's stand on G-B being a part of the Indian state of J & K has been consistent. The demography of the area has been changed and outsiders were settled in this area to achieve this objective. In 1948, Shias and Ismailis constituted 85 per cent of the population, but today only 50 per cent, which is evident from comparisons between the last two censuses in 1998 and 2017, because whereas the population of Pakistan increased by 56 per cent, in the same period that of G-B doubled; the desire of the people of G-B to be connected with India has been prevented by Pakistan despite the fact that two land routes— Kargil and Leh—on the Indian side of the LoC connect with Skardu and Khaplu (POK) side; Northern Areas were separated from the rest of POK to ensure greater federal control. There has been pandering to China's concerns as China, since 1962 and after the Sino–Pak agreement of 1963, occupies 19 per cent of the territory of J & K which includes some vital territory of POK which both have been using to the detriment of Indian interests.

Pakistan's Nuclear Programme

Narasimha Rao took interest in Pakistan's nuclear programme. On different occasions, we discussed both its commencement and ongoing developments. Pakistan took the decision to go nuclear in January 1972, at a meeting convened by Bhutto, of officials and nuclear scientists, in Multan. Mobilization of resources started thereafter. Negotiations with France for a plutonium reprocessing plant in 1973 ended in an agreement in March 1976. In May 1972, the Pakistani Metallurgist, Dr A.Q. Khan, joined Physics Dynamics Research Laboratory (in Dutch FDO), a subsidiary of Almelo Enrichment Consortium, a Dutch company, and returned to Pakistan in 1975 after obtaining details of the gas centrifuge enrichment process and a list of supplier firms in Europe for various assemblies.

In 1975, the 'Special Works Organization' was established in Islamabad under then Brig. Anees Ali Saeed, which began ordering items required for the nuclear programme through Pakistani embassies in Paris and Brussels, as also through various fictitious firms established for this purpose in West Germany and elsewhere in Europe. This was later confirmed in a BBC documentary. The pace and scope of both overt and covert activities of Pakistan from 1972 onwards made amply clear the hollowness of western propaganda that India's peaceful explosion in 1974 instigated Pakistan to go nuclear.

The Nuclear Programme not only continued unabated under President Ziaul Haq but later assumed a new priority. Pakistan's secret purchases since 1977, though denied by President Zia and his government, were well known. In addition to acquisition of nuclear technology information from Almelo in Holland, Pakistan obtained equipment and raw materials for a huge gas centrifuge at Kahuta (near Islamabad), a uranium fuel fabrication plant near Karachi and two pilot plants outside Rawalpindi. These plants produced plutonium 239 and uranium 235—essential ingredients for nuclear weapons or explosive devices. In 1981, the Canadian government intercepted supplies from a Canadian supplier of Pakistani origin. The supplies had reached Canada from the USA and were detected when they were being sent to Pakistan through a Middle Eastern country. In October 1981, the American customs detected a supply of zirconium, used to provide outer covering for fuel rods, used in the Karachi reactor. In 1982, there were credible reports of a Pakistan test in a Chinese location.

I told PM Narasimha Rao that I had written in my handover report as deputy chief of mission in Islamabad in September 1982 that Pakistan conceives its nuclear programme to subserve its strategic military interests, which would necessitate an explosion. It would, however, take time for it to suit both its internal and external compulsions. Pakistan preferred to wait until acquisition of military equipment from the USA, particularly the F-16 planes. He inquired whether this assessment had been shared with others. When I responded that I doubted it had been read by more than two people, he smiled and asked me to continue.

On New Year's Day in 1983, President Ziaul Haq said, 'Pakistan is not making a bomb,' and later on 6 September, he reiterated, 'Pakistan will not conduct such a test even for peaceful purposes.'[46] On 27 February 1985, he declared that Pakistan's nuclear project was for meeting its energy shortage. Around the same time, A.Q. Khan made his disclosures to Kuldip Nayar. A change was indicated in President Zia's public statement on 27 November 1987, 'Pakistan does possess the requisite technology to make an atom bomb but would not do so nor has it already made one.' On 22 May 1989, the civilian government under PM Benazir Bhutto approved a twenty-year plan for developing nuclear power generation. On 5 June 1989, Benazir Bhutto announced, 'Pakistan will not allow anyone to inspect its nuclear installations.' This was repeated by President Ghulam Ishaq Khan on 25 August 1991 when he declared, 'We will not accept any conditions about our nuclear programmes.'

I had kept the prime minister informed both about public statements and other information regarding Pakistan's nuclear programme. On 7 February 1992, foreign secretary, Shahryar Khan, in an interview to the editorial board of the *Washington Post*, acknowledged that Pakistan possessed elements which, if put together, could become a nuclear device. He confirmed that these elements included potential weapon cores fashioned from highly enriched uranium. Prime Minister Sharif, in an interview to CNN on 13 January 1993, said that there was no gainsaying the fact that Pakistan had achieved nuclear capability. He added, 'We are developing it for peaceful purposes, and we have no intention of making a nuclear device.' Significantly, on 10 March 1993, Pakistan's nuclear scientist A.Q. Khan said that the armed forces were kept in the dark about Pakistan's nuclear programme for the first three years of its existence. He said President Ghulam Ishaq Khan, in different capacities, was the head of the programme since its inception in 1976 and had to face 'unbearable external pressure' on account of his role in the nuclear programme. Interestingly, on 23 July 1993, in an interview to Awaz International of London, former army chief Gen. Mirza Aslam Beg claimed that Pakistan had crossed the nuclear line in 1987. He was quoted as saying, 'Pakistan carried out the test in cold laboratory conditions and it was very successful. No one should have any doubt about that.'[47] Five days later, on 28 July, a Pakistan foreign office spokesman denied that Pakistan had tested any nuclear device in 1987 and added that Gen. Aslam Beg had already clarified that he had been misquoted. Much later, when I asked Gen. Aslam Beg at a social function about his statement, he laughingly said generals make statements, diplomats make both statements and denials. On 30 July 1993, at a press conference in Washington, following his meetings with U.S. vice president Al Gore, Pakistan caretaker prime minister Moeen Qureshi said, 'It is correct that so far as nuclear capacity is concerned, Pakistan has the technical capacity to prepare a nuclear facility. It is not our intention to move to any next stage or acquire nuclear weapons. In other words, we have the capacity to make one within a reasonable period of time.' It is evident that the Pakistan foreign office clarification two days earlier was made keeping the meeting with the U.S. vice president in mind. Immediately after her election and taking over as prime minister for the second time, Benazir Bhutto, in her first broadcast on 20 October 1993, said, 'We will safeguard the nuclear programme of Pakistan and will not allow any damage to our national integrity.' In a policy statement to the National Assembly on 28 November 1993, Foreign Minister Sardar Asif Ali said that Pakistan had acquired some technical capability in the nuclear field; however, a political decision had been taken at the highest level to use the technical capability for peaceful purposes only and not to produce nuclear weapons. He also stated that Pakistan would, under no circumstances, roll back

its peaceful nuclear programme. A few days later on 11 December
1993, in an article in the government-controlled *Pakistan Times*,
former army chief Gen. Aslam Beg repeated that Pakistan had
acquired nuclear capabilities in 1987. He added that during a
meeting in the presidency in January 1989, attended by President
Ghulam Ishaq Khan, Prime Minister Bhutto and Army Chief
Aslam Beg, the unanimous assessment was that Pakistan had
acquired the nuclear capability vitally needed for its security and
that it had significantly added to its defensive strength by achieving
a 'credible deterrence'. Shortly thereafter, on 10 January 1994, PM
Bhutto, in an interview to the Associated Press of America, stated
that Pakistan needed a nuclear deterrent against India. On 7 April
1994, at an impromptu press conference in the premises of the
Pakistan National Assembly, on the eve of the visit to Pakistan
of U.S. deputy secretary of state, Strobe Talbott, PM Bhutto, in
response to a question whether Pakistan was ready for 'verifiable
capping', said, 'We believe in non-proliferation and we will
consider every proposal presented to us but it is clear that we are
not going to open our installations unilaterally as there is a national
consensus on this issue.' Ten days later in the course of a private
visit to Pakistan, former caretaker PM Moeen Qureshi said at a
news conference in Islamabad that Pakistan's nuclear programme
had been 'capped four years ago', adding, 'Let us not add to our
arsenal of nuclear weapons.' In reply to a separate query from the
correspondent of the *Dawn* as to whether Pakistan actually had a
nuclear arsenal, Moeen Qureshi said, 'Yes, we have something.'
PM Rao was kept fully informed of these developments and
wanted additional information about M-11 missiles which was
given separately to him.

India had always been carefully monitoring reports about
China's assistance to Pakistan in the nuclear field. Rao, when
he was minister of external affairs, as early as 30 March 1984,

made a statement in the Lok Sabha expressing concern on Sino–Pakistan nuclear collaboration. He extensively quoted from statements of senior U.S. functionaries, who had testified that China had transferred sensitive nuclear weapon design information to Pakistan.

As it emerged later, Narasimha Rao, who I found always wanted me to inform him of Pakistan's nuclear programme, had been paying close attention to India's nuclear programme. Arunachalam, the head of Defence Research and Development Organisation (DRDO) had separately informed him in 1991 that Pakistan had the capability to produce ten atomic bombs.[48] There had been reports about India conducting nuclear tests during Prime Minister Rao's tenure. It is mentioned in Rao's biography, that 'two days after Narasimha Rao's body was cremated in 2004, an emotional Atal Bihari Vajpayee, paying his old friend a startling tribute, stated that Rao was the "true father" of India's nuclear program. Vajpayee said that in May 1996, a few days after he had succeeded Rao as prime minister, Rao told him, "*Samagri tayyar hai*", (the ingredients are ready). "You can go ahead, Rao told me that the bomb was ready. I only exploded it."'[49]

Sitapati, an Indian journalist and author, later writes,

The BJP's Atal Bihari Vajpayee took over as prime minister on 16 May 1996. Narasimha Rao, Abdul Kalam and R. Chidambaram went to meet the new prime minister 'so that', in Kalam's telling, 'the smooth takeover of such a very important programme can take place'. Vajpayee's revelations of 2004 make clear what was discussed. Immediately afterwards, Vajpayee ordered nuclear tests, but rescinded that order when it was clear that his government would not last. In 1998, back as prime minister for the second time, Vajpayee was able to finally 'go ahead' and explode.[50]

Visit of Arjun Singh and Srinivasan to Pakistan

Towards the end of 1994 and early 1995, there were some interesting visits between India and Pakistan in both directions. Foreign Secretary K. Srinivasan, led an Indian delegation to the Commonwealth senior officials' meeting in Islamabad, at a time when the Pakistan government was not engaging in any bilateral discussions (21–25 November 1994). Virtually back to back, India's senior minister in charge of human resources and development, Arjun Singh, visited Pakistan (26–29 November) to attend the twelfth Conference of Commonwealth Education Ministers. He was given priority placing at functions connected with the conference. To enable the two visitors to get acquainted with public opinion in Pakistan, I hosted large receptions of over 100 people each for both, in the same week and tried to ensure no duplication of guests. It was even more necessary for Foreign Secretary Srinivasan, as this was a low point of India–Pakistan relations, when Pakistan did not interact with the Indian foreign secretary on his visit to Pakistan on bilateral relations. The reception provided him an opportunity to meet and exchange views with leaders of political parties and think tanks. A former Pakistan foreign secretary told Srinivasan that his interaction at the reception undoubtedly gave him a much better idea of developments in Pakistan than he would have got from his counterpart. It is interesting that people-to-people contact continued at the same period. Pakistan–India People's Forum, a non-official body, held a conference in New Delhi (24–25 February 1995), and a month later the ninth session of the India–Pakistan Neemrana dialogue was held in New Delhi (13–14 March 1995). Shri I.K. Gujral, on a visit to Pakistan to attend a seminar by three NGOs, met President Leghari, Prime Minister Benazir Bhutto, opposition leader Nawaz Sharif and

POK PM Abdul Qayyum. Our attempt was to keep contact at non-official levels as active as possible. In May, President Leghari visited India for the eighth SAARC summit in June 1995. Benazir Bhutto decided to abstain and sent Leghari as the conference is technically a meeting of heads of state or governments. Her policy backfired as Leghari, thereafter, started projecting himself as an independent authority rather than an obedient President and eventually dismissed her in November 1996. In between, Pakistan tried to create an issue over the visit of Pakistan artist Abida Parveen in March 1995, who was to have visited India for a performance on the occasion of Pakistan Day. Pakistan claimed she was denied a visa. The factual position was that a visa was given even though she gave an incomplete visa application.

P.V. Narasimha Rao once summed up the core of India's foreign policy as a 'role of persuasion'. With Pakistan, it was a role he consistently sought to exercise at three levels. One, with Pakistan itself, seeking to persuade it that a relationship with India that was stable and secure, even if not necessarily cast in the idiom of shared history, song and literature, was in its own national and global interest. Two, with his own government and party, which all too often and understandably, sought to view the relationship in the specific and limited context of the subject at hand, whether security, commerce or the management of common waters, or cultural exchange. And third, with the broader national community beyond, including parties in opposition particularly, to avoid the temptation to use the issue of the bilateral relationship to challenge or criticize the performance of the government itself, and so hold it hostage to factors partisan and irrelevant.

As prime minister, he added a fourth element, using imagination in foreign policy to enhance powers of persuasion at home. The access given to external observers to Jammu and Kashmir, and his broadcast from Ouagadougou, are instances in point, in which he was very clear he was acting as the leader of India, in relation to political processes within the Union of India. He was acutely aware of the many points of brusque congruence, and at times messy overlap, between domestic and foreign policy, a situation sharpened, in the case of Pakistan, by two factors. One, its clandestine efforts within India to diminish the Indian state, and two, the frequent, often violent, changes in its government, in stark contrast to India's own, where every prime minister was elected to office and was, or had been, a member of a political party.

In the very first public speech of Mr Rao's that I heard, at the Pakistan Institute of International Affairs in Karachi on 11 June 1981, he made an assertion in which he genuinely believed that India had 'an abiding interest, even a vested interest, in the stability of Pakistan'. Even casual reflection would attest to the truth of that affirmation, particularly in the context of the human and financial costs to India from a neighbour that did not possess the stability of self-assurance and a clear focus on compulsions within its own borders, the costs of which he became particularly conscious as prime minister, costs which he saw in complete contrast to the possibilities of bilateral economic development, which he felt the reforms he had initiated within India would allow.

This was not a new conviction. A long eight years earlier he had, in his hand, drafted a paragraph for Prime Minister Indira Gandhi's address to South Asian leaders,

> We have had our political differences in the past and have even now, but economic cooperation will give a strong impetus to closer friendship and greater stability in South Asia. We should avoid bilateral differences and aim at concentrating on what unites us and helps us in our common quest for peace and

development. We are all equals. We are against exploitation
and domination. We want to be friends with all on a footing
of equality. We should ever be vigilant against the attempts of
external powers to influence our functioning.[51]

That last line was to be reflected in the last line of the last speech
he was to deliver at the United Nations in October 1995, when
he concluded, 'I have deliberately kept bilateral matters out of this
short intervention,'[52] a bilateralism vivid in its many possibilities,
of open dialogue and back channels, of a stable network of
agreements and accords governing specific aspects of the
relationship, of a community of interest and competition in sports
and the arts, and yet, as Pakistan's policies proved, a bilateralism
susceptible to sacrifice to internal and external ambitions.

5

Professional Engagement, Personal Interactions

General Ziaul Haq

When I arrived in Islamabad on my first tenure in Pakistan as deputy chief of mission (1978–82), Gen. Ziaul Haq was already in power. Though hand-picked by Bhutto, because he believed him to be obedient and easy to manipulate, it was Gen. Ziaul Haq who engineered the July 1977 coup against him. Bhutto was framed for murder and subsequently executed. Gen. Ziaul Haq's (later President) promise to hold elections within ninety days never materialized and he held the reign of power until his death on 17 August 1988.

As the second-in-command at the embassy, and by virtue of the absence of an ambassador, I was chargé d'affaires for seventeen months of my tenure. During my posting in Islamabad and later in Delhi, as head of the Pakistan–Afghan desk in the MEA, I was present at different sessions in President Zia's meetings with the Indian president, prime minister, ambassador and my own, making it a total, at a rough estimate, of over a hundred hours.

President Ziaul Haq avoided saying 'no', but at the same time was slow in taking action on what he had agreed.

On one occasion, I observed that both President Ziaul Haq and Foreign Minister Sahabzada Yaqub Khan addressed each other as 'sir'. I came to know that this was because Zia had served under Yaqub Khan in the army, and by irony of fate, now as President was his superior. Soon both adjusted to their new roles.

In February 1982, President Ziaul Haq attended the Indo–Pak hockey match in Peshawar. I was chargé d'affaires at that time. Through his secretary, he requested me to join him. Our initial conversation was on the game, and his reference to my paternal grandfather being president of the municipal committee showed how well briefed he was. I broached the subject of the forthcoming visit of the commerce secretary, Krishnaswamy Rao Sahib, to discuss trade. His immediate response was that this would create a pro-India lobby, to which I responded that this would help to improve relations. He quickly retracted his words by saying this would, on the contrary, create a lobby against trade with India. Normally, for a man who was careful with his words, this was a rare slip of indiscretion which I observed. When I left Islamabad at the end of my posting, I got a call from his powerful chief of army staff, Gen. Arif, to convey to me the President's best wishes. Few heads of state would do this to a departing number two of a diplomatic mission.

President Ziaul Haq was born in Jalandhar (India) and had studied in the prestigious St Stephen's College in Delhi. As President, he visited his alma mater and identified his hostel room. I was among some ex-Stephanians present on that occasion. When he invited a delegation of the college that included his teacher, Prof. Kapadia, to Pakistan, I received them at the Attari border. The Pakistan government had hired a bus for the delegation, but a car had been put in attendance for his teacher. Prof. Kapadia was head of the department of history when I had studied in college and had taught me too. On hearing a separate car was awaiting him, he said he would prefer to travel with the rest in the bus. The military liaison officer said he could lose his job if standing orders to him were not adhered to. With a compromise reached, Professor Kapadia travelled in the bus throughout his stay while the car followed regardless. Three Stephanians from the embassy and consulate, ambassador Natwar Singh, the consul general from Karachi, Mani Shankar Aiyar and I too attended the functions.

As chargé d'affaires, my wife and I were invited for a farewell tea for military adviser, Brigadier Srikant and his wife, at the residence of the President in Rawalpindi. This was hosted by the President in his capacity as chief of army staff. Before entering the premises, I instructed the chauffeur to keep the engine of the car running after half an hour as the official diesel Mercedes took a while to start. Knowing the President's penchant for seeing off visitors, I did not want to keep him waiting. The others felt I was overreacting, but the President did come to our car to see us off.

Perhaps because he was the son of a maulvi, he was the first army chief to openly praise Islamic groups. He developed political ties with the Jamaat-i-Islami and provided arms and economic support for the radical Afghan militia. During this period, there was a significant increase of madrasas which became centres for the ethos of violence inspired by promotion of jihad as a righteous duty. The Afghan proxy war against the Union of Soviet Socialist Republics (USSR) resulted in Pakistan becoming a frontline state, receiving generous donations of arms and money from the USA and Saudi Arabia. President Zia had a shrewd political mind, and under him Islamist extremism acquired legitimacy.[1]

President Zia's personal life was without blemish. He was the subject of caricature and derision but was not a fool. His traits of ruthlessness and deviousness were camouflaged with a display of humility and courteousness. His seeing off visitors to the car and discreetly placing a gift for them, usually a carpet, disarmed them and boosted egos. This was also evident in the case of George Fernandes, who had emphatically claimed he would raise the issue of Benazir with him, but had instead returned full of praise for the man. At the meeting, the President won over Fernandes by saying, 'Sir, I want to learn about labour issues from you.'

On a transit stopover in Delhi, he had a meeting with PM Indira Gandhi. The ministerial-level discussions, led by Foreign Minister Narasimha Rao and Pakistan Finance Minister Ghulam Ishaq Khan, to discuss the Indian proposal for establishing a joint commission, was rejected by the Pakistan delegation, but agreed to by President Zia at his meeting with Indira Gandhi. The agreement was signed during Zia's visit to India in March 1983.

At a meeting with President Zail Singh in March 1983, when President Zia attended the nonaligned summit, he expressed a desire for peace with India. This was a time when help was being provided to militants in Punjab by Pakistan.[2] Zail Singh astutely responded in Punjabi that a woman cannot do two things at the same time (*Akh bhi maare, tey gungat bhi kaddae*) she cannot wink provocatively and cover her face at the same time. Laughter followed his words but he had made his point.

President Zia, during the nonaligned summit, while staying at the Oberoi Hotel told me that he did not know what the protocol officials had brought for me, but he and his wife had selected some gifts for my wife, which she might be missing after her stay in Islamabad.

Mangoes were a part of his diplomatic overtures, and it was ironical that mangoes might have led to his death on 17 August 1988. A bomb hidden in a crate of mangoes aboard the PAF C-130 plane could have been responsible for the crash that ended his eleven-year rule.

Benazir Bhutto

My first meeting with Benazir Bhutto was at a reception at the Saudi Arabian Embassy in 1978, when Zulfikar Ali Bhutto's murder case was before the Supreme Court of Pakistan. She told me the judges were divided five to four in her father's favour. Her assessment was correct. The eventual four to three judgment against Bhutto became possible only after the retirement of one judge and disqualification of another. Meeting Benazir was difficult during President Zia's time, as she was either under house arrest or in prison. However, I did manage to send her some reactions of the Indian media on the execution of her father. The Indian government had preferred to remain silent on the issue. Many years later while posted to Hungary, I was presented her autobiography, *Daughter of the East*, by visiting Miraj Khalid, then speaker of the Pakistan National Assembly, and later prime minister for a brief period. He said Benazir had asked him to give a copy to me. The hardships she had suffered in those years made her a survivor. Through sheer grit and determination, she carved a political niche for herself in a male-dominated society. Tall, imposing and elegant, she was intelligent, articulate, confident and bravely spoke her mind. Some called her arrogant. Being politically savvy, she inherited Bhutto's mantle and led his Pakistan Peoples Party (PPP). A good orator, she instinctively knew how to appeal to the masses. I recall being on the same table as her at the wedding of the son of Gen. Beg, and observed she certainly did not mince words to make a point. She married Asif Zardari and had three children in quick succession, including during her tenure as prime minister too. This resulted in her being referred to in jest as perpetually pregnant prime minister, by people in Pakistan.

On my first posting to Pakistan, we got to know Asif Zardari's father, Hakim Ali Zardari very well. He was a regular visitor to our house during his visits to Islamabad. In fact, when we were having trouble with the insurance company, in respect of car insurance, he advised us to shift the insurance policy of the car to the Federal Insurance Company of which he was a director. It worked well. However, during my second tenure, as high commissioner, when his daughter-in-law was the prime minister, he did not meet us.

On my first visit to Karachi as high commissioner in early 1992, Benazir arrived at the reception hosted by Consul General Mani Tripathi and his wife Shashi, who was deputy consul general, claiming the invite had been only for her mother, but she had come to meet me even though she was not invited. The consul general insisted she was, but she held her ground.

During my meeting with her in Islamabad, when she was leader of the Opposition, I observed her little children peeping into the living room where we were seated. She waved them aside, adding that whenever she had meetings, visitors were more engrossed in discussions than the cakes and savouries offered. As the children looked forward to the leftovers, she always ordered what they liked.

After becoming prime minister, initially she did not meet me for some time, the reason being, I was told informally by her political associate, that she was unhappy about my close association with her political rival, Nawaz Sharif, when he was prime minister. Conveying this to Prime Minister Narasimha Rao, I suggested he should appoint someone else as high commissioner for better access. This was dismissed with the words, 'You are our high commissioner, not theirs.'

However, before my departure on completing my tenure, she hosted a lunch for me, following my farewell call on her—this was the first time any Pakistan prime minister had ever hosted a meal for a departing Indian envoy. As the lunch was after the meeting, she inquired about the colleague who had accompanied me for the meeting. When told he was not invited, she insisted he must join. The list of guests included the defence minister and foreign and defence secretaries. She inquired about foreign minister, Sardar Asif, who had excused himself on some pretext.

After lunch we all sat in different areas of the room. She and I spoke alone. She made no significant statement on bilateral relations in the first few minutes but suddenly dropped a bombshell, saying laughingly, 'Why don't you send the missile man to us?' (She was referring to Abdul Kalam, who a decade later became President of India). I said I hoped she did not mean this seriously as I would not be reporting this in my conversation with her. I told her that Muslims in India were held in high esteem and were holding high positions in the country. This was unlike her own home province of Sindh, where the Mohajir Muslims who came from India were still treated as second-rate citizens. She realized she had committed a mistake and changed the subject.

I mentioned this conversation verbally to PM Narasimha Rao, who was surprised and said my response had been appropriate. The only other person I mentioned this to was my good friend, Ronen Sen, who was ambassador in Moscow, during a chance meeting in Delhi shortly thereafter. He too felt I had done the right thing by not putting her comment on paper.

News of the lunch she had hosted for me travelled fast. On reaching Germany, my next posting, the Pakistan ambassador in Germany, Lt Gen. Durrani, former head of ISI, expressed surprise and wondered if Pakistan was changing its policy towards India.

Nawaz Sharif

On my first visit to Lahore, after joining the embassy in Islamabad in 1978, a common friend introduced me to a young businessman. Luckily for me, it was Mian Nawaz Sharif. He received me at the airport in his sports car and was my first guide to Lahore. The primary purpose of my visit was to attend a meeting Ambassador Shankar Bajpai was addressing, at the Lahore Chamber of Commerce. Nawaz Sharif too attended.

Later, en route to Murree, he, together with his family, stopped in Islamabad and spent an afternoon with us. On a subsequent visit to Lahore, we spent time with his family in their large house. He showed us the five identical houses his father, a leading businessman in Punjab, had made for him and his brothers. He was also a keen cricketer.

On a subsequent visit to Lahore, we were with him when President Ziaul Haq announced denationalization measures that benefited his steel industry. Congratulatory calls to him started pouring in.

Even after the completion of my tenure in Islamabad, I remained in touch with Nawaz Sharif. He came on a private visit to Delhi with Governor Qureshi of Punjab, Pakistan. At that time, I was heading the Pakistan/Afghanistan/Iran desk. I took Nawaz Sharif for dinner at the Taj Hotel Chinese restaurant, House of Ming, where a waiter accidentally dropped soup on his white suit. The hotel apologized and offered to dry-clean it, but he remained cool and declined the offer. I arranged a call, for both him and the governor, on President Zail Singh where the governor stated there ought to be good relations between the two countries, bemoaning this was impossible due to the negative approach of bureaucrats. The President cryptically responded in Punjabi that bureaucrats were like horses: if kept under control they ran well, but if the rider was weak, they overthrew him, conveying it was the leadership rather than the bureaucrats to blame. A lunch at the state guest house, Hyderabad House, was hosted for them too.

In April 1985, I had accompanied Foreign Secretary Romesh Bhandari on a visit to Pakistan. On reaching Lahore, I was informed that Nawaz Sharif had been appointed chief minister of Punjab that very day. I took some of the sweets to Nawaz Sharif from those we were carrying for President Zia. Though I was unable to meet him because he had already left for the governor's residence to discuss the formation of his cabinet, I left the sweets with a congratulatory note and rushed back to the airport to catch the flight to Islamabad with the foreign secretary.

When told of my appointment as high commissioner, Nawaz Sharif told his foreign secretary, Shahryar Khan, to give an agreement the same day, which was unusual.

On my arrival in Islamabad to take over as high commissioner, a pleasant surprise awaited me. There was a call from the prime minister's office inviting my family and me for lunch after presenting my credentials. This was postponed by a day to enable his wife, Kulsoom, to attend on her return from Lahore. The conversation at the lunch included our past contacts, emphasis on highways in Pakistan and appreciation of his interaction with former PM Chandra Shekhar at the recent Malé SAARC summit. His wife praised the educational system of India. As instructed by PM Narasimha Rao, I specifically raised the issue of Pakistan support for Sikh extremists, saying that India had controlled the situation, but if Pakistan also changed its attitude it would help. Interestingly, he responded he would do as much as he could. After lunch, we were shown around the residence. All the rooms were tastefully done by different designers, some of whom we knew. They wanted to know which was the best. He asked what he could do for me in Islamabad. My only request was that I should be able to meet him whenever there was need. He designated an official in his office and shared his phone number with me for this purpose. This helped in arranging many meetings. The only day I could not contact him was when Babri Masjid was demolished.

Following his dismissal as PM, when Nawaz Sharif was reappointed PM by the Supreme Court, I was the first foreign envoy to meet him with a congratulatory message from PM Narasimha Rao. He lost the elections in October 1993. Later, as leader of the Opposition, he hosted a farewell lunch for me in July 1995 at his Murree house, which was attended by the top leadership of his party. He told me he would like to see me at his swearing-in ceremony when he was again appointed prime minister.

When he did again become prime minister, Mushahid Hussain, who was at that time a leading member of his party, came to my house in Germany where I was ambassador, conveying greetings from PM Nawaz Sharif which I reciprocated warmly. I later met Nawaz Sharif under unusual circumstances in Jeddah in 2004. When he was re-elected as prime minister in 2007, I, as special envoy to PM Manmohan Singh, visited Lahore for a day to convey greetings from the Indian PM. We revived memories and hoped for a better future.

I was fortunate to know Nawaz Sharif as prime minister, leader of the Opposition, PM elect, businessman and in exile. The common denominator was the dignity he maintained throughout. His temperament was that of a businessman; he was astute, hospitable and easy to talk to. In discussions, despite differences of opinion on some issues, he showed maturity and understanding of the other's position. He always wanted better relations with India.

Wali Khan

Wali Khan, a freedom fighter, was opposed to the partition of India, and with the creation of Pakistan, agitated for Pashtun autonomy. During presidential elections, he supported Fatima

Jinnah against Ayub Khan, leading to his imprisonment and disqualification from elections. He referred to his political rival, Zulfikar Ali Bhutto, as Adolph Bhutto, while Bhutto accused him of collusion with India and Afghanistan to ruin Pakistan.

He was the son of Khan Abdul Ghaffar Khan, (1890–1988) who was popularly known as Badshah Khan and had started the Khudai Khidmatgars (servants of God) in 1929 to bring about social reforms in society. His relentless nonviolent struggle against the British earned him the title of Frontier Gandhi. Respected and adored, he had the courage to believe in and work for his convictions. He attended the Karachi Congress in 1931 and was arrested and kept in a Bihar jail. I have vague memories of his arranging Mahatma Gandhi's trip to Peshawar, where women donated jewels for the national movement. I was present in Delhi when the Nehru Peace Award was conferred on him in 1969, and again at the Delhi airport when PM Rajiv Gandhi received him when he came for the Congress party's centenary meeting in 1985. I also spent some time with him at the residence of Muhammad Yunus, where he stayed for some time, before proceeding for the Bombay Congress session.

I recall an incident when Wali Khan had invited Ambassador Natwar Singh, his wife and us to his ancestral home in Charsadda. In accordance with Pakistan regulations for Indian diplomats, the embassy applied for permission for our travel to Charsadda. At the last moment, the Pakistan foreign office rejected the application. In those days, calls to Charsadda were difficult, so Natwar Singh asked the chief of protocol to inform Wali Khan, which he did not. Wali Khan later told us there was no need for us to feel guilty. He had in any case, not prepared lunch because he heard the news of permission not granted on the BBC.

Later, when I returned to Pakistan as high commissioner, we met regularly. Once the foreign minister, Agha Shahi, Wali Khan and we were present at Shaukat Hyat's house. Wali Khan related an instance when President Zia offered him the post of prime minister of the country which he refused. Turning to Shahi, he asked whether he was aware of this. The response was negative. Wali Khan mischievously added that he hardly expected President Zia to discuss such serious political matters with him. When Shahi left, Shaukat questioned Wali for pulling Shahi's leg in the presence of an Indian diplomat.

He and his wife, Nasim, were our guests on several occasions. A well-read and intelligent leader, he maintained good relations with Indians. His knowledge of the history of NWFP and Afghanistan was an education. I also knew his son Asfandyar, who became the party leader after him. Both felt the 1972 Simla Agreement was the basis to bring India and Pakistan together. I was among those who had met the leaders of three generations—Frontier Gandhi Ghaffar Khan, his son Wali Khan and grandson Asfandyar.

Mir Afzal Khan

Mir Afzal Khan was an important player in the politics of NWFP (now Khyber Pakhtunkhwa). His father, Sarfaraz Khan, had married the granddaughter of Amir Dost Mohammad Khan, the Afghan ruler who had challenged the British on several occasions.

After 1947, Mir Afzal owned the Premier Sugar Mills in Mardan, of which my maternal grandfather had been director since its inception till his death in 1958. My mother had a few shares which were held by my father. In 1978, on my first posting to Pakistan, Mir Afzal on meeting me in Islamabad, presented me a box of sugar, which he said was in lieu of the dividends for the shares which had been declared enemy property after the 1965 war. In 1992, when I returned as high commissioner, Mir Afzal was the sixteenth chief minister of the province. On a visit to

Peshawar, I asked for an appointment and was promptly requested to reach the chief minister's residence by 6 p.m. as it would be followed by dinner. On arrival, I was surprised that the cabinet of NWFP was there to welcome me. Mir Afzal, introducing me to his colleagues, said this was a rare opportunity to meet a diplomat from Peshawar, born in the city and now representing what newspapers described as an enemy country, adding the subcontinent requires the enemy country to be treated as friendly. He talked of the Premier Sugar Mills, my maternal grandfather and his house in Peshawar where I was born, which became the residence and office of the British deputy high commissioner, from 1947–67 and thereafter the Cantonment House. Another minister spoke of how my paternal grandfather, as chairman and owner of the Peshawar Electric Company, gave rebates to people who complained of excessive billing. He even showed a photocopy of the bill in which he had given a rebate of four annas (25 paise), to explain the increase in inflation from the early 1940s to 1990s. Another mentioned a cinema hall called Picture House, owned by my father. Another interesting revelation by one of the ministers, which I was neither aware of nor able to confirm, was that the British government had asked Khan Bahadur Kuli Khan Khattak and my maternal grandfather to resolve with the Pashtun tribes in the border areas the issue of building a railway line between the settled and tribal areas of NWFP. They did so. However, when the first train went, the Pashtun tribal leaders objected, saying the agreement never mentioned movement of trains and only pertained to the building of a railway track. The two negotiators were again sent and another agreement was reached involving a further payment to the tribal leaders. Everyone laughed, and the ministers happily mentioned that the Pashtuns always had the last word. I was humbled by the welcome and research some of the ministers had done on my family. When they left, Mir Afzal, a generous host, offered a splendid array of frontier dishes. It was a unique evening, which perhaps no diplomat from any other country would experience.

Mian Ziauddin

Pakistan's high commissioner in the late 1950s was, before Partition, a leading lawyer, my paternal grandfather's legal adviser and my father's senior at the bar. On a visit to Peshawar in early 1979, and after initial pleasantries he humorously set the rules for future meetings with him and his family. He said his son-in-law, who was also present and had been a prisoner of war in India in 1971, would meet me whenever he visited Islamabad, and it was expected I look after him and his daughter well. His son in the Pakistan foreign office should be treated as any other diplomat. As regards his elder son, who was at that time vice chief of air staff and not in President Zia's good books, I should show no sign of recognition in public. Thereafter, he took me for a drive to a house which my paternal grandfather had bought on his advice a few months before Partition. He put both his hands on his waist, saying he always felt guilty when he saw the house and asked what I thought of his advice. Clearly nobody had expected the partition. I responded it was sincere and my grandfather would have got some compensation for it. We both laughed. The next day, at a pre-wedding function of Gen. Habibullah's son Reza, he mentioned in my presence to some guests that he had got some good news from Iran that the generals had all been shot. There was pin-drop silence. His audience were senior serving generals of the Pakistan Army. Some people were surprised that this was said in the presence of an Indian diplomat. This was typical Pashtun candid outspokenness.

General Habibullah

Gen. Habibullah was the son of Khan Bahadur Kuli Khan Khattak, one of the closest friends of my maternal grandfather R.B. Dina Nath Kakar. He would have become army chief in Pakistan in the 1950s, had Ayub Khan not extended his tenure. Later, his daughter married Ayub's son, Gohar. The general subsequently became one of Pakistan's richest industrialists and moved to Karachi. He was in Peshawar when I, together with my mother Kunti, her sister Sheila and husband Kishan Chand Khatri, my wife and children, visited the city. Informed of our visit, the general lost no time in coming to the hotel saying the biggest insult to a Pashtun was that his sisters stay at a hotel, and on his instructions, the hotel staff started collecting the baggage. He said I could stay on at the hotel as I was chargé d'affaires of India, but the rest were going to his house. My children, Vikram and Diya, enjoyed their stay in 10, Fort Road, which offered the facilities of a swimming pool and riding. Ten years later, when I returned to Pakistan, I was told that when the general took my family to his house, he had created a problem for his younger son, a serving fighter pilot for the F-16 planes in the Pakistan Air Force. He told his father he was not even given time to inform his superiors that Indians were going to stay in the same house. His father suggested a simple solution. He should shift with his family to his father-in-law's house for the duration of the stay of the Indian guests. On visits to Karachi, I always met the general, but on the visit after the demolition of the Babri Masjid, he specially came to meet me despite being unwell. Later in 1995, we went to Peshawar to attend his grandson's wedding and were told he could not come due to ill health. He passed away on the day of the wedding, and his body was flown to Peshawar in an army plane by his son. I attended his funeral.

Aslam Khattak

Aslam Khattak, elder brother of Gen. Habibullah, former governor of NWFP and Pakistan's ambassador to Iran, was a senior minister in Nawaz Sharif's government when I arrived in Pakistan as high commissioner. My call on him at his office was made informal as he invited some members of his family to it. Discussions covered no official subjects. However, the following day newspapers covering the meeting wrote that the senior minister had criticized India's policy in respect of Kashmir. Even before I could react, I received a call from him apologizing that his office had issued an earlier prepared statement, and he invited me to a private breakfast the following week. At breakfast, he asked me to look closely at a photograph on the wall of his study. It was a group photograph where I immediately recognized both my grandfathers. A week later he sent me a framed copy of the photograph with names of all those in it. I had several informal meetings with him, both in Islamabad and Peshawar. Just before leaving Pakistan on completion of my tenure in July 1995, as a private citizen, he invited my wife and me to his house in Abbottabad. On arrival at the NWFP frontier, there was a confrontation between the security guards trailing me and the local police. Aslam Khattak had, in a thoughtful gesture, requested the governor to give me a special escort as this was to be my last visit to the province as high commissioner. It took a while for matters to be sorted out. However, we spent a memorable evening where he recounted several stories of the past. He explained the reason he had invited us to Abbottabad was to see his house built by his father in 1925. In those days there were hardly any architects, and the house had been designed by my maternal grandfather, an engineer and close friend of his father. The following day the newspapers mentioned that Lambah and Aslam Khattak were schoolmates, regardless of the fact that there was a thirty-year age gap between the two![3]

Kulsoom Saifullah

Kulsoom Saifullah, the matriarch of the Saifullah family and daughter of Khan Bahadur Kuli Khan, was a leading figure in NWFP. All her sons held important positions in different political parties and business concerns. The family were among the pioneers in bringing mobile phone technology to Pakistan. Two of them, Salim and Anwar, held important ministerial posts in different governments. She told me that the house she was staying in, which had been bought from the Evacuee Trust Property Board, had originally belonged to my paternal grandfather. We had interesting discussions on different visits with the family.

Just after the Babri Masjid episode, on a visit to Islamabad, she told my wife that she had met President Ghulam Ishaq Khan (whose daughter was married to her son Anwar), and told him that he should ensure that no harm was done to the Indian high commissioner, explaining our close family ties. The President told her she need not worry as the Indian high commissioner was among the most protected individuals in Islamabad.

Shireen Wahab

Sir Qazi Mir Ahmed, Chief Justice of NWFP, and my maternal grandfather were close friends. They were also neighbours, as the rear entrances of their homes were adjoining. I recall there was gloom in our house the day he passed away in 1945. I managed to get the address of his daughter, Shireen Wahab, and on my visit to Peshawar on my first posting, we paid her a visit. She was in the garden and greeted us warmly. Asking us to remain at the entrance, she hurriedly went inside. Surprised, we waited a while. She re-emerged at the door carrying sweetmeats and money on a silver platter. She explained she had gone to put on the lights of the house so that she could welcome me and my wife, as a bride of the family. She felt Kunti's daughter-in-law must be welcomed in true tradition. We spent time with her, and she recounted several stories and incidents of the past.

This was in total contrast to several other experiences we had, including being disinvited to a New Year's Eve function on the grounds that senior army officers present would be embarrassed by our presence.

Station House Officer (SHO), Peshawar

During my first posting to Pakistan, my maternal uncle, Joginder Nath Kakar came on a visit to revive youthful memories of his hometown. He and his wife Purnima accompanied me to Peshawar. According to regulations, Indians are required to register their passport at the local police station on arrival. The head of the police station received us. On reading my uncle's father's name in the passport, he told us that thirty years ago he had been recruited to the police on the recommendation of my grandfather. The registration ceremony was converted into a feast with kebabs and sweets being served. Two policemen formally handed over the passport to us. On our return to the hotel, we discovered my uncle's passport had not been stamped, which resulted in another visit to the police station. The SHO profusely apologized, and with the registration completed, he escorted us back to the hotel.

Three Remarkable Brothers

We had the good fortune to know Syed Amjad Ali, Syed Wajid Ali and Syed Babar Ali.

Syed Amjad Ali (1906–95). A few months after my arrival in Islamabad as deputy commissioner of mission in the Indian Embassy in mid-September 1979, I got a message that Syed Amjad Ali wanted to meet me. On entering the room, he clarified he had come neither for a business deal nor a visa request. He had come to pull my ears for not having contacted the family in Lahore. My wife, as the granddaughter of R.B. Ram Saran Das, would have been welcomed warmly. I said we would make amends on our next visit, which we did. He was a gracious host. Over the next few years, he sent me several interesting dispatches on the role of civil servants in international affairs. He was Pakistan's ambassador to the USA, Pakistan finance minister and member of the United Nations civil service. His son, Yavar, maintained good relations with us.

Syed Wajid Ali (1911–2008). Once introduced to the family, I came to know Syed Wajid Ali, chairman and director of several Pakistan public listed companies, member of the International Olympics Committee, chairman Pakistan Red Cross Society and chairman Pakistan Olympics Committee.

Recently, when Air India was given back to the Tatas by the Government of India, a reference to the Maharaja logo did the rounds on social media. Bobby Kooka, inspired by the moustache of Syed Wajid Ali, used it as a symbol on the Air India Maharaja. When my wife informed Syed Babar Ali about this, he responded, he 'knew it when the Maharaja was created by Bobby Kooka before 1947'.

Syed Babar Ali (1926), whom we were fortunate to know during both my tenures in Islamabad, was a multifaceted personality. He was of immense help to my wife in collecting information on a book on her grandfather, *R.B. Ram Saran Das of Lahore.*

Like his elder brother Amjad Ali, he too had been finance minister. He was chairman of several Pakistan public listed companies, president of the World Wildlife Fund International which he took over from the Duke of Edinburgh, and a member of the American Academy of Arts and Sciences. His greatest gift to Pakistan was the setting up of the famous Lahore University of Management Sciences (LUMS).

Eqbal Ahmad

Eqbal Ahmad is considered one of Pakistan's renowned academicians and a leading political scientist. Edward Said mentions him among the two most significant influences on his intellectual development. Kabir Babar described him as one of the most outstanding thinkers to originate from the subcontinent. He spent over three decades in the U.S. and Europe studying and teaching. From 1990 onwards, he spent more time in Pakistan, which included his failed efforts to start a liberal arts college named after Ibn Khaldun. Since his death in 1999, a memories lecture has been instituted in his honour in Hampshire University. Speakers included Kofi Annan.

I was fortunate to meet him through Raza Kazim and Mubashir Hasan. We spent several evenings discussing history, the Algerian Revolution in which he had taken part, Vietnam, which he had meticulously studied and Indo–Pak relations. On the last day of my tenure in Pakistan, he spent time in my hotel room in Lahore. He never mentioned the article he was writing for the *Dawn*, which the Indian High Commission faxed me a few days later, titled, 'Farewell to an Adversary'. I was touched.

The article gives a perception of problems and prospects of Indo–Pak relations (See Appendix for the complete article).[4]

Sadequain

Sadequain (1930–87), born in Amroha, is considered one of Pakistan's most famous painters and calligraphers. In a recent article commemorating his ninetieth birth anniversary, Raza Naeem wrote that Sadequain is among the four gifted names in the field of art and culture in Pakistan.

I met Sadequain, shortly after my arrival in Islamabad in 1978 on my first posting to Pakistan, at the house of a common friend, Naeem Jaan. My initial introduction to his art was through the boldly exhibited paintings of four nude nymphs depicting the seasons, on the glass panels of Naeem Jaan's living room doors. This attracted more attention because of the two strategically placed broad black stripes across the body of each figure. These stripes were the contribution of the lady of the house, who felt that with three growing daughters there was a need to maintain an element of decorum. Our friendship grew over the next four years of my tenure.

On one occasion he sought my help for his visit to India, where he was taking part in an exhibition. His request was threefold: a meeting with Prime Minister Indira Gandhi, the Indian government should pay for his train fare from Delhi to Amroha, and that the Public Works Department (PWD) guest house should be reserved for him although he would not stay there. The air ticket for his international travel between Delhi and Islamabad would be paid by himself. Each request stemmed from his childhood memories. By being booked in the PWD guest house, where as a child he was prevented from playing as he was told only important people lived there, he wanted to exhibit to the people of his birthplace, relatives and friends, his new standing. On his return, he thanked me for fulfilling all his wishes but added he had a major regret. He had been invited for an early-morning meeting by PM Indira Gandhi, but as no photographer was present at that hour, a photograph with the PM could not be taken.

Sadequain, a frequent visitor to our house in Islamabad, made a portrait of my wife, which has since travelled with us to all our postings. I was told by an art critic that Sadequain had made very few portraits. Sadequain was, at times, referred to as the M.F. Husain of Pakistan. On a visit to Karachi, when told of this, Husain responded he would like to be called Sadequain of India. Sadequain told me this was the best compliment paid to him.[5]

Ahmad Faraz

Ahmad Faraz (1931–2008), among the most famous Urdu poets of Pakistan, was a fierce critic of military and authoritarian rule. He was jailed and exiled on different occasions. Mohinder Singh Bedi Sahar, the Indian Urdu poet, was a common link between us. During my first tenure in Pakistan, Bedi made several visits to attend literary events. According to Faraz, Bedi treated him like a son. During our discussions, the idea to publish a book on the selected works of Mohinder Singh Bedi emerged. After Benazir Bhutto came to power, Faraz was appointed chairman of the government publishing house. In my foreword to the book, it was mentioned that this book was only possible due to his determined efforts.

My last meeting with Ahmad Faraz was at my farewell reception. He remained till the end and recited some of his Urdu couplets to the delighted guests. One of these, which he composed on the spot, mentioned that I was born a decade after him, but the cities of our birth, Kohat and Peshawar, were only 50 miles apart.

Determined and strong-willed with clear-cut likes and dislikes, Sadequain and Ahmad Faraz took pride in their artistic achievements. Both were in favour of increased contacts with India in the field of art and culture.[6]

Sirdar Shaukat Hyat

Shaukat Hyat was the eldest son of Sir Sikander Hyat, the erstwhile prime minister of undivided Punjab (1936–42). After being in the army, he joined politics in 1947. A follower of Muhammad Ali Jinnah, founder of Pakistan, he supported Jinnah's sister Fatima Jinnah in her campaign against Ayub Khan. By the time we arrived on our first posting he was leading a retired life in Islamabad. Keeping in view his father's closeness to my wife's family, we sent him a message but got no response for several months. An invite to his daughter's wedding brought us together, and thereafter we got to know him and the family very well. We became good friends with his children and as his grandchildren were around the same age as our children, it resulted in their spending a lot of time at his home. When he and his younger son met with an accident, we received a frantic call from his daughter late evening, asking us to rush to the hospital. With the family away in Lahore, she was too agitated to handle the situation alone. We had just returned from a reception, and on receiving her call, we immediately left without changing into something simpler. On arrival we found both had serious injuries. Shaukat Hyat had broken a few ribs and was in excruciating pain while the son lay unconscious. The doctor, who was known to us, could not fathom our active presence, and that too in formal evening attire, inquired of my wife if we were the cause of the accident. She said we were there to help out in friendship. Once things were more in control, the daughter wanted to inform the family in Lahore. She asked my wife to drive her to Uncle's place, which was nearby, so that she could make the call. Uncle, who was related to them by marriage, turned out to be Agha Shahi, then foreign minister. That was also the only time my wife visited his home.

We met different leaders at the Shaukat Hyat house on several occasions where a variety of interesting subjects were discussed. Whenever he had an argument with his wife, she would in anger leave in the car. At times he would call to inquire if she was with us, and if not, would laughingly say, she is taking revenge by using my credit card liberally. When he was writing his book, his wife whom we fondly called Aapa, warned him not to write anything that could cause problems for the family. Eventually he followed her advice. He died while we were posted to Germany. Aapa called us as his body was being taken out and tearfully informed me that he was leaving the house for the last time.

Kaiser Monnoo

Kaiser Monnoo was the elder member of the leading industrialist Monnoo Group. We spent time with him on our visits to Lahore and often celebrated pre-Basant evenings with him. He arranged for us to get an old, beautifully carved door from his village provided we replaced it with a good sturdy teak door, which we did. The carvings adorn our front door in Delhi. He loved Japanese food which we often enjoyed on our Lahore visits to his home. Even after leaving Islamabad, we continued meeting him in London, Delhi, Bonn and Moscow. He remained in touch even while visiting remote areas of the world. Warm, generous and affectionate, he always had a place in our hearts.

6

Firm Hand in a Soft Glove

Inder Kumar Gujral (4 December 1919–30 November 2012), born in undivided Punjab in a family of freedom fighters, was the twelfth prime minister of India (April 1997–May 1998). Earlier, he was foreign minister in the V.P. Singh and Deve Gowda governments. Being the first prime minister hailing from what is now Pakistan, he knew Pakistan well. During the early 1980s, I was often invited to his house for discussions with visiting Pakistanis. My first lecture at the Saturday Club in 1985, before I became a member, was as his guest. When he became prime minister, I was ambassador in Germany. Discussions with him, at that time, were primarily on Pakistan. He ensured that Foreign Secretary Salman Haidar met me in Germany before visiting Islamabad. I hosted him in his two favourite capitals, in Islamabad as former minister of external affairs and in Moscow as a former prime minister. He was well liked in both countries.

I.K. Gujral's specific contribution to Indian foreign policy was the Gujral Doctrine on neighbourhood, and his refusal to sign the Comprehensive Nuclear-Test-Ban Treaty (CTBT) in 1996.

Gujral–Yaqub Clash

In the summer of 1990, when I.K. Gujral was foreign minister in the V.P. Singh government, a crisis developed over Kashmir. Pakistan Foreign Minister Yaqub Khan visited Delhi and gave a nuclear threat to Gujral. Walking in the corridor of South Block, Khan told Gujral, 'This war won't be like any other, that India's mountains and rivers will be caught in an all-consuming fire, of the kind never seen before, and on the very first day of the year.'[1] Gujral responded by saying, 'You should avoid talking recklessly, because we have all been brought up on the same rivers as you.'[2] This shows that the mild-mannered Gujral could be tough when required. He extensively covered this episode in a personal diary which he maintained. The Gujral family shared the diary with me. The following extracts explain the above incident explicitly.

Extract from the Diary of I.K. Gujral

Begins 23 January 1990 (Tuesday 6.30 a.m.)

My talks with Yaqub (one-to-one) began at 10.00 a.m. yesterday in my office, and we talked for nearly one hour and forty minutes. With a straight face he delivered me the message that had been taken at a very high level in Islamabad. He said that he was instructed to say that the situation in Kashmir was 'perilous' and could lead to 'perilous consequences', and that 'we meet under dark clouds', and there were critical differences: in our perceptions regarding Kashmir, and that led to 'resentment, animus, may I say hatred, and it could lead to prospects of hostilities and confrontation'.

Though he did not use the word ultimatum, the hard message conveyed that effect. My effort was to make him appreciate that what he was saying could lead our countries, once again, to the path of war. His main purpose was to communicate that Pakistan had not accepted that Kashmir was a settled issue. 'It is a disputed territory, and our claims to it are very much there. The Simla Agreement itself recognizes this.' I pointed out that the Simla Agreement, while stating this fact, was also prescriptive. It had emphasized peaceful means and bilateral talks, etc. 'You know full well under what circumstances even the mention of it was conceded, and Benazir should surely know the background since she herself was present at Simla.' My oration caused little effect. Though, after delivering the initial message, his style was relaxed. He said that the '*josh wallahs* on our side were now centre stage. They sometimes talked of the '65 war, and sometimes they talked of the war of 1971.'

My style continued to be persuasive. I did not get provoked nor did I lose my cool. I invited him to understand what raising of tempers and slogans could ultimately lead to. 'The situation at the edge of a precipice takes its own course that may be beyond recall.' Though his style was friendly and easy, it had no effect. I had to ultimately tell him, 'I hope you realize and appreciate that my pleas for peace are not out of weakness or lack of political will to confront the situation, and hope you, being a military man, do not underestimate the strength and tenacity of the Indian state.' He said he did but, 'we are talking of 1965 style. Please be assured we are not thinking nor planning any such steps. But as you know, the sympathies of our people are with the Kashmiris and they have relatives and friends on our side and that affect their sentiments.' Earlier in the day, I had seen reports of Benazir's TV talks wherein she had talked of concerns of the 'Umma'. I told Yaqub that there was a vast 'Umma' in our country too, and any situation in Kashmir could affect adversely the Hindu–Muslim relationships here. We talked for a while about it but came back again to his brief that their perception and our perception regarding the territory of J & K were different, and they are forced to tell the world about it. 'It will lead to tensions but let us try to manage it,' was his remark. 'And for this it would be useful to keep open and activate all channels of communications.'

The picture that emerged was dismal and full of ominous prospects.

Our second round, at about 11.30 a.m. was formal in the midst of delegations wherein we talked mainly about the SAARC and prospects of the next summit. This was followed by his call on the PM at 12.30 p.m. Since I had no time to brief V.P. Singh in the interregnum, I also went along. Once again, he was hawkish. Both his language and style were challenging, and he said what he had told me earlier in the day. The PM chose not to respond.

At 1 p.m. we had our weekly meeting in the defence ministry where I reported briefly about my talks and we discussed the prevailing situation in the Valley.

I had earlier planned with Yaqub that we would have one more (one-to-one) session the next morning over breakfast, but later I decided to shift it since I had invited some MPs from our alliance parties to share with them the foreign policy initiatives in various spheres. So I phoned Yaqub to ask him if we could prepone the talks to after dinner, which was being hosted by the Pakistan ambassador. He readily agreed.

The Central Consumer Protection Authority (CCPA) meeting lasted for the best part of two hours and ended at nearly 9 p.m. So, I was late for the dinner by nearly an hour, but my staff had conveyed this to him.

On reaching the dinner venue, S.K. Singh whispered to
me that Yaqub had earlier in the day met a group of Indian
intellectuals and told them that they (Pakistan) believed that
the Simla Agreement needed to be renegotiated in the changed
circumstances and conveyed their perception of Kashmir.

We had another session of one-to-one talks from 10.40
p.m. for about one hour in the ambassador's library at
his residence.

This time I took the initiative and told him in a firm tone,
'We had a high-level meeting to discuss what we believed was
your ultimatum and I have been asked to tell you that you
would be well-advised to appreciate the strength and resilience
of the Indian state. We have both the will and the strength
to safeguard our interests.' I told him clearly that though he
had not used the word 'ultimatum', what in reality he had
conveyed was that. In a way he relented. He said, 'No, it was
not meant to be any ultimatum'—if by his enunciation, we had
understood that Pakistan was about to launch an adventure like
that of 1965, then it was not his intention. He was sure that
his side had no such intention, though in the morning he had
said, 'We don't want war and surely you don't want it either,
but if it is thrown at us, we will take it as surely you would.'
He was keen to assure me that he meant to give no ultimatum.
He said, 'Why, no, but surely we are in for an era of tension
and we should try reduce the damage, though some damage
is inevitable.' We went round for quite some time, and in the
end, I summed up that what I had understood him to mean
was: (1) no war and (2) the tension was inevitable and it may
lead to talk about it in other countries, and that channels of
communication must be kept open to cut the damage. He
confirmed that was what he meant.

On the way back home I briefed our ambassador and asked him to record it.

Yes, I had told Yaqub that he must know the Indian psyche carried on its shoulder the history of a thousand years, and it would go through anything but not permit any cession.

On the whole, it is obvious we are on the confrontationist path that may lead even to a war, but the key lies within the Valley and how speedily we can overcome the agitation.[3]

This episode has been widely talked of and discussed in the media. Yaqub Khan, when asked to comment, did not offer a reply. Maybe this was on account of his ill health. At times he liked to keep quiet. For instance, it was not known in Pakistan that he had a brother, Sahabzada Yunus Khan, who was in the Indian Army. He met him after a gap of four decades in Delhi in 1982. Yaqub never spoke about his elder brother Yunus Khan. His reluctance can perhaps be explained by the fact that both the brothers, who served in the British Army before the independence of India, split after the partition of the country. While Yaqub joined the Pakistani Army, Yunus chose to stay with the Indian Army. During the Kashmir war in 1948, the brothers leading battalions of opposite forces came face to face and shot at each other. Yaqub was wounded whereupon Yunus told him 'not to grieve, Chotey' (reference to a younger sibling), 'we are soldiers and we did our duty.' After that, the two reportedly met only once, in 1982 when Yaqub visited India as foreign minister of Pakistan.[4]

In his autobiography, I.K. Gujral has also mentioned this incident and added:

More than a year later, Benazir Bhutto visited New Delhi to condole Rajiv Gandhi's death. He had died on 21 May 1991. She came to meet me at our Maharani Bagh home.

I took the opportunity to complain to her about Yaqub's 'ultimatum'. Her response is quotable: 'God is my witness. I never knew about it till I saw your public statement. I had asked Yaqoob about it. He denied that there was any such exchange between yourself and him!' The veracity of what she said remained unverified. I knew that Benazir's foreign minister did not belong to her party. Such was the oddity of Pakistan's policy.[5]

Did He End R&AW Operations?

It was believed in India that I.K. Gujral was soft on Pakistan. This, as mentioned above, is not corroborated by this incident. It has also been said that during his tenure as prime minister, he terminated some of the alleged R&AW operations in Pakistan, leading to a gap in India's intelligence capabilities. Some analysts feel this was one of the factors responsible for intelligence failure before the Kargil war. However, I have been told by a key member of the Kargil Committee that the report nowhere blamed Gujral for ending R&AW operations. Perhaps it attributed the failure to the lack of coordination among the main intelligence agencies of the country, who did not share information with the joint intelligence committee. In spite of I.K. Gujral not having been blamed in the report, perceptions matter, and this is a cross which he will have to bear.

Gujral–Nawaz Sharif Meetings

During his tenure, he met his Pakistan counterpart, Nawaz Sharif, four times: in May 1997 at the Malé SAARC summit, in September at the United Nations General Assembly (UNGA) in New York, in October in Edinburgh during CHOGM, and in

January 1998 at the trilateral meeting between India, Pakistan and Bangladesh in Dhaka. There are some interesting comments on the conversations with Nawaz Sharif in Gujral's handwritten personal diary. For instance, he recorded the following on 1 October 1997 (Wednesday midnight).

> Situation was sensitive today as well, only the scare shifted to Uri side. So, I decided to speak to Nawaz Sharif on the hot line. This was done at 11.30 p.m. I reminded him about our agreement and told him that the civilian casualties on both sides was heavy. His response to my proposal regarding level talks was evasive. The impression was that he was not master of the show. He has promised to speak to his people and phone me tomorrow.[6]

There is another interesting entry in Gujral's diary on Tuesday, 13 May 1997 (Maldives), 5.15 a.m., in which he rejected Nawaz Sharif's suggestion to have a working group on Kashmir as a part of the foreign secretary-level talk. He recorded,

> Nawaz wanted that the foreign secretaries (FSs) may be asked to set up a number of working groups, including Kashmir, to expedite progress spheres of travel, trade, Siachen, etc. The list had been made available earlier by FS Shamshad (Pakistan Foreign Secretary) to Salman Haidar. I told him the better formulation would be to ask the foreign secretaries to 'identify the subjects and set up working groups'. This was initially resisted by him but later conceded. In a brief prior to lunch, we talked about it. I told Nawaz Sharif that his formulation would be strongly objected to by our Parliament so I could not agree.[7]

This was a firm measure which he took at that time—not to have a working group on Kashmir in the foreign secretary-level discussions on account of conditions in J & K.

When Nawaz Sharif met Gujral in New York on 28 September 1997, Gohar Ayub and Mushahid Hussain, information minister, were with him. Gujral writes, 'When he arrived at my hotel I shook his hand warmly but resisted his attempt to embrace me as I felt this gesture would be misunderstood back home, because of the increased tension on the border.'[8] It is likely Gujral had in mind the adverse publicity he got after embracing Saddam Hussein in Iraq. In fact, his son Naresh Gujral later told me that he had advised his father not to embrace Nawaz Sharif.

On 25 October 1997, when Gujral met Nawaz Sharif on the sidelines of CHOGM, he was accompanied by P. Chidambaram. Nawaz Sharif had Foreign Minister Gohar Ayub and Foreign Secretary Shamshad Ahmad with him. Nawaz Sharif started the conversation by offering to sell India surplus electricity, but his colleague shot down the proposal on the plea that other issues were pending. Gujral observed, 'What was surprising was that the prime minister's own colleagues could, in a brazen style, defy him in our presence.'[9] In the one-to-one meeting that followed, Gujral told Nawaz Sharif that 'the Inter-Services Intelligence [ISI] of Pakistan had planned to assassinate Farooq Abdullah, the chief minister of J & K. (I had earlier passed on this information to him via Thomas Pickering, the U.S. undersecretary of state). Sharif was aghast after I had made my statement. His response was, "It would do us immense harm." I then highlighted the activities of the group called "Al Faran". He feigned ignorance and wanted me to give him more information . . . He did not deny anything, but said that the uprising in Kashmir was "internal from 1989 onwards."'[10]

These are some episodes of the discussion between Gujral and Nawaz Sharif. No significant agreement was reached at these meetings.

The Gujral Doctrine

I.K. Gujral is known for his five-point doctrine which is a set of principles for conduct of foreign relations with India's immediate neighbours. This was first formulated when he was external affairs minister in the Deve Gowda government and later improved when he was prime minister. In his Chatham House speech in London in September 1996, he outlined the details of the doctrine.

> The United Front Government's neighbourhood policy now stands on five basic principles: First, with the neighbours like Nepal, Bangladesh, Bhutan, Maldives and Sri Lanka, India does not ask for reciprocity but gives all that it can in good faith and trust. Secondly, no South Asian country will allow its territory to be used against the interest of another country of the region. Thirdly, none will interfere in the internal affairs of another. Fourthly, all South Asian countries must respect each other's territorial integrity and sovereignty. And finally, they will settle all their disputes through peaceful bilateral negotiations. These five principles, scrupulously observed, will, I am sure, recast South Asia's regional relationship, including the tormented relationship between India and Pakistan, in a friendly cooperative mould.[11]

It will be observed he did not include Pakistan in all aspects of his doctrine, particularly in respect of the principle of reciprocity. Later, in his autobiography, he has explained the rationale. To quote him, 'The logic behind the Gujral Doctrine was that we had to face two hostile neighbours in the north and the west, so we had to be at "total peace" with all other immediate neighbours in order to contain Pakistan's and China's influence in the region.'[12] His policy on Pakistan was realistic.

He once explained his doctrine to me in simple terms. In the neighbourhood, India should be seen as a good neighbour rather than a big brother. Some observers have pointed out that Gujral's successors followed his doctrine without mentioning or subscribing to it, in respect of their neighbourhood policy. There may be an element of truth in it.

A gentleman politician, I.K. Gujral during his short tenure as prime minister, presided over the fiftieth anniversary celebrations of India's independence. He will be remembered for his contribution in suggesting a neighbourhood policy for India.

7

The Persistent Statesman with a Vision of Peace

Atal Bihari Vajpayee was prime minister of India from 1998 to 2004. Born in 1924, he began to make a mark in public life soon after India's independence with his outstanding oratorical skills and ability to connect with people. A prominent member of the Jan Sangh since its early days, a parliamentarian par excellence since the 1950s, a founding member of the Bharatiya Janata Party, a statesman with a deep interest in global affairs and India's role, and a minister of external affairs in the short-lived Janata government from 1977 to 1979, he was always regarded as a leader with excellent credentials, and for many a natural choice to be the prime minister of India.

It would not be until he was in his seventies that he occupied the office of prime minister. But, as someone who had spent a lifetime thinking about India's foreign policy, he acted with speed and left an important, and in some respects transformative, legacy on India's foreign policy. When he died in 2018, the outpouring of grief in India and tributes from around the world reflected the impact he had in India and in our relations with the world.

Weeks after he became prime minister for the first time, he ordered five nuclear tests on 11 and 13 May 1998 and launched India into an exclusive club as a nuclear weapons state. Soon after that, India announced the policy of No First Use (NFU), thus making India the second country after China to adopt this policy. In addition, he took up the challenge to design a nuclear doctrine and strategy. In January 2003, in a short and crisp statement, the prime minister's office highlighted the main markers of India's nuclear doctrine. The National Security Advisory Board (NSAB) was established with the legendary strategist, K. Subrahmanyam, as its first convener. A few years later, I held this post in 2004–05.

Vajpayee also began the process of transforming ties with the United States, which had long been strained, but had also slipped into a crisis after the nuclear tests. Even as the United States was imposing a wide range of punitive sanctions and was bringing the full force of its diplomatic weight to censure India (and Pakistan), Vajpayee declared India and the USA were natural allies in a speech to the Asia Society in New York in September of that year. The Jaswant Singh–Strobe Talbott talks, which had perhaps been one of the most intense dialogues between the two countries, commenced immediately thereafter, leading to a broader understanding and normalization of relations between the two countries without compromising on the newly established nuclear status. Less than two years after the nuclear tests, President Bill Clinton became the first U.S. President to visit India in twenty-two years in March 2000, and Vajpayee reciprocated the visit in September, when he also addressed the U.S. Congress. That was the beginning of the journey that has culminated in a strong strategic partnership between the two countries.

He wanted improved relations with China, too. His visit to China in 2003 resulted in the signing of the Declaration on Principles for Relations and Comprehensive Cooperation, and a decision was taken to appoint high-level special representatives to settle the Sino–Indian boundary question.

Russia, too, was uppermost in his mind. When I was appointed ambassador to Russia in 1998, his clear directions were that all attempts should be made to restore the traditional warmth in relations with Moscow. The visit of President Putin in 2000 to India resulted in several landmark decisions. As ambassador to Moscow, I was witness to an impressive convergence of views on different subjects. An annual summit between the two countries was agreed to, which is continuing. The strategic partnership agreement signed during this visit remains the guiding document for relations with Russia in the twenty-first century. President Putin also consented to support India's investment in Sakhalin, for an oil and gas project. I had spoken to the prime minister and Principal Secretary Brijesh Mishra regarding this investment, to which many, both in Delhi and Moscow, were opposed. When it was signed a year later, it became India's largest investment abroad in any single project at that time.

Vajpayee's human touch and grace always left a deep impression. I first saw this as a young undersecretary on the Americas desk in MEA in 1971, when I had gone to cover his meeting with Senator Edward Kennedy of the United States in the central hall of the Parliament. I was to see it again a few years after my retirement. When I was ambassador in Moscow, my wife had developed a good rapport with President Putin's wife, Lyudmila Putina in October 2000, during the Putins' visit to India. When we were leaving Moscow at the completion of my tenure in the end of July 2001, Mrs Putin hosted a one-to-one lunch for my wife at the President's dacha. The Russian protocol official who accompanied her mentioned that, according to memory, this was the only instance she could recall of a Soviet or Russian First Lady hosting a meal for the wife of a departing ambassador. In December 2002, when the Putins were again on an official visit to India, at the Moscow airport departure lounge, Mrs Putin expressed a desire to our embassy official that she would like to meet my wife during the visit. Due to shortage of time in her one-day schedule, a meeting could not be fixed. However, Prime Minister Vajpayee graciously invited my wife and me to a small private dinner he hosted for the Putins on the day of their arrival.

His years as prime minister were marked by swift and sweeping developments in Afghanistan. For all the complications and uncertainties, Vajpayee and the external affairs minister acted with speed and clarity to restore India's relations with Afghanistan after the fall of the Taliban in November 2001. Soon after my retirement and immediately after 9/11, I was appointed special envoy of the Government of India for Afghanistan. The Vajpayee years witnessed a transformation in relations with Afghanistan.

Despite his many achievements as prime minister, Vajpayee is remembered most for his policy towards Pakistan. An obituary I wrote for the newspaper, two days after his death, was published under the headline, 'Always a Peace Maker. As Foreign Minister, Leader of the Opposition and Prime Minister, Vajpayee tried to repair ties with Pakistan.'[1]

Painstaking research by A.S. Bhasin revealed that, on taking over as foreign minister in 1977, Vajpayee assured the Pakistan ambassador there was not going to be any change in policy towards Pakistan as the existing foreign policy 'was based on more or less a national consensus'[2]. This reflected both pragmatism and statesmanship on his part.

Vajpayee always had a realistic approach with regard to his dealings with Pakistan. On a visit to Pakistan in February 1978 as external affairs minister, he was questioned as to how he reconciled his present commitment to the Simla Agreement with his highly critical stance when it was signed in 1973. In his inimitable style, he responded, 'I am trying to forget my past and I urge you to do the same.'[3]

Two months after Vajpayee's visit as foreign minister to Pakistan, the agreement on Salal Dam was signed in April 1978. If we believe the claims made by Nasim Zehra in her book,[4] there was apprehension in India about signing the agreement even as Agha Shahi, the Pakistan President's adviser on foreign affairs, was in India for the signing ceremony, possibly because of change in the government in India. She claims that Foreign Secretary Jagat Mehta informed Agha Shahi that the agreement could not be signed. I have not seen any evidence of this in our own records. In any case, it is widely recognized that Vajpayee had facilitated the signing of the agreement.

Few could defend India's interests as eloquently and effectively as he could. As leader of the Opposition, Vajpayee agreed to the request of Prime Minister Narasimha Rao to lead the Indian delegation in 1994 to the UN Human Rights Commission in Geneva. I have written in greater detail in an earlier chapter how his leadership of the delegation played an important role in the Indian victory in Geneva.

Vajpayee made two visits to Pakistan as prime minister. Of the fourteen prime ministers of India, nine did not visit Pakistan during their tenure. Jawaharlal Nehru, Lal Bahadur Shastri (who made a stopover in Pakistan), Rajiv Gandhi and Narendra Modi visited Pakistan, when they had a majority in Parliament. The exception was Vajpayee, who visited Pakistan twice, despite leading a coalition government.

His first visit to Pakistan as prime minister was the historic bus journey to Lahore on 19 February 1999. The visit generated great excitement and interest in India, Pakistan and the rest of the world. The atmosphere and the outcomes of the visit had a positive impact, both in India and Pakistan. In fact, Foreign Minister Jaswant Singh informed Parliament that 'the bus journey captured the imagination of the people of India and Pakistan, indeed of the world'[5]. Important bilateral agreements were signed in Lahore. The joint statement mentions a commitment of both countries to intensify efforts to resolve all issues, including that of Jammu and Kashmir, condemnation of all forms and manifestations of terrorism, and to undertake measures to reduce the risk of accidental or unauthorized use of nuclear weapons.

The visit was replete with great symbolism that itself spoke unequivocally of Vajpayee's mission. Vajpayee, founder of the Bharatiya Janata Party (BJP) and leading light of the Jan Sangh and RSS, significantly placed a wreath at the Minar-e-Pakistan where the resolution for the creation of Pakistan in 1940 was signed. He wrote in the visitor book, 'From the Minar-e-Pakistan, I want to assure the people of Pakistan of my country's deep desire for lasting peace and friendship. I have said and I say this again, a stable and prosperous Pakistan is in India's favour. Let there be no doubt about this.'

At a speech at the governor's house in Lahore, he concluded by reciting his own popular poem,

'Jang na hone denge'
Bharat Pakistan padosi, saath-saath rehna hai
Pyar karein ya war karein, dono ko hi sehna hai,
Jo hum par guzari, bachon par na hone denge,
Jang na hone denge (India and Pakistan. We are neighbours. We
have to live together, whether we love or fight each other, we both

*have to face the consequences. What we had to endure we shall not
let our children suffer the same. We shall not let another war break
out between India and Pakistan.)*

In Pakistan, his visit to Lahore was opposed not only by the
right-wing political party Jamaat-e-Islami, which organized
violent demonstrations, but also, significantly, by the chiefs
of the three armed forces of Pakistan. They did not receive
Vajpayee at the Wagah Border, despite Prime Minister Nawaz
Sharif having asked them to. That did not dilute the enthusiasm
and expectations generated by the Lahore summit. But, the
position of the three chiefs could well have been the sign of other
developments elsewhere.

However, unfortunately this initiative was soon overtaken
and overshadowed by the Kargil war that followed Pakistan's
intrusion and occupation of posts across the LoC.

What embarrassed Vajpayee later—and, perhaps, his Pakistani
interlocutors, too—was that the Kargil operation, launched by
the Pakistan military, was already in full swing even before the
commencement of his visit.

Kargil Operation

In May 1999, Foreign Minister Jaswant Singh visited Moscow
during my tenure as ambassador in Russia. He apprised me of
the seriousness of the situation in Kargil. India felt betrayed
that preparations were afoot in Pakistan for their misadventure,
even while the Lahore visit was on. Foreign Secretary Raghunath
constantly briefed Jaswant Singh from Delhi on the deteriorating
state of affairs. At one point, Jaswant Singh thought the situation
may not be as bad as it appeared, because Gen. Ved Malik, India's
army chief, was continuing with his visit to Eastern Europe.

However, subsequent feedback from Delhi convinced him that conditions on the Line of Control in the Kargil region were alarming. Jaswant Singh briefed the Russian leadership and got their support.

During Jaswant Singh's visit, I arranged a call on the Secretary of the National Security Council of Russia, Vladimir Putin. Some journalists accompanying Jaswant Singh wondered why so much time was allocated to this meeting. I explained that in the Russian hierarchy the secretary of the National Security Council ranked above the foreign minister and was one of the five leaders entitled to a plane at his disposal. Jaswant Singh was very happy with his meeting, which he said was one of the best during his visit. A few months later, Putin became prime minister and shortly after President.

The U.S. Deputy of State Strobe Talbott was in Moscow to consult Russia on the Kosovo crisis. Jaswant Singh and Strobe Talbott met in the dacha where the foreign minister was staying. Though he was able to convince his interlocutors about the gravity of the situation in Kargil, Jaswant Singh left Moscow a worried man. Events in Kargil resulted in a rupture of the Lahore spirit and disrupted the implementation of the agreements and understandings in Lahore. As the situation evolved, there was broad international consensus that Pakistan had violated the Line of Control.

Further confirmation came from the leakage of the recording of a telephone conversation between Pakistan army chief, Pervez Musharraf who was on a visit to China, and his chief of staff, Lt Gen. Aziz Khan in Pakistan, which coincided with Pakistan's Foreign Minister Sartaj Aziz's visit to India in June 1999. It confirmed Pakistan's involvement and also established 'that the Army Chief was waiting to see how not only would Delhi react to the operation, but also how

Pakistan's elected prime minister would react and how would the whole thing really blow up'.[6]

In her very well-researched book, Nasim Zehra, a Pakistani journalist and author, has provided facts from Pakistani sources, of the root of the confrontation, the details of the Kargil operation and the final exit. According to her, the Kargil operation started earlier, but was formally approved on the last Friday of Ramadan as it was considered auspicious. This was thirty-six days before the Vajpayee–Nawaz Sharif Lahore summit. According to Pakistani sources, their troops had by this time infiltrated about 7 kilometres in different directions. Their plan was to choke the Dras–Kargil sector. Their hope was that the Zojila Pass would be snowbound in winter. The other route, Leh–Manali, under construction, and at an altitude of 5000 metres, traversing five mountain ranges, would not be feasible for a sustained supply line. The objective was to cut off the lifeline of the Indian troops in Ladakh and Siachen without having to attack Siachen, as it was well protected. Between March and April, they claimed to have occupied 140 posts and pickets across five areas, including watersheds across the LoC in Meshkat, Dras, Kaksar, Batalik and Turtok. The prime minister of Pakistan and the civilian leadership were unaware of these developments. The three Kashmir-related briefings given to Nawaz Sharif on 29 January, 5 February and 12 March made no mention of the Kargil operation. It was only on 17 May 1999 that he was briefed on the operation in Kargil.

After foreign ministers Jaswant Singh and Sartaj Aziz met on 12 June 1999, the Niaz Naik (former foreign secretary of Pakistan)–R.K. Mishra back-channel negotiations commenced. The objectives of the two sides was at variance. India wanted Pakistan to retreat from Kargil, and Pakistan desired an announcement of talks on Kashmir. During that period, R.K. Mishra visited Pakistan five times. On one of his visits from

Delhi on 25 June, he returned in a Pakistani special aircraft. The next day Niaz Naik reached Delhi, and a meeting was held at the Imperial Hotel.

Later, he called on Vajpayee, where, according to Pakistani sources, Vajpayee asked Niaz Naik, 'We started the journey from Lahore. How did we reach Kargil?' Niaz Naik is reported to have said that we will see how we can come back from Kargil to Lahore. To which, Vajpayee is reported to have replied, 'Very simple. You should just withdraw.'

Nawaz Sharif visited China but found the response lukewarm. Niaz Naik, on his return from India, reported 'all on board', resulting in Nawaz Sharif curtailing his visit in China by a day to enable him to visit Delhi to announce the deal. However, on 27 June, word came from Delhi that he could come, but not on the invitation of Vajpayee. It was later denied in India that any deal had been agreed to.

What became clear to Pakistan was that India was uncomfortable with the proposed simultaneity of the withdrawal and the agreement to enter into a time-bound negotiation on Kashmir, particularly since Pakistan had violated the Indian demand for unconditional withdrawal. There are also other extensive details of the back channel. Pakistan had kept these negotiations secret from the U.S. Even Foreign Minister Sartaj Aziz was kept out, because some officials suspected that he could pass on details to the U.S. Eventually, Niaz Naik himself mentioned the back channel to a senior U.S. embassy official, according to Pakistani sources.

On the battlefield, India reacted fast after discovering Pakistan's perfidy, and on 26 May, the Indian Air Force entered the battle, restricting activities to the Indian side of the LoC. It took the Indian Army and Air Force a few weeks to ensure Pakistan's retreat.

After suffering casualties and humiliations, Nawaz Sharif hurriedly visited the U.S. Following the now famous 4 July meeting with Clinton at Blair House in Washington, he was advised to withdraw, which Pakistan finally did.

For Pakistani observers, President Clinton's conversations with Vajpayee on the phone during and after his meeting with Nawaz Sharif in Washington, D.C. was an act of U.S mediation. India did not see it that way. Jaswant Singh made that famous statement, 'I do not accept this as mediation or even as playing the role of an intermediary. We have consistently said no mediation is necessary. We don't need interpreters because we speak the same language.'[7]

While Pakistan may have seen the conclusion of the Kargil conflict as Washington-engineered withdrawal of Pakistani troops from Kargil, it was, in the final analysis, Vajpayee's firm policy combined with strategic restraint that led to both a military and diplomatic victory for India in Kargil.

There was considerable speculation and some unanswered questions on the Niaz Naik–Mishra talks, reported in the media of both countries, much of which came from accounts from Pakistan. This was essentially whether the two were discussing, with authorization from their leaders, a Chenab plan, which would lead to the relocation of the Line of Control along the Chenab River. This would have had the effect of dividing Jammu and Kashmir into a Muslim-majority area to the north of the river and the Hindu-majority area to the south of the river, resulting in the Muslim-majority areas, including most parts of the Valley, being under Pakistan's control, and the southern area, together with Ladakh, remaining with India.

Most of this is attributed to Niaz Naik, who reportedly spelled it out in an interview to a Pakistan Geo TV programme, and the newspaper, the *News*, on 15 May 2003, the following day carried headlines, 'Naik Divulges Details of Talks with Vajpayee'. According to the paper, he revealed the details of this formula for the first time in Geo TV's programme, *Capital Talk*. Naik said the Indian Prime Minister showed a lot of interest in that formula. According to this formula, the Chenab River was to be adopted as the new line of division between India and Pakistan, the whole city of Jammu went to India, many districts of Jammu province also went to India because the majority of the population of these areas comprises Hindus, but the city of Srinagar and most parts of Kashmir valley were to come to Pakistan as the population of these areas consists of Muslims.[8]

The Chenab Formula

The genesis of the proposal of India ceding the Chenab basin to Pakistan emanated from the then U.S. Ambassador J.K. Galbraith and the then British High Commissioner Sir Paul Gore-Booth between the fourth and the fifth rounds of the Swaran Singh–Zulfikar Ali Bhutto talks on the Kashmir issue held during the first half of 1963.[9] It appears that the then U.S. Secretary of State Dean Rusk, U.S. Assistant Secretary of State Averell Harriman and the then British Foreign Secretary Duncan Sandys, had earlier broached the Chenab proposal with their Indian counterparts. It had been explained to them that the defence of Srinagar and Ladakh would get severely compromised without the Chenab valley remaining in Indian hands. Further, the Indus Waters Treaty had taken adequate care of Pakistan's water requirements. Before the commencement of the fifth round of talks, the Anglo-American non-paper defining the contours of a settlement on Kashmir gave the Chenab valley to the Pakistanis.[10] As a result, during the fifth round of talks, which commenced in Karachi on 21 April 1963, Pakistan pressed their claim to the Chenab basin.

From there, Bhutto proceeded to say that the '[Kashmir] valley was indivisible', and that they must have the whole of it.[11]

Two and a half decades later, in 1990, when he was a brigadier, General Musharraf prepared a paper for the Royal College of Defence Studies in London, linking the India–Pakistan conflict to water issues. These documents, however, somehow give credit for the Chenab formula to General Musharraf and the Pakistan Army. The formula received attention and prominence when it was purportedly discussed in the back channel by the Indian and Pakistan intermediaries, Niaz Naik and R.K. Mishra. Niaz Naik is quoted as having said, 'On the 27th of March, I met R.K. Mishra in Delhi's Imperial Hotel where I was staying under a different name, and without knowledge of the Pakistani High Commission. On behalf of our respective prime ministers, we entered into frank discussions on what could be done to make headway on Kashmir.'[12] In these meetings, nine in all between 7 March and 27 June, the basic parameters of the dialogue between the two countries were decided. These, according to Naik, were as follows:

1. Both sides will go beyond their stated policy positions;
2. The interests of Pakistan, India and the Kashmiris ('above all the Kashmiris' is how Vajpayee modified this point later) will be at the heart of any solution to the Kashmir problem; and
3. The solution will be feasible and will be sincerely implemented.

'Later, during a meeting with both of us, Mr Vajpayee added another clause to the discussions, which stipulated that any solution to the Kashmir problem would be final and not partial,' Naik wrote. It was during the course of their discussions that Naik displayed the contours of the Chenab solution to Mr Mishra on a tourist guide map, which he had picked up from the same hotel. Mishra showed keen interest, but wanted to discuss the matter with Vajpayee first. 'During our second meeting, the Indian prime minister asked me to have blown-up maps of the area ready as "they may come handy,"' Naik said. No corroborative evidence is available to support the veracity of Naik's account.

The idea was to make the River Chenab a geographical boundary between the two countries. Nawaz Sharif had apparently asked Niaz Naik to get a briefing from Musharraf. The Chenab formula had always been unacceptable to India as it encouraged another partition on religious lines and meant giving up their claim to the Valley.

* * *

G. Parthasarthy, high commissioner of India in Pakistan during the Kargil conflict, contributed an article in the book, *Diplomatic Divide* on this subject. He wrote, 'According to his Pakistani counterpart Niaz Naik, Mishra had indicated in one of their meetings in Delhi, during the Kargil conflict, that New Delhi would agree to adjustments in the Line of Control that would eventually lead to the Line of Control being moved to the Chenab river basin . . . Mishra vehemently rejects this assertion of Naik, but refused to appear and testify about his role before the Kargil Committee . . .', and G. Parthasarthy finally says, 'Naik is too accomplished a diplomat to go so wrong in his account of what had transpired.'

Another Pakistani account, this time by Shuja Nawaz, brother of a former Pakistani army chief, in his book on the Pakistan Army, *Crossed Swords: Pakistan and Its Army and the Wars Within*, Nawaz has written about discussions that are supposed to have taken place between Jaswant Singh and Pakistan Foreign Minister Sartaj Aziz in Sri Lanka to explore an agreement on Kashmir.

According to Shuja Nawaz, in March 1999 during a foreign ministers' meeting at Nuwara Eliya in Sri Lanka, the two met privately on a bench overlooking a lake, without any notes or other participants, and made great progress, identifying issues on which they had unacceptable options as well as those that had a common good. Shuja Nawaz claims,

> Singh said he wanted to avoid division on the basis of religion. He was open to the idea of geographic division, coming closer to the idea of the Kashmir Study Group. They agreed to continue their exchanges privately in the months ahead, using Pakistan's High Commissioner or Ambassador to India, Ashraf Jehangir Qazi, as the contact.

The fall of the BJP government in India on 17 April and the Kargil adventure put an end to that initiative, says Sartaj Aziz. Later, when he met Vajpayee, he says the latter had 'tears in his eyes'. He said to me, 'Sartaj Sahib! *Yeh aap ne kya kiya?*' Aziz believes that the military coup in October 1999 put an end to the idea of progress on Kashmir with India.

On the Indian side, Kuldip Nayar wrote in his book, *Scoop*,

> When I met Vajpayee after the coup in Pakistan, he said, 'He [Nawaz Sharif] sacrificed himself for us.' Regarding the settlement on Kashmir, Vajpayee said, 'We were almost there.' He was referring to the behind-the-scene talks between former newspaperman R.K. Mishra and Niaz Naik, the former foreign secretary of Pakistan. I failed to scoop on what the agreement was which made Vajpayee say. 'We were almost there'. R.K. Mishra has not opened his mouth.[13] Niaz Naik has said in subsequent press interviews that the settlement still had a lot to cover. So, exactly what direction the talk between Mishra and

Niaz took, for Vajpayee to remark 'we were almost there' is not known yet.[14]

If the discussions on the Chenab formula did take place, there being no clear indication from the Indian side, except by inferences, it would have been to our disadvantage, because it was communal and territorial. Swaran Singh had instantly rejected it when it was suggested during his discussions with Bhutto in 1963.

All efforts were made after the fall of the Vajpayee government to review the records of the negotiations. Unfortunately, there were none available in government records. When later I told Brijesh Mishra that we could not trace the papers in the PMO, MEA or cabinet secretariat, he smiled and pointed a finger to his head, indicating it was all there, hinting that they were either destroyed or not kept. It is hard to say conclusively if the Chenab formula came up, or was mentioned as an option, or was discussed as a basis for an agreement. At any rate, it would not have found traction in Vajpayee's own party.

Hijacking of IC 814 to Kandahar, 24–31 December 1999

An Indian Airlines Airbus A 300, flight IC 814 from Kathmandu to Delhi, was hijacked on 24 December 1999. It touched down in Amritsar for refuelling, where unfortunately it was not immobilized. This remains a major failure on our part. The plane flew to Lahore and Dubai before the hijackers forced it to land in Kandahar, which, like the rest of Afghanistan, was under Taliban control at that time. During the course of its flight, one hostage was killed and twenty-seven released in Dubai. The remaining 176 passengers reached Kandahar.

At the height of the Kandahar hijacking, I received a call from Delhi inquiring whether I knew any Taliban representative in Moscow. At that time there was none. With pressure from the families of the hijacked passengers, desperation was mounting. Negotiations were difficult as the Taliban government was being supported by the Pakistan ISI. The Indian team of negotiators included Ajit Doval, a senior IB official, later National Security Advisor (NSA) in the Modi government, and Vivek Katju, joint secretary dealing with Pakistan, Afghanistan and Iran, in the MEA. The hostage crisis lasted a week, ending only when India agreed to the release of three militants. As the Taliban administration wanted the presence of a high-level Indian representative, Foreign Minister Jaswant Singh accompanied the militants on the same plane to Kandahar. The released passengers and crew of IC 814 were brought back safely to India.

The three militants released were later involved in activities inimical to India and the rest of the world. Maulana Masood Azhar, who founded Jaish-e-Mohammed in 2000, was involved in the attack on the Indian Parliament in December 2001, the Mumbai attack in 2008 and, most recently, in the Pulwana attack in 2019, which resulted in the death of forty-four Central Reserve Police Force (CRPF) personnel. The second, Ahmed Omar Saeed Sheikh, was under arrest in India because of his role in the kidnapping in 1994 of foreign tourists in Kashmir. He was later arrested in 2002 by the Pakistan authorities for the murder of journalist Daniel Pearl. The third, Mushtaq Ahmed Zargar, had since his release been active in POK.

Intense debate followed the release of the three militants. According to A.S. Dulat, former head of R&AW, in his book, even deputy prime minister, L.K. Advani, was against the release of the terrorists and hijackers, but did it smartly, by absenting himself from the meeting when the decision was taken. The release of the terrorists proved embarrassing for the Vajpayee government then and thereafter.

I received a call in Moscow from Foreign Minister Jaswant Singh on his return to Delhi on the evening of 31 December. He had himself dialled my number. Later, through officials, I gathered that K. Subrahmanyam, India's strategist, was with him when the call was made. Jaswant Singh, clearly under great strain, inquired whether he had done the right thing. I responded I was not aware of the situation under which he had acted and wondered if the militants could have been taken in another plane. He said that an additional plane was not available at short notice. Second, he said the negotiating team were convinced of the risk of great harm to the hijacked passengers if their demands were not met. We could not speak longer as we were talking on an open line.

International opinion on Pakistan's violation of the LoC and support for militancy in India was crystallizing now. It was articulated clearly by President Bill Clinton during his five-day visit to India in March 2000, which was contrasted with only a five-hour stopover in Pakistan.

Musings from Kumarakom, 1 January 2001

From 26 December 2000 to 1 January 2001, Prime Minister Vajpayee spent his annual vacation at Kumarakom Resort on the famous backwaters of Kerala. In two articles, popularly called 'Musings from Kumarakom', he expressed some thoughts on the Kashmir issue, relations with Pakistan and the Babri Masjid dispute. He also shared his vision of how a better legacy could be left for future generations. He wrote, 'A self-confident and resilient nation does not postpone the inconvenient issues of yesterday to a distant tomorrow . . . India is willing and ready to seek a lasting solution to the Kashmir problem. Towards this end, we are prepared to re-commence talks with

Pakistan, including at the highest level, provided Islamabad gives sufficient proof of its preparedness to create a conducive atmosphere for a meaningful dialogue.'[15] He added,

> My heart shares the agony of the grieving mothers, sisters and widows who have lost their near and dear ones in the violence that has bloodied the beautiful Kashmir Valley. I also feel the pain and anguish of those Kashmiris who have become refugees in their motherland. The New Year is the time to heal their wounds. The Government will soon initiate talks with various representative groups in the State. We are prepared to take further steps to respond to Jammu and Kashmir's deep longing for peace, normalcy and accelerated development. In our search for a lasting solution to the Kashmir problem, both in its external and internal dimensions, we shall not traverse solely on the beaten track of the past. Rather, we shall be bold and innovative designers of a future architecture of peace and prosperity for the entire South Asian region. In this search, the sole light that will guide us is our commitment to peace, justice and the vital interests of the nation.[16]

At the same time, there was also criticism of Vajpayee and Advani's policy in respect of Kashmir. Writing just after Vajpayee's Red Fort speech on the fifty-fourth anniversary of Indian Independence, journalist Inder Malhotra complained,

> From the moment he took over as home minister, L.K. Advani had been bragging about following a 'pro-active' policy in combating Pakistan's sponsored terrorism in Kashmir and denouncing previous governments for being 'only reactive'. And yet . . . all that it seems to have yielded is a spate of newspaper reports that the main target . . . is not terrorists in Kashmir, but

the prime minister's principal secretary and national security advisor, Brijesh Mishra . . . This is one hell of a way of crushing terrorism in Jammu and Kashmir.[17]

He concluded,

Mr. Vajpayee's fundamental task is to regain a credible measure of control over the ground situation in Jammu and Kashmir. Until that is done negotiations with Pakistan . . . would remain a sideshow.[18]

This viewpoint was widespread, but Vajpayee was determined to proceed with a mission to which he was devoted. Willingness to recommence talks with Pakistan, in spite of the deception at Kargil following his initiative to go to Lahore by bus, speaks volumes of his large-heartedness.

Agra Summit, July 2001

When Foreign Minister Jaswant Singh visited Russia in 2001, he laughingly stated my date of birth was incorrect, adding he had studied details of some senior officers and found I would be retiring a few months before Chokila Iyer, who was to later be appointed as foreign secretary (March 2001). In other words, I could not be appointed foreign secretary. He then said that after my retirement, he would like to use my expertise on Pakistan by designating me as special envoy for Central Asia. I responded that this could be discussed in Delhi after my retirement. However, soon thereafter, I received a communication to start work on Central Asia by visiting different capitals. The following day, some of our ambassadors in Central Asian countries sent me messages suggesting dates for a visit, welcoming my assignment.

I called the foreign secretary, Chokila Iyer, and told her, that in my opinion, it would not be appropriate for an ambassador in Moscow to go as special envoy as it would undermine the position of our resident ambassadors and may not be appreciated by some host countries, who may feel they were being imposed on. My suggestion was accepted, and it was decided that this could be discussed once I retired a few weeks later. In early July, I received a call from Foreign Minister Jaswant Singh, if I recall correctly, from Australia where he was on an official visit, to tell me that Prime Minister Vajpayee would like me to come to Delhi immediately for pre-Agra preparatory discussions for General Musharraf's visit to India.

I took part in all discussions held in the Race Course office of the prime minister. Those attending the meeting included deputy Prime Minister Advani, Foreign Minister Jaswant Singh, Mr K.C. Pant, Brijesh Mishra principal secretary to the prime minister, Ex-Foreign Secretary Mansingh (who was Ambassador to USA), Joint Secretary in MEA Vivek Katju, and on occasions, Defence Minister Fernandes and Information Minister Sushma Swaraj. The strategy for deliberations with Pakistan was reviewed and there was agreement that emphasis would be on normalization of relations, with discussions on all issues including J & K. With everyone expressing their views, there appeared to be an overall consensus, with no hint of differences, as reportedly took place later in Agra.

The Agra summit can be briefly summarized as: Big Expectations. Large Delegations. No Agenda. Attention to a Single Issue. No Joint Communiqué. The above gives the substance of the failure of the Agra summit held between 14 and 16 July 2001. Four one-to-one rounds of discussion were held, some of which lasted over five hours. Media of the two countries spoke of two issues as the source of dispute, obviously with different lenses in both countries—with cross-border terrorism and the freedom struggle as core issues. The initiative of PM Vajpayee to invite the Pakistan President was marred by the latter's insistence on only taking into account what, in his view, was the core issue. Even during the summit, Indian media and others were expecting a breakthrough. *The Hindu* said, 'Hopes rise for a productive Summit.'[19]

The *Times of India* went even further, stating, 'The expectation is soaring . . . breakthrough is possible; history in the making.'[20] The remarks of President Musharraf at the media breakfast meeting were later described as one of the causes of the failure of the meeting. While at the meeting, India stressed the need for normalization of relations including discussions on J & K, Pakistan wanted discussions to be as far as possible solely restricted to the Kashmir issue.

India was willing to discuss Kashmir as part of the overall agenda as was stated by Vajpayee in his opening remarks at the plenary of the summit. He said, 'We remain committed to the establishment of trust and confidence to develop mutually beneficial cooperation and to address all outstanding issues, including Jammu and Kashmir.'[21] However, on account of Pakistan's obduracy, the result was that the summit failed even to produce a joint declaration. The Pakistani viewpoint was that Vajpayee and his cabinet hard-liners, led by Advani, were on different wavelengths.[22] As expected, media of both countries described the cause of the failure differently. The *Indian Express* attributed it to Pakistan's 'support to cross-border terrorism'.[23] And Pakistan's hard-liner newspaper *Nawaiwaqt* mentioned, 'Pakistan should give more patronage to jihad movements.'[24]

Pakistan failed to recognize that the summit had taken place despite Kargil and the hijacking of the Indian aircraft to Kandahar. Perhaps there was no intention to engage constructively with

Vajpayee. Musharraf may have had other objectives. He had just declared himself President a few days before, and for Pakistan, India's acceptance was most important. He wanted this through this visit. His hard-line position was also essential to retain the support of the military and hard-liners in Pakistan.

What followed was intensification of terrorist attacks in India, including on the J & K Legislative Assembly in Srinagar (1 October 2001) followed by the attack on the Indian Parliament (13 December 2001). Two well-known terrorist organizations, Lashkar-e-Taiba and Jaish-e-Mohammed, which had been outwardly banned, started functioning under different names. Around the same time, Pakistan was peeved that the International Court of Justice had ruled against it on their complaint regarding the shooting down of Pakistan's naval aircraft in August 1999. The court advised Pakistan to resolve the matter bilaterally in terms of the Simla Agreement and Lahore Declaration.

The U.S. and the Region

In January 2001, President George W. Bush was sworn into office with a clear intent to transform relations with India. In fact, his deputy secretary of state, Richard Armitage, made Delhi his first stop on a three-nation tour of India, Republic of Korea (ROK) and Japan to explain President Bush's New Strategic Framework. The Bush administration's position on Pakistan was hard. Indeed, they were sceptical about President Musharraf's intentions when Vajpayee invited him to Agra.

However, 9/11 changed all that. The U.S. needed Pakistan to attack Al-Qaeda and the Taliban in Afghanistan. As the U.S. military deployment and diplomatic engagement with Pakistan intensified, it coincided with two major incidents that rapidly escalated tensions between India and Pakistan and led to risks of an all-out war—the attack on the Indian Parliament on 13 December 2001 and the Kaluchak massacre in May 2002.

The U.S., keen to avoid a distraction from its Afghanistan mission and prevent a possible conflict, began a shuttle diplomacy that brought secretary of state, Colin Powell, secretary of defence, Donald Rumsfeld and deputy secretary, Armitage on a number of missions to India and Pakistan. Even as they applied a measure of pressure on Pakistan to take action on terrorism and terrorist groups, without jeopardizing their own mission, they also urged India to show restraint and engage in a dialogue with Pakistan. This would go on until the end of Operation Parakram.

Tempers in India were so high that U.S. missions had virtually no influence on India's decisions, despite the now growing ties between India and the U.S., and it would eventually be the operational assessments that were to dictate the course of developments for over the next ten months.

Attack on Parliament, 13 December 2001

After retirement, I was appointed special envoy for Afghanistan, which resulted in visits to Rome (to meet the ex-King of Afghanistan), New York and Kabul. I led the Indian delegation to the Bonn Conference on Afghanistan (26 November–5 December 2001). The leader of the Afghan delegation, Minister Qanooni, travelled back with me on the flight to Delhi. As no commercial flights were operating on the Delhi–Kabul sector, I was able to give that assurance because Foreign Minister Jaswant Singh had said an air force plane would always be available for my visits to Afghanistan. On 12 December, I took Qanooni to Kabul, and after meeting Afghan leaders, returned the same evening with Foreign Minister Abdullah, who broke his Ramadan fast in the plane. Within a fortnight of the Bonn Agreement being signed, two important ministers came to Delhi after a long gap. More Afghan ministers followed later. Delhi, and the rest of the country, was shaken by the attack on Parliament on 13 December 2001. Ajai Raj Sharma, the then commissioner of police in Delhi, in his memoirs written two decades later, has given a graphic description of the event,

> Shots were fired in the Parliament House. There are 'terrorists in here', screamed a frantic voice, laced with fear and panic. It was 12.15 p.m. on 13 December 2001, when I took the call . . . I was sitting in my office. The information was terrifying and unthinkable. A chill ran down my spine. The first thought was that I had met with my 'Waterloo'. On reaching the scene, I saw several dead bodies littered at several places. The dead included terrorists, policemen and a couple of unfortunate civilians. AK rifles, pistols, grenades, mobile phones and several items were all lying scattered on the ground around the dead terrorists. The highest political figures of the nation—the prime minister, the home minister and other ministers as well as the members of the parliament—all were struck by shock, disbelief and anxiety. I could not help imagining the disastrous consequences, had the Pakistan terrorists succeeded in their mission.[25]

The attention of the entire country was focused on events in Parliament. Sonia Gandhi, president of the opposition Congress party, spoke to Prime Minister Vajpayee and inquired about his welfare. There was countrywide indignation. This attack dealt a blow to the prospects of any positive developments in India–Pakistan relations. Speaking in Parliament, deputy Prime Minister L.K. Advani said, 'This time the terrorists and their mentors across the border had the temerity to try to wipe out the entire leadership of India.'[26]

Afghan Foreign Minister Abdullah Abdullah's meetings started on 13 December, the day of the attack on the Indian Parliament. His meetings took place as scheduled. My meeting with the parliamentary consultative committee, to brief them on the situation in Afghanistan and the Bonn conference, had been scheduled for 14 December. To exhibit that normality prevailed despite the Parliament attack, there was no change, except the venue was moved to the annex of the Parliament building. There was a slight postponement of my meeting with the principal secretary to the prime minister, Brijesh Mishra, scheduled for 13 December.

A few days later, India withdrew its high commissioner from Pakistan and took some other measures—the reduction of the strength of the Pakistan High Commission in Delhi, ban on overflights by Pakistan aircraft and termination of both the Delhi–Lahore bus service and the Samjhauta Express train. A few months later, following the terrorist attack on Kaluchak in May 2002, India asked Pakistan to withdraw its high commissioner from Delhi.

Relations between Vajpayee and Advani had been traditionally close but on many occasions, they held different points of view. In his book, *My Country My Life*, Advani wrote, 'I was in close contact with a senior Pakistani diplomat, with Karan Thapar, a noted journalist whom I had known for many years, acting as intermediary.'[27] Immediately after the publication of the book, Karan Thapar came out with details in his article in which he mentions that 'there were perhaps 20 such clandestine meetings', where he drove the Pakistan high commissioner to Advani's house.[28] Two meetings mentioned in the article are significant. One was a secret meeting between Advani and the Pakistan high commissioner a day after the attack on Parliament. The timing and nature of the meeting after such an event is surprising. The last meeting, according to Karan Thapar, was just the evening before Jehangir Ashraf Qazi was withdrawn from India. According to Karan Thapar, on this occasion, 'tears welled up in Advani's eyes', allowing emotion to overtake the '*lahu purush*'.

Operation Parakram

Immediately after the attack on Parliament, a decision was taken to have a full-scale mobilization of the Indian Army for the first time since 1971. Operation Parakram was launched on 15 December 2001, after the approval of the cabinet committee on security. The formation required to defend the border normally takes three to four days to complete mobilization. However, Strike Corps 1, 2 and 21 took three weeks as they were based at long distances from the border, and it was finally on 3 January 2002, that the troops were in their new operative positions. Operation Parakram came to an end on 16 October 2002, when it was announced that the troops were being strategically relocated. During this period, there were a few occasions when tensions were high. In January 2002, there was a possibility of offensive action on the borders with Punjab and Rajasthan, but Musharraf's speech of 12 January 2002, stating that Pakistan would not permit any terrorist activity from its soil, prevented the Indian Army from taking action. Again, the attack on Indian army garrisons at Kaluchak on 14 May 2002 was another occasion for possible action, but the military strike was not approved by the government. The total cost incurred on Operation Parakram, as reported to Parliament in 2002, was Rs 8,000 crore, excluding Rs 300 crore paid as compensation to people in border areas where deployment of troops took place. The total casualties during Operation Parakram were 798 as reported by the defence minister in Parliament in July 2003.

Strategic analysts felt that India gained little from the expensive operation. Brahma Chellaney, an Indian columnist and author on geostrategic affairs, critically mentioned, 'The harsh truth is that the government played a game of bluff not just with Pakistan but also with its own military.' He further added that Vajpayee ended up practising coercive non-diplomacy.[29]

General Karamat of Pakistan and I were in a small group at Stanford University to discuss nuclear issues. He told me that as a result of Operation Parakram, India was able to conduct elections in the state of Jammu and Kashmir.

The elections to the J & K State Assembly were conducted in September–October 2002. Before proceeding with the prime minister on a visit abroad, Brijesh Mishra, principal secretary to the prime minister, asked me to supervise the briefing of foreign correspondents covering the election. The information minister, Sushma Swaraj, however, felt this job should be done by her ministry. Brijesh Mishra, on the telephone from Frankfurt, discussed this with me, and it was agreed that the briefing could be handled by Information & Broadcasting (I&B) officials. The election results showed a turnaround of 44 per cent in J & K; in the Valley, it was 31 per cent. This was not impressive compared to the rest of the country, but it was a huge improvement from the past. The elections were described as fair by the international media. The victor was the Congress–Peoples Democratic Party (PDP) coalition and not the ruling BJP–National Alliance coalition.

SAARC Summit, Islamabad, January 2004

Vajpayee was determined to go ahead with his desire for improved relations with Pakistan, and despite Kargil, had not hesitated to invite Musharraf to India. Even after the attack on Parliament,

he sought opportunities to move ahead. The result of the J &
K elections encouraged him, and on 18 April 2003, in a public
meeting in Kashmir, he spoke of *Insaniyat, Jamhooriyat and
Kashmiriyat*—Humanism, Democracy and Hindu–Muslim
Unity in Kashmir. He also extended a hand of friendship to
Pakistan, provided they reciprocated without guns. The Pakistan
Prime Minister, Jamali, invited him to Pakistan to which he
promptly responded. There were other developments—ceasefire
on the Line of Control on 26 November 2003, resumption of
overflights on 30 November, and a decision to restore diplomatic
relations to high commissioner level. The SAARC summit in
Islamabad on January 2004 was the first important international
event in Islamabad after Musharraf took over as President. For
him, Vajpayee's presence at the summit was essential.

Vajpayee's decision to attend the SAARC summit was
another important initiative. Prior to Vajpayee's departure for
Islamabad in 2004 for the SAARC summit, I was asked to meet
him. On inquiring from his secretary as to how much time had
been earmarked for the briefing, I was informed there was plenty,
as Mr Vajpayee had a dentist's appointment only much later
that evening, thereby ensuring no inconvenience caused to the
public as regards traffic arrangements. His emphasis during the
conversation was that we should work towards making Pakistan
realize that it needed to cease help to terrorists so that discussions
on bilateral relations could move forward. He thanked me for
my few suggestions as was his gracious nature. Two hours later,
I received a call to the effect that I had made seven points, which
should be sent in writing. He remembered the number.

The seven points included: strengthening ceasefire line of
2003, ensuring no harm to India through Pakistan jihadi or
official action (the final wording of the joint declaration was more
elegant), diplomatic missions to function in accordance with

agreed code of conduct, resumption of economy, trade and travel, need for change in Pakistan policy on Afghanistan—instead of negating India's efforts, it should consider working together for reconstruction of Afghanistan, and making SAARC more effective and giving it a more economic content.

Before the summit, discussions took place between the national security adviser to Prime Minister Vajpayee, Brijesh Mishra, and adviser to the Pakistan President Tariq Aziz. The back channel was being institutionalized. Both agreed that the Islamabad SAARC summit was an opportunity for a breakthrough.

At the conclusion of the SAARC summit, the Islamabad Declaration was issued. The framework agreement on South Asian Free Trade Area (SAFTA) was described as a major milestone. Besides regional cooperation, the declaration concentrated on poverty alleviation and combating terrorism.

The important achievement was the bilateral joint press statement issued on 6 January 2004, which mentioned,

> Prime Minister Vajpayee said that in order to take forward and sustain the dialogue process, violence, hostility and terrorism must be prevented. President Musharraf reassured Prime Minister Vajpayee that he will not permit any territory under Pakistan's control to be used to support terrorism in any manner. President Musharraf emphasized that a sustained and productive dialogue addressing all issues would lead to positive results.[30]

This commitment by Pakistan and the earlier agreement on a ceasefire on the LoC helped to improve relations between the two countries for the next decade.

For both the SAARC summits held in Pakistan in 1988 and 2004, India was represented by Prime Minister Rajiv Gandhi and

Prime Minister Vajpayee. However, in the three SAARC summits held in India, Pakistan was never represented by the effective head of government. During the second SAARC summit in Bangalore (November 1986), Prime Minister Muhammad Khan Junejo represented Pakistan. President Zia attended the first SAARC summit in Dhaka. During the fourteenth SAARC summit in New Delhi in 2007, Prime Minister Shaukat Aziz represented Pakistan. President Musharraf attended the Kathmandu summit. In both cases, it can be argued that Pakistan did not have a prime minister at that time. However, at the eighth SAARC summit in New Delhi in May 1995, Prime Minister Benazir Bhutto deliberately absented herself and instead sent President Leghari. When Prime Minister Modi convened a video conference of SAARC leaders on 15 March 2020 to discuss the Coronavirus crisis, it was attended by heads of government of all countries with one solitary exception. On behalf of Pakistan's Prime Minister Imran Khan, his special assistant on health, Dr Zafar Mirza, attended. Pakistan has been diluting its presence at SAARC summits held in India.

My last meeting with former Prime Minister Vajpayee was on 10 June 2006. The purpose was to brief him on the back-channel discussions with Pakistan. Thereafter, I continued briefing Brijesh Mishra, who was in regular touch with him. Every meeting convinced me that his policy towards Pakistan was based on pragmatism and realism.

Visit to Saudi Arabia to Meet Nawaz Sharif

One of the last important decisions taken by Vajpayee as prime minister, in respect of relations with Pakistan, was to send me as his special envoy to meet Nawaz Sharif, who was in political exile in Saudi Arabia. He was keen to maintain India's contacts with the civilian leadership in Pakistan. I was told that this decision was also on account of my past close contact with Nawaz Sharif. The visit, in April 2004, was arranged in such a manner that no one was aware of it. I travelled as a private citizen to Jeddah and booked myself in a hotel. I spent the following full day with former Prime Minister Nawaz Sharif and his family. Immediately on my arrival at their home, they spoke to my wife in Delhi asking why she had not accompanied me. She told them she was unaware of my visit but was glad that I was with them. During the course of the day, there were expansive discussions on the political situation in the subcontinent, developments in Iraq and India–Pakistan relations. He was glad there was improvement after the prime minister's visit to Islamabad to the SAARC summit, but hoped for much more. There were discussions on Kashmir, too. He was deeply touched that Prime Minister Vajpayee had sent me to meet him in his difficult moments. Personally, he said, he was comfortable, but to be away from his country was traumatic. Next morning before my departure, he sent gifts for Prime Minister Vajpayee, Foreign Minister Jaswant Singh, Principal Secretary Brijesh Mishra and me. This was a few weeks before the elections that brought the UPA under Sonia Gandhi and Dr Manmohan Singh to power.

Pakistan's Favourite Indian Prime Minister

Every prime minister in India has been the subject of intense discussion in Pakistan at all levels. For historical reasons, prime ministers belonging to the Nehru–Gandhi family are not their favourites, but there is healthy respect for them. Nehru bore the burden of pre and post-Independence developments. Indira Gandhi was seen as responsible for Pakistan's defeat and loss of East Pakistan in 1971 and the takeover of Siachen in her second tenure, though they did admire her for her stand against Bhutto's hanging. Rajiv Gandhi initially evoked interest, which turned to disappointment because he made no concessions, as was expected, on Siachen or Sir Creek.

Lal Bahadur Shastri became unpopular because of the 1965 war. Morarji Desai was liked in Pakistan and was even awarded the Nishan-e-Pakistan, the highest award for foreigners, from General Zia. Chandra Shekhar and I.K. Gujral were liked, but were seen as ineffective because they led minority governments.

There is genuine admiration for Manmohan Singh, but he was seen as being under the influence of Congress president Sonia Gandhi. There was much regret that he did not travel to Pakistan in ten years in office.

The most popular PM was, of course, Vajpayee, who is seen as a man of peace, who visited Pakistan three times, including once as external affairs minister, and despite many disruptions and disappointments, kept up efforts to engage with Pakistan. He genuinely sought to find a solution to one of India's greatest challenges, while keeping India's interests in mind.

After Vajpayee's death, sociologist and writer Dipankar Gupta rightly observed in the *Daily O* on 21 August 2018, 'The spirit behind Vajpayee's Pakistan overture dominates our appreciation of Vajpayee, much more than the many successes of his government.' He further writes that this theme was also echoed by people and commentators covering Vajpayee's funeral. He added, 'Time and again the Pakistan peace progress was recalled with an occasional aside on Pokhran or the Golden Triangle.' According to Sudheendra Kulkarni, a close aide of Vajpayee, 'The best tribute to Mr. Vajpayee would be to continue his peace mission until it is crowned with success.'[31] In Pakistan, too, warm tributes were paid to Vajpayee on his death. Mushahid Hussain, a Pakistani Politian and journalist, described him as an 'icon of peace . . . who had the vision, will and moral courage to walk the talk with Pakistan'.

Raza Rumi, editor of the *Daily Times,* described him as a bridge between the two countries.[32]

History always records both successes and failures. Vajpayee will be remembered for his efforts to bring about better relations with Pakistan. Magnanimous, he reached out equally to supporters and foes.

8

From Nowhere to Centre Stage

Afghanistan is an amazing and absorbing country. Over the years, it has been transformed from a monarchy to a dictatorship, from a pliant state to a chaotic revolutionary regime and later from a medieval theocracy to an alleged fledgling democracy. An important centre of civilization, it has given the region and the world the richness of Dari and Pashto literature, the Sufi tradition of the Chishtis, the legacy of Buddha, the Buddhist art of Bamiyan and the Gandhara school of art. It has always been a coveted area for strategic influence, a junction between South and Central Asia and a frontline state. Alexander invaded it in 327 BC, Babar in 1504 and the British in 1836. In 1843, it became the first country in the region to gain independence from the British, a hundred years before India. In 1979, the Soviet Union occupied Afghanistan, and left it defeated a decade later. North Atlantic Treaty Organization (NATO), and U.S. forces occupied it in 2001, and spent two decades in another costly and deadly war before leaving Afghanistan in August 2021.

India and Afghanistan have had millennia-old civilizational and economic linkages. Till 1947, they were immediate neighbours. Even today there is great mutual warmth, affection and goodwill between the two people. Indians hold Afghans in high esteem. This can be seen in the characterization of Afghans in popular Indian cinema.

As early as 4 January 1950, a treaty of friendship was signed between the Government of India and the Royal Government of Afghanistan, which also provided for appointments of consulates in each other's country. Interestingly this agreement was signed by the Afghan ambassador on behalf of his country and Jawaharlal Nehru, as prime minister and minister of external affairs, on behalf of India. When it was pointed out that the agreement could be signed by a senior official, Nehru responded that Afghanistan was a valuable neighbour and that he would sign it himself. This was the degree of importance attached right from the beginning to India–Afghanistan relations. India has always supported the emergence of a strong, stable, democratic and prosperous Afghanistan.

Thereafter, relations between India and Afghanistan grew in all areas, despite the changed circumstances that the two countries were no longer neighbours, but separated by a country that was deeply hostile towards India, hegemonic towards Afghanistan and deeply suspicious of India–Afghanistan relations. India did not seek to use its relations with Afghanistan or the differences between Afghanistan and Pakistan, especially over the Durand Line, as an instrument against Pakistan. By the 1970s, Afghanistan had emerged as one of the largest recipients of India's development assistance and capacity-building programme. People-to-people contacts also continued to flourish.

Relations were ruptured in the 1990s, in the violent chaos that followed in the aftermath of the Soviet withdrawal and then by the takeover of Afghanistan by the Taliban. After this temporary disruption, India became Afghanistan's first strategic partner. Since 2001 India had been Afghanistan's partner in reconstruction and development. The cooperation started by providing immediate humanitarian, food and medical assistance, from restoration of vital telephone services to grant of buses and civilian aircraft and to urgent repairs and upgrading of educational institutions. In 2003, the two countries signed the Preferential Trade Agreement and in 2007, India facilitated Afghanistan's entry into SAARC at the Delhi summit. In addition to humanitarian assistance and capacity building, India helped in setting up community development projects, described officially as Small Development Projects (SDP) in all provinces of Afghanistan, which were implemented by local contractors at the grassroots level in six to twelve months. Their success was evident in the sense of partnership and ownership they created in the local community.

The most impressive feature of the development partnership has been India's help in the infrastructure sector. Some examples of this are the over 125-mile-long transmission line built on very challenging terrain and a substation that connects various transmission lines from Central Asia to Kabul, enabling Kabul to enjoy nearly twenty-four hours of power supply now; the over 125-mile-long Zaranj–Delaram road; the 42-MW Salma Dam for power and irrigation; the Afghan Parliament building and the upgrading and restoration of telecom and television broadcast links in Afghanistan.

These projects have been implemented in a spirit of solidarity and friendship, despite the hurdles put up by Pakistan, and have been successful because of widespread political and public support in Afghanistan. President Hamid Karzai told me, when he graciously invited me to a private dinner on a visit to Delhi, that these changes in the first decade of the century, after decades of conflict, had to be seen to be believed.

My links to Afghanistan go back to Peshawar in undivided India, where I was born and spent my early childhood.

Interestingly, when the Indian Embassy in Kabul was established, the first ambassador, a political appointee, was my wife's uncle, Wing Commander Rup Chand, and the two political officers were J.C. Kakar, my maternal uncle, and Girdhari Lal Puri, the husband of my paternal aunt's adopted daughter.

In 1982, as head of the Pakistan/Afghan desk in the MEA, I dealt directly with Afghanistan and also co-chaired the Indo–Afghan Commission. In addition, during my two postings in Islamabad, I had an opportunity to deal closely with Afghanistan.

Soon after I retired from the foreign service, end July 2001, and returned to Delhi from Moscow, the horrifying tragedy of 9/11 (September 2001) took place in the United States. The U.S. and global attention turned to Afghanistan, the base of Osama Bin Laden and Al-Qaeda under the patronage of the ruling dispensation in Afghanistan, the Taliban. A U.S. and NATO invasion of Afghanistan looked imminent. It was clear that India's neighbourhood would once again be at the centre of great geopolitical turmoil.

In November 2001, our foreign minister, Jaswant Singh, informed me that the Government of India had decided to appoint me as special envoy for Afghanistan. He said Prime Minister Vajpayee had approved the proposal within hours of receiving the suggestion. He observed that in spite of our close association with the Northern Alliance, we were nowhere on the international scene in respect of Afghanistan, as the Taliban rule had excluded us from any role, be it in the UN or in ad hoc groups like Six plus Two. He wanted India to play a pivotal role in the expected developments with regard to Afghanistan and told me to accompany him to New York, where Afghanistan was to be discussed in the UNGA. He agreed to my suggestion that I should meet ex-King Zaheer of Afghanistan in Rome. He mentioned that the USA and UK had appointed special envoys and was concerned that India was missing from the international processes on Afghanistan, though he added we had occupied some space through our assistance to the Northern Alliance. His objective now was to go from nowhere to a place of influence.

Realizing that developments in Afghanistan, and the role the international community would play in that, would have a profound impact on India's security and our regional interests, and conscious of our responsibility to the people of Afghanistan, Prime Minister Vajpayee and Foreign Minister Jaswant Singh were keen for India to participate in shaping the future of Afghanistan.

Meeting with Ex-King Zaheer Shah, before and after, and with his Delegation during the Bonn Conference

My immediate objective was to establish contact with all actors including the ex-king, who had earlier shown reluctance to meet an Indian representative. After being appointed special envoy, I asked Siddharth Singh, our ambassador in Rome, to fix a meeting as I wanted to start with an audience with the king. His last meeting with an Indian representative was with minister of state, Natwar Singh, on 5 February 1988, months after the Soviet departure from Afghanistan. At that time, the king was not in favour of either assigning any role for the People's Democratic Republic of Afghanistan (PDPA), which had played a role in his overthrow in 1973, or considering even a minor role for the PDPA's general secretary, then President Mohammad Najibullah, in the coalition. Natwar Singh sought to persuade the king by bringing to his notice that Najibullah had in December 1987 said that he considered the king 'a father figure'. The king, however, did not relent.

I met King Zaheer Shah on 9 November 2001 in Rome. Times had changed, and in my discussion with him, he was very positive about an Indian role. I met the king a second time after the Bonn Conference on 1 February 2002. By then, he was convinced about India's intentions, objectives and cooperation.

New York (11–18 November 2001)

After the Taliban regime refused to accept the U.S. and UNSC demand to hand over Osama Bin Laden, the U.S.-led coalition began bombing Afghanistan on 7 October 2001. The ground invasion started after the bombing had sufficiently softened the Taliban defences and forced the remaining Taliban forces and Al-Qaeda members into hiding. The ground advances were led largely by the Northern Alliance with the support of coalition air power and ground forces.

Those were the days of fast developments on the ground in Afghanistan. Every day, every hour the Northern Alliance made progress and the Taliban retreated, leading to dramatic changes. As I reached New York, the Northern Alliance was marching into Kabul, which was taken over as the first hint of Afghanistan's bitter winter entered the air, on 11 November.

My first meeting in New York, on 11 November 2011, was with Richard Haass, the then U.S. special envoy on Afghanistan. He had stayed on in New York to meet me, before going to Washington. A few days later at the Bonn Conference, the Americans realized they needed India in their interaction with the Northern Alliance. Later, after establishing their own contacts with the Northern Alliance, they did not need us to the same extent. Before leaving for Kabul, in my assessment of my visits to New York and Rome, I conveyed to the external affairs minister on 19 November 2001, that both Richard Haass and the UN special envoy for Afghanistan, Lakhdar Brahimi, understood India's role, but with the objective of succeeding in Afghanistan, they did not wish to annoy Pakistan, and in the process would be willing to bypass India if it suited them. This approach on the part of the U.S. remained valid till the end of its presence in Afghanistan.

There were many other meetings with foreign ministers, Brahimi and other UN officials and Afghan representatives. More importantly, I represented India in the first G-21 meeting on Afghanistan held in New York after the recent developments.

Our immediate aim to re-establish bilateral relations after the fall of the Taliban government were conveyed in my recommendations sent on 15 November 2001 from New York:

a) Start the process of identifying suitable officials for establishing diplomatic presence at an early appropriate time in Afghanistan.

b) Restore Ariana (Afghan Airlines) air links between Delhi and Kabul as early as feasible.

c) Establish and strengthen our medical presence in areas where it is needed and feasible.

d) Initiate the process for sending a technical evaluation team to visit our hospital in Kabul (Indira Gandhi Children's Hospital) to ensure its earliest reopening.

e) Provide artificial limbs (Jaipur foot) to the needy in Afghanistan as early as feasible.

f) Immediate visit of an Indian delegation to Kabul.

On my return to Delhi, and following discussions with External Affairs Minister (EAM) on the eve of the departure of the first Indian delegation to Kabul, these objectives were refined on 19 November 2001, to a short-term six-point programme.

i. Visits to Kabul, Herat and Mazar-i-Sharif.

ii. The process of identifying suitable personnel for establishing diplomatic presence in Afghanistan.

iii. Measures for reopening our hospital in Kabul and providing facilities for Jaipur foot and medical presence elsewhere in northern Afghanistan.

iv. Establish contacts with Pashtun leaders.
v. Establish air links between Kabul and New Delhi as early as possible.
vi. Contribution for reconstruction of Afghanistan.

Visit to Kabul, 21 November 2001

India was the first country to reach Kabul, five days after the fall of the Taliban. It had been decided on 19 November 2001, immediately on my return from New York, that I should lead the delegation to Kabul. Foreign Minister Jaswant Singh put former defence secretary, Naresh Chandra, in charge of making the necessary arrangements, including security. It was decided that to maintain secrecy, the visit would be through Iran. An IAF plane was readied. A small delegation was selected. A quick search was conducted to identify a senior official who would volunteer to stay back in Kabul. Gautam Mukhopadhaya was selected, who as a student, had crisscrossed Afghanistan and enjoyed it. Immediate consultations were done with authorities in Afghanistan. The anti-Taliban, Northern Alliance welcomed the visit. The Americans objected. The government, however, decided that I should go ahead. Interestingly, in her well-researched book, *The Struggle for Pakistan*, Ayesha Jalal, a Pakistani–American historian and author, writes about what happened on the same day when the U.S. tried to discourage the Indian delegation's visit to Kabul.

On November 21, 2001, the United States halted air strikes on Kunduz to allow Pakistan's military planes to airlift more than 1,000 Pakistani soldiers and agents who had been fighting alongside the Taliban and Al Qaeda in the besieged city. The ISI is known to have used the opportunity to fly out senior

Al Qaeda members as well as Chechens, Uzbeks and Afghans considered to be strategic assets.[1]

The IAF plane flown by Air Vice Marshal Menon, (who I later discovered was the son of my favourite English schoolteacher) left for Kabul on the night of 20 November. The plane refuelled in Iran and landed at Bagram airport near Kabul—as expected, without any communication from the Air Traffic Control (ATC), which was under American control. On arrival, there was further confusion because the welcoming party, and the vehicles from Kabul, had not reached Bagram. These eventually arrived two hours later. The Kabul airport was not operational, and the drive from Bagram to Kabul, through a circuitous route, as a result of damaged roads and broken bridges, was overwhelming. There were constant calls on the satellite phone from external affairs minister, Jaswant Singh, who wanted to inform the Parliament about the historic step that symbolized a significant change in India's re-engagement with Afghanistan. He had to wait till we reached Kabul. After considerable delay, we arrived, and the external affairs minister immediately made the following announcement in the Rajya Sabha (21 November 2001).

I am happy to inform Hon'ble Members that a diplomatic Mission to Afghanistan landed at Bagram Airfield near Kabul at 0955 hrs this morning. This Mission Team comprises Special Envoy for Afghanistan, senior officials of the Ministry of External Affairs, interpreters and other essential staff. It also has a medical and nursing component, which will stay on in Kabul along with the Liaison Officer of the Ministry of External Affairs, Government of India. Members are no doubt aware that the Indian Embassy in Kabul closed on September 26, 1996. This is the first Indian Diplomatic Mission, thereafter.[2]

During my stay in Kabul, I had discussions with President Burhanuddin Rabbani, Defence Minister Mohammad Qasim Fahim, Interior Minister Yunus Qanooni and Foreign Minister Abdullah Abdullah. The Indian Embassy was reopened and the India-aided Indira Gandhi Children's Hospital was also made operational.

We also discussed the forthcoming Bonn Conference. During these discussions, the Afghan leaders indicated their preference for Hamid Karzai as head of the new Interim administration. Foreign Minister Abdullah told me that the Northern Alliance delegation to the Bonn Conference would be led by Qanooni and would consist of eleven delegates, which would be 50 per cent of the total delegates. The Rome process (ex-king of Afghanistan) would have a representation of five out of the remaining eleven.

Rabbani's briefing was different from the others. He mentioned his plans of a Loya Jirga, grand assembly or grand council, and said that changes in the administration should take place after elections were held, hinting nothing ought to be done at this juncture. No other member of the Northern Alliance mentioned this. The warmest meeting was with Fahim, held jointly with Qanooni, who acted as the interpreter. They did not rule out a symbolic role for the ex-king and said they were in touch with his grandson, Mustapha Zaher, who was present at my meeting with the ex-king in Rome on 10 November. While Fahim and Qanooni supported Karzai, they said there were indications that Pakistan was also in favour of Deputy Prime Minister Abdul Samad Hamid. Qanooni agreed to remain in close touch with me in Bonn. Fahim was emotional, and while embracing me, said he was thrilled to welcome the representative of friendly India at the headquarters of the defence ministry.

We also visited the Indira Gandhi Children's Hospital where we were warmly welcomed. We gave them the medicines we had carried, received requests for future requirements and assured them of salary payments and arrangements for the provision of artificial limbs (Jaipur foot). We visited both the embassy residence and chancery and introduced Gautam Mukhopadhaya, chief liaison officer, to them. All promised help in his work and gave him the security cover to enable him to renovate the chancery building and start repairs to the residence. On our return to Delhi in the evening, a report was given to the prime minister and the external affairs minister, to approve the suggested follow-up action. This was, as mentioned above, the first visit of a foreign delegation to Afghanistan, after the fall of the Taliban.

Bonn Conference

Within four days of my return from Kabul, preparations commenced for my departure for Bonn. I led the Indian delegation for the conference on Afghanistan and arrived in Bonn on 24 November, a city where I had represented our country as its ambassador from 1995–98.

For the moment the global attention had shifted from New York and Kabul to Bonn. After the U.S.-led military intervention and the spectacular victory of the Northern Alliance, its United Front had come into power by mid-November 2001, and Rabbani was once again the President, leading an interim administration. The country he now presided over was not a functioning state by even the most liberal definition. No one doubted that a greater challenge lay ahead for the international community and the Afghan people to create a functioning state, a new government acceptable to the widest cross section of Afghans, a country that could reintegrate itself into the international community, and a nation united in a common pursuit of peace and prosperity, no longer serving as a factor of regional instability and a haven for terrorism. It would be international diplomacy's hardest challenge, but its success would ultimately depend on the will of the Afghan leaders themselves. No sooner had the Taliban fallen, but not disappeared, the UN set about the task of getting the different Afghan factions under one roof to decide on a government and the future of Afghan polity.

The meeting was originally supposed to take place in Germany's capital, Berlin—a city that was itself in the process of overcoming the scars and divisions of history and regaining its international stature as the capital of reunified Germany. Since it could provide no venue that met the criteria of size, seclusion and security, the German government fell back on the city that it had left behind. Bonn, a charming little town located on the banks of the Rhine, had served as the capital of post-war West Germany.

A short distance away, atop a hill covered with dense forests, was the Guesthouse Petersberg, which was selected as the location of the Bonn Conference. Petersberg traces its history to 3500 BC and was a hotel at the end of the nineteenth century and no stranger to historic accords. It had served as the official guesthouse when Bonn served as the capital of West Germany.

The UN had invited four major Afghan factions to meet in Bonn to establish a new government in Kabul and define a new political future for Afghanistan. It also invited interested countries to send delegations as observers. Seventeen countries sent their representatives at different levels. These were Austria, Belgium, Canada, China, France, India, Iran Italy, Japan, Norway, Pakistan, Republic of Korea, Russian Federation, Turkey, the Netherlands, United Kingdom, the United States, Switzerland and the European Union.

The U.S. delegation was led by the State Department's special envoy for Afghanistan, James Dobbins, and the White

House point man for Afghanistan, Zalmay Khalilzad, an American of Afghan origin with a doctorate from the University of Chicago and many years of experience in Rand Corporation, who would continue to play a decisive role at different stages, including at the end of U.S. withdrawal from Afghanistan in 2021. Both played a pivotal role in achieving a successful conclusion at Bonn. Foreign minister, Joschka Fischer, led the host government's delegation. The Iranian delegation was led by Deputy Foreign Minister Javed Zarif, who joined the conference after the talks began and stayed till the end. His arrival gave a higher profile to the Iranian delegation and his help was crucial, because it was at his suggestion that the word democracy was added in the Bonn agreement at the last moment. It appeared that a beginning was being made in the U.S.–Iran relations but it was not to be so.

Reflecting shock and confusion in its policy establishment, due to the sudden turn of events after 11 September, Pakistan, which had sought to build strategic depth in Afghanistan through the Taliban, was represented by Arif Ayub, ambassador in the Taliban's Kabul. Perhaps it was the only country represented by a person who had been accredited to the Taliban. Farooq Afzal, an ISI officer, was there to assist him, making Pakistan the only delegation to publicly field an intelligence officer at the conference. This was not surprising since ISI was the architect of Pakistan's Afghan policy and the Taliban's chief supporter.[3]

The UN team was led by special representative of the secretary general, Lakhdar Brahimi, and included Dr Ashraf Ghani, a Pashtun anthropologist at the World Bank, and Barnett Rubin, a New York university professor and an expert on Afghanistan. He was earlier with the council on foreign relations. Another key figure in the UN delegation was Francesc Vendrell, a Spanish diplomat who later served as head of the UN special mission on Afghanistan and then as the EU's special representative for Afghanistan. However, it was Brahimi who was the focus of attention.

The first shock for us on arrival in Bonn was to learn that there was no room for me or the Indian delegation at Petersberg. We had to initially stay at a hotel in Bonn, which was some distance from Petersberg. To be in the immediate vicinity was essential, to enable us to participate in parleys and consultations as these did not follow any fixed schedule or pattern, and to join in spontaneous meetings late at night or discussions in small groups held on the margins of such meetings. Staying away from Petersberg put us at a disadvantage. There is something strangely fertile and productive in diplomats' minds late in the night, which leads to new ideas or solutions, so it was important to be present in what I had anticipated would be many late-night consultations.

Ambassador Matussek of the German foreign office mentioned to Ambassador Ronen Sen in Berlin on 27 November that the UN—actually Brahimi—took all decisions on accommodation. Brahimi had decided that only the 'Six plus Two' countries and the remaining P-5 countries would be accommodated at the venue. It is interesting that after rejecting an initial Chinese démarche for a special role for the 'Six plus Two,' the UN special representative, Brahimi, made a gesture of this nature. In any case, the representation of the six neighbouring countries was limited. Three Central Asian countries—Uzbekistan, Tajikistan and Turkmenistan—were not participating. China was represented by an embassy official at the inaugural function. Pakistan kept a low profile. Only the Iranians had a high-profile representation. Perhaps Brahimi gradually realized that Six plus Two was no longer relevant.

There was an exchange of messages between the UN and Germans about allotment for a room to the Indian delegation, and each tried to shift the responsibility on the other. It was both

Ambassador Sen's persuasive powers and the recognition of the potentially important role that India would have to play in the conference, that resulted in the allotment of a room for the Indian delegation in Petersberg, thus enabling us to be effective at the conference. The room allotted to me was the only one available and smaller than a normal single room with just enough place for a bed and table—perhaps a room for an attendant. Nonetheless, it enabled me to be an active participant of the conference.

Immediately after our arrival, Ambassador James Dobbin, the U.S. State Department's special envoy for Afghanistan, invited me for lunch. The discussions revealed that there was more convergence than divergence between Indian and American positions for the conference. Contacts were also established with all other delegations, particularly Russian, Iranian and European.

At the same time, extensive contacts were maintained with the four Afghan factions participating in the conference. One, the Iran-supported Cyprus process of Afghan technocrats living abroad, led by Humayun Jareer, son-in-law of Gulbuddin Hekmatyar, a former Mujahideen leader and prime minister twice in the 1990s; two, the Peshawar group led by Syed Hamid Geelani, son of Peer Geelani. His daughter, Fatima Geelani, was an adviser to the Peshawar delegation, while her ex-husband, Nasir Zia, Afghan chargé d'affaires in Rome, was with the United Front faction—the group that Fatima's faction was most suspicious of. Three, the Rome group, regarded as the former king's faction, led by Professor Abdul Satar Sirat, was the largest but was also a divided house. My contacts with the king in Rome enabled us to keep in close touch with them.

The fourth—and the most important group—was the United Front, which had by this time taken over the reins in Kabul. It was led by Interior Minister Qanooni. As a result of our earlier meeting in Kabul, we began meeting on a daily basis in Bonn, and this had an impact on the ultimate decision. In addition, there was regular contact with UN officials, including Brahimi. Satish Mehta, from our UN mission in New York, had been included as a member of the delegation, because I had observed he had once worked with Brahimi. This proved helpful in Petersberg. Arun Singh, joint secretary for the PAI (Pakistan, Afghanistan and Iran) division in MEA, came for the first two days. Second Secretary Shambhu Kumaran from the embassy in Bonn was an asset throughout the conference. We had intensive consultations with the missions of the United States, Russia, Iran and Italy. The Americans were the dominant players and they clearly recognized the value of keeping India on the inside track.

The conference kept on dragging. Till the last day the outcome hung in balance. It was like a day alternating between bright sunshine and grey clouds. The uncertainty increased with every passing day. On 30 November, the spokesman for Brahimi said at a briefing that the deal would hopefully be concluded in the original time frame of 1 December. The conference lasted till 5 December. Later, at the press briefing on 4 December, the spokesman of the conference said that the four Afghan groups had concurred on the text of an agreement that would pave the way for the establishment of an interim administration in Kabul as soon as possible. He added that the four Afghan groups had submitted a total of 150 names to Brahimi who would suggest a short list of twenty-eight names for the approval of all groups. Even after this announcement, uncertainty prevailed. It had been agreed that German Chancellor Schröder would attend the concluding session, but by the time he went to bed in Berlin, it was not certain if he would need to fly to Bonn for the concluding session in the morning on 5 December.

During the Bonn Conference, I maintained close relations with the Rome group representing the king. At the conference, the king's delegation got overambitious and created problems, particularly his grandson, Prince Mustapha. Eventually, the king intervened, and it was agreed that while the new head of administration could be from his group, conflict should be avoided. The Rome process had no problems in finalizing the interim administration in Bonn or in presenting their list of candidates. After internal consultations, they suggested the name of Abdul Satar Sirat, who was close to the king and leader of the Rome process faction, as head of the interim administration. As had been agreed, the new head of administration would be a member of the Rome group, and they met to decide who should head the new Afghan administration. Though the ballot was secret, it was widely believed at the conference that there were eleven votes for Sirat, two for Karzai and one for Arsala (an economist and a prominent politician in Afghanistan).

This was not acceptable to the United Front as well as some others. The ex-king was approached in Rome and his intervention sought. The U.S. delegation wanted, and got, Hamid Karzai to lead the interim administration, leaving some Rome process participants grumbling. There had actually been no doubt from the beginning that Hamid Karzai would head the government. This was also the distinct impression we got from the United Front leaders, when the Indian delegation visited Kabul on 21 November 2001, prior to the Bonn meeting. Dobbins had also mentioned his name to the Indian delegation at the meeting before the conference started. James Dobbins commented in his book, *After the Taliban: Nation-Building in Afghanistan*, 'Both Lambah and Kabulov had spoken positively about Karzai with me earlier that day. Now with the Iranians proposing him as well, a bandwagon seemed to be rolling.'[4]

The Afghans were by and large prepared for Hamid Karzai to head the new administration, but in the nine days in Bonn, the representatives of different Afghan factions did their best to advance the claims of their candidates. There was also an unwritten understanding that the new leader would be a Pashtun. Karzai was. Sirat was of Uzbek origin.

The Rome process, determined to get as enlarged a role as possible for the ex-king, and in the belief that he enjoyed very high popularity in Afghanistan, wanted the creation of a body that would serve as some sort of Parliament leading up to a Loya Jirga. Some representatives of the Rome group, including Prince Mustapha Zaher, made a strong pitch for a role for the former monarch. At a press conference in Bonn on 29 November, Sirat answered questions that were supplemented often without his request by the prince, Sayed Mansur Naderi and Mrs Sima Wali, who later became highly regarded globally as a human rights activist. They made the point that King Zaheer Shah was the spiritual leader of the Afghan people and he should play a central role in the future of Afghanistan, either as head of state or head of the supreme council for national unity of Afghanistan. They clarified they had no plans to restore the monarchy.

Midway through the negotiations, it became clear that the concept was controversial, with the United Front as well as the Iran-backed Cypress process opposing the idea. Both did not see any role for the ex-king beyond a minimal symbolic one. To bring back the focus to the main issue of an interim administration, the idea of a supreme council was jettisoned. In its place, it was agreed to create a twenty-one-member special independent commission for the convening of an emergency Loya Jirga. The final Bonn statement handled the situation neatly when it mentioned, 'The participants in the UN talks on Afghanistan have invited His Majesty Mohammad Zaher, the former King of Afghanistan, to chair the Interim Administration. His Majesty has indicated that he would prefer that a suitable candidate acceptable to the participants be selected as the Chair of the Interim Administration.'⁵

Midnight Session

The final deal on the composition of the interim administration was struck at a meeting that took place well past midnight on the last day in Brahimi's room. Dobbins had organized the meeting. Besides Dobbins, Khalilzad and Brahimi, Interior Minister Qanooni (Afghanistan), Zamir Kabulov (Russia), Deputy Foreign Minister Zarif (Iran) and I attended the meeting. In other words, among P-5 of the UN Security Council, only the USA and Russia were present. From the 'Six plus Two', only Iran and Afghanistan were there. The only non-member from Six plus Two and P-5 was India.

The objective was to persuade Qanooni to agree to accept fewer ministerial berths than he was asking for. The American proposal to him was to take over 50 per cent of the crucial posts and less than 50 per cent of the total posts.

Recalling the midnight session in his book, James Dobbins wrote, 'Fifteen minutes later we assembled around Brahimi's dining room table. In addition to Brahimi, the group consisted of Kabulov, Lambah, Zarif, Matussek, Khalilzad and me. Qanooni arrived, looked around the room, and saw that he was in for a difficult session. For the next two hours, we took turns explaining to him why the Northern Alliance could not expect to retain the three power ministries while also insisting on holding most of the others.'⁶

Eventually, he got more than what was originally offered. He clinched the three crucial posts that he was interested in and over 50 per cent of the total posts. In the early hours of 5 December, the Germans were told that they could make arrangements for their chancellor to reach Bonn for the concluding session, which he did.

It was interesting from the Indian point of view, that the delegation which had initially not even been provided accommodation in the conference hotel, was eventually included in the crucial midnight session attended by a select few where the ultimate decision was taken.

T.C.A. Raghavan, who was at that time director of the office of external affairs minister, Jaswant Singh, said the minister was elated when he saw the cable about the midnight session. This was rightly so because it was his idea that the Bonn Conference should be used to project India's vital role in Afghanistan, which had been ignored in the recent past.

The decision of the Bonn Conference was to transfer the power on 22 December to an interim authority, and an emergency Loya Jirga was to be convened within six months to be opened by the ex-king. Hamid Karzai was to head the interim administration, and the composition of the interim government was finalized. The agreement provided for a new constitution to be framed and a legal framework and judicial system to be established.

I spoke on satellite telephone to Hamid Karzai, then in Kandahar, through his brother and congratulated him. He recalled our meeting at my house in Bonn and we looked forward to meeting each other in Kabul.

I persuaded Qanooni to come with me to Delhi. With no Delhi–Kabul flights at that time and Foreign Minister Jaswant Singh having said I could use the IAF plane when necessary, I took Qanooni to Kabul on 12 December, and on the return flight, I brought Foreign Minister Abdullah with me to Delhi. After a long time, Delhi became a favourite destination for Afghan leaders. At that time, it was the only capital which had been visited by two-thirds of the thirty-member Afghan interim cabinet, including a visit of Chairman Karzai in February 2002.

The Indian delegation left Bonn satisfied with the successful conclusion of the Bonn Conference. Our basic objective had been met: a broad-based interim administration with effective control in the hands of India's friends had been hammered out in Bonn. The international community appreciated India's role in the process. U.S. Secretary of State Colin Powell expressed appreciation for the Indian delegation's role in the conference to the external affairs minister on 20 December 2001, stating, 'The engagement of Ambassador Lambah and his colleagues was important to the success of the meeting, and to realizing our hopes for an end to war and the beginning of a peaceful era in the history of Afghanistan.' The U.S. State Department's director for policy planning, who was also involved in the Afghanistan affair, was in Delhi at that time and publicly praised India's contribution at the Bonn Conference. Later, Robert Blackwill, the U.S. ambassador in Delhi, mentioned that Indo–U.S. cooperation in Bonn was the first practical result of the Jaswant–Talbott discussions.

Dobbins also expressed appreciation for the work of the Indian delegation in his book.

India sent a distinguished senior diplomat who had been brought out of retirement for the purpose. White haired, elegant, soft-spoken, with an English diction I could only envy, Ambassador S.K. Lambah had earlier served in the most demanding of New Delhi's diplomatic postings, as the Indian envoy to Pakistan. Lambah explained to me his government's long-standing ties to the Northern Alliance leadership. He was ready to draw on these relationships to ensure the success of the upcoming conference. I knew that India's interest in Afghanistan stemmed largely from its competition with Pakistan. Lambah understood, however, that the United States needed Islamabad's support to prosecute the war in Afghanistan and was careful not to adopt an anti-Pakistan tone. On the contrary, he spoke rather fondly of his years in Islamabad. When the Pakistan delegate to the conference arrived, later than the rest, Lambah was one of the few people to show him any kindness.[7]

After the Bonn Conference, India took quick steps in rebuilding relations with Afghanistan. The opening of the Indian diplomatic mission in Kabul on 21 November 2001, and its formal opening on 21 December 2001, during Foreign Minister Jaswant Singh's visit, again placed India among the first few countries to have a diplomatic presence in Kabul. This was followed by the opening of consulates in Herat, Mazar-i-Sharif, Jalalabad and Kandahar. Afghanistan also chose India as the first destination for the revival of the Ariana flights. The inaugural flight reached Delhi on 24 January 2003. The first business delegation of any country that visited Kabul was from India, when the Confederation of Indian Industries (CII) delegation went there on 17 February 2002. The CII became the first trade/industry organization to open an office in Kabul.

On 14 December, soon after returning from Bonn and a day after the 13 December attack on the Indian Parliament, I briefed the standing committee on external affairs on India's re-engagement with Afghanistan. On 19 December, Dobbins visited Delhi.

On 30 December 2001, I again visited Kabul and met Chairman Karzai. When I asked about the kind of aid he would like from India, his response was that India was the first to ask this question. The others were giving what they wanted. He asked for Tata buses, so that the city transport system could restart, as they had these buses in the past. This was done within weeks.

* * *

First UN Conference on Afghanistan in Delhi

Unlike in the past, when the UN ignored India, it now started inviting India to all major conferences on Afghanistan. The United Nations Development Program (UNDP) joined India in co-hosting a conference on south cooperation and the reconstruction of Afghanistan in New Delhi from 23–24 May 2002. Mark Malloch Brown, administrator of UNDP, and I jointly issued the invitation for the conference on 22 April 2002. This conference also gave a signal that the UN accepted that India had a role to play in Afghanistan. Departing from the past practice of keeping Indians away from Afghanistan-related jobs in the UN, now they started giving some assignments to Indian nationals.

Emergency Loya Jirga

I visited Kabul again from 10–16 June 2002, to attend the emergency Loya Jirga. The highlights of the Jirga included the strengthening of the position of Karzai, who secured 80 per cent of the votes (1295 out of 1567); the role of the ex-king was defined, and he was designated, Baba-e-Afghanistan (Father of Afghanistan); the Pashtuns and the Northern Alliance played an important role, paving the way for a political process. So did the women. Massooda Jalal, who contested the election for President, obtained over 10 per cent of the votes. I had an interesting conversation with her about the future role of women. Both Khalilzad and Brahimi, who were also present in Bonn, involved India in their strategy sessions.

On my return to Delhi, I told Foreign Minister Jaswant Singh I was going to Cordova (Spain) for a conference on Afghanistan, after which my work was completed. I requested him to accept my resignation. He was reluctant. When I returned, he had been transferred to the finance ministry, and Yashwant Sinha had taken over as external affairs minister. Yashwant Sinha asked me to stay on, but I told him I had already taken a decision. On learning of my resignation, Jaswant Singh wrote a gracious letter to me.

* * *

2003 Onwards

The period 2003 onwards for the next six years was difficult for Afghanistan as the U.S. diverted its attention to Iraq. It must be said, to America's credit, that their diagnosis of the situation was correct. The treatment, however, was wrong. Dobbins, the chief American negotiator on Afghanistan after 9/11, wrote in his book:

> The decision to invade Iraq in 2003 diverted American manpower and money from Afghanistan. More important, it distracted Americans from what is the true central front in any war on terror. The central front is neither in Iraq nor Afghanistan but in the border regions of Pakistan. Al-Qaeda, after all is now headquartered in Pakistan. The Taliban also operates out of Pakistan, as do several other terrorist groups seeking to expel international forces from Afghanistan. In the 1990s, Pakistan assisted the North Korean and Iranian nuclear programmes. Potential terrorists in western societies still travel to Pakistan—not Iraq, not Afghanistan—for inspiration, guidance, support and direction.[8]

These concerns are still relevant and should determine the policy of the international community towards the Afghanistan–Pakistan region.

During the same period, India worked assiduously on its efforts for Afghanistan's development in the fields of infrastructure (transmission line, roads, dams, Parliament building), humanitarian assistance (supply of high-protein biscuits to 2 million schoolchildren, gift of 250 metric tons of wheat, medical mission, children's hospital, vehicles for mass urban transportation) capacity building, scholarships, training of professionals, women vocational training and special courses for women. One of the most successful schemes undertaken by India was the SDP relating to quick-impact, small-scale projects in sectors such as agriculture, rural development, education and health—with a budget, typically, of less than US$1 million per project. These were implemented in six to twelve months, conceived at grassroots levels and implemented by local contractors. They brought visible benefits to the local community in the vulnerable border districts in the southern and eastern provinces of Afghanistan. Nearly a hundred small projects were implemented in nineteen provinces of Afghanistan. It brough India closer to the Pashtun population too.

These projects were implemented despite hostility from Pakistan and scepticism about our intentions among several donor countries, whose perceptions were shaped by proclivity to see the situation from the perspective projected by Pakistan.

As the U.S. focused on an increasingly complex war in Iraq, and as reliance on Pakistan to achieve the goals in Afghanistan increased, the Taliban began to regroup in Pakistan, and together with various groups supported by Pakistan, including the dreaded Haqqani Network, began to wage attacks in Afghanistan, both on foreign troops, Afghan forces and the civilian population.

Indian interests, too, were subject to direct attacks. The most egregious among the many attacks that the Indian Embassy, consulates and projects faced, was the terrorist attack on the

Indian Embassy on 7 July 2007, which took a number of lives, including that of a senior Indian diplomat.

Besides the deteriorating security environment, there were governance and economic problems in Afghanistan, as also the persisting challenge of forging unity in the multiethnic society.

As the Bush administration approached the end of its second term in 2007–08, it began to recognize that the situation in Afghanistan was slipping and sought to increase pressure on Pakistan and the government in Afghanistan.

By this time a view was gaining bipartisan consensus in the U.S. Congress that the U.S. needed to provide more economic and military assistance to Pakistan to induce stronger cooperation in Afghanistan. There was a growing sense of doubt, even pessimism, about the direction of the military operations in Afghanistan, the financial and human cost, and prospects for success.

There were growing talks, especially among the Democrats, about a political settlement in Afghanistan. A section of the strategic community and leadership of the Democratic Party was of the view that there was an external dimension to the problem which lay in Pakistan's security concerns, specifically its fear of India using Afghan territory against Pakistan through a regime favourable to India. Therefore, the argument went, the real problem was the competition between India and Pakistan. To resolve it and achieve a peaceful political settlement within Afghanistan, these American experts believed that India–Pakistan relations needed to be improved.

They, thus, began to see the problem as a triangular one, involving India, Pakistan and Afghanistan. This view was also quite strong in the camp of Democratic presidential hopeful and later President Barak Obama.

The mountain of evidence regarding Pakistan's support for terrorist groups and for the Taliban, their killing of U.S. and allied forces, not to mention the attack on the Indian Embassy in Kabul, did not dampen western support for Pakistan or seeking a solution in Afghanistan through addressing Pakistan's perceived concerns. The 2008 Mumbai terror attack did not lead to any change in that thinking. Nor, as we learnt later in May 2011, did Osama Bin Laden's presence in Pakistan in the vicinity of a major Pakistan military establishment in Abbottabad.

Once President Obama came into office in January 2009, a review of the Afghan strategy began, which eventually crystallized into a military surge with a clear intent and timeline for withdrawal. On the diplomatic side, President Obama appointed a veteran diplomat, Richard Holbrooke, who was close to Secretary of State Hillary Clinton, as special envoy for Afghanistan and Pakistan (Af–Pak). They probed India on the possibility of Holbrooke including India as part of this portfolio. With our strong advice against it, which I conveyed during a Track II Strategic Dialogue and our embassy conveyed officially, the idea was dropped.

Throughout this period, Indian, Afghan and international observers found it hard to understand why the U.S. was relying so much on Pakistan, ignoring its activities instead of exerting genuine pressure on it, and not focusing more on strengthening Afghan capacity. Further, anyone with a cursory reading of history would have realized that India had never used the tensions in the Afghanistan–Pakistan relationship to its advantage.

Before going into the new phase of diplomatic activism on Afghanistan by the new Obama administration, it is worth recalling a brief history of the U.S.–Pakistan relations and also of relations between Afghanistan and Pakistan.

* * *

U.S.–Pakistan: A Brief History Review

The U.S. has always been partial towards Pakistan. This was clear when Dulles confused Gorkhas with Pathans. Pakistan's alliance with the U.S. and UK during the Cold War, starting with membership of Southeast Asia Treaty Organization SEATO and Central Treaty Organizations (CENTO) in the 1950s, and the role Pakistan played in brokering the U.S.–China rapprochement and in supporting the fight against the Soviet occupation in Afghanistan in the 1980s, had created a strong political and institutional relationship, including with Pakistan's military and intelligence. In a cable to all U.S. embassies in April 1981, titled 'U.S. Policy towards Pakistan', U.S. Secretary of State Haig[9] stated, 'Pakistan security is inextricably linked to our own security and to that of industrialized democracies, primarily because of Western and Japanese dependence on Persian Gulf oil.' The United States had 'concluded that a stronger, more self-confident Pakistan' was 'essential for the enhanced deterrence to Soviet expansionism which we seek'.

After meeting President Ziaul Haq on 7 December 1982, Reagan preferred not to highlight Pakistan's nuclear programme, in view of its frontline role in confronting the Soviet Union. Being soft on Ziaul Haq, Reagan wrote in his diary, 'He's a good man. Gave me his word they were not building an atomic or nuclear bomb. He's dedicated to helping the Afghans and stopping the Soviets.'[10] Such an approach, of which there are many instances, despite complete knowledge of the reality, indicates how the U.S. permitted Pakistan to continue with its mischievous activities, by ignoring it.

The Americans were always aware of the role of intelligence agencies in Pakistan, 'The intelligence service had become

Pakistan's kingmakers in addition to controlling insurgencies in Afghanistan and Kashmir.'[11] According to Steve Coll, nearly everyone of prominence in Pakistan believes that his or her telephone is bugged by the intelligence agencies. The Secretary of State James Baker in May 1992 sent a letter to Prime Minister Nawaz Sharif stating, 'We have information indicating that ISI and others intend to continue to provide material support to groups that have engaged in terrorism.'[12]

The U.S. was also aware of Pakistan help to the Afghan Taliban. Pakistan nationals constantly bolstered the ranks of the Afghan Taliban. 'At one point the U.S. Embassy estimated that 20–40 per cent of Taliban soldiers are Pakistani. U.S. diplomats acknowledge that the presence of Pakistani volunteers in Afghanistan "solidifies Pakistan–Taliban relations".' But the United States still adopted the formal position that 'this does not indicate outward or official Pakistani government support'.[13] Even after 9/11, when Mehmud, the then ISI chief, made two trips to Kandahar to meet Mullah Omar, he advised the Americans not to act in anger and told them, 'If the Taliban are eliminated, Afghanistan will revert to warlordism. The ISI did not want the Taliban defeated militarily.'[14] We have always been told that the U.S. started helping Pakistan after Soviet intervention in Afghanistan, 'but Carter signed the first authorization "to help Mujahideen covertly" on July 3, 1979, almost six months before the Soviets invaded Afghanistan. And Pakistan had been recruiting and training the Mujahideen for years before that.'[15]

After 9/11, the United States and India had common objectives in Afghanistan. What both sought at that time was an Afghanistan that contributed to rather than undermined international peace, security and stability, and which empowered its people rather than oppressed them. However, due to Pakistan's concerns, the U.S. had reservations about India's political and diplomatic role in Afghanistan. The U.S. had even advised India not to open consulates in Afghanistan.

In the initial aftermath of 9/11 and the runup to the attack on Afghanistan, the U.S. had been careful about Pakistan's interests in Afghanistan. For instance, the Pentagon persuaded the Northern Alliance not to enter Kabul on 13 November 2001, in order to give Pakistan two to three days to withdraw its assets. In fact, as James Dobbins confirms in his book, 'it had largely been at Pakistan's behest that President Bush had pressed the Northern Alliance leadership not to enter Kabul until a UN or Pakistan force could be organized'. The Northern Alliance wisely felt that a vacuum after the Taliban retreat was not desirable, and they entered Kabul on 16 November 2001.

American eyebrows were raised when Afghan leader Rashid Dostum made a private visit to India for medical treatment. Shortly thereafter the U.S. reportedly encouraged him to visit Pakistan.

After the Mumbai terror attack in 2008, the then ISI chief, Pasha, visited Washington and had discussions with U.S. officials. The assessment of the then Pakistan Ambassador Husain Haqqani was that 'there was clearly no intention to act against LeT'.[16] After the detection and killing of Bin Laden, Lt General Douglas Lute, the U.S. National Security Council coordinator for Afghanistan and Pakistan, in his discussion with the Pakistanis, made veiled threats that 'countries have been designated state sponsors of terrorism on less evidence than that available on Pakistan'.[17] The U.S. Navy SEALS, he said, 'had found a whole treasure trove of material' at the compound where Bin Laden was killed'.[18] Nothing happened. Economic and military aid resumed a couple of years later.

Pakistan's Relations with Afghanistan

Rifaat Hussain, a Pakistani scholar, has written, 'Despite shared geography, ethnicity and faith, relations between Afghanistan and Pakistan had never been smooth. With the sole exception of four years of Taliban rule over Afghanistan, successive governments in Kabul have displayed varying degrees of disaffection towards Islamabad.'[19] The reasons for this are I) the Durand Line; II) divergent strategic outlook and 'dissimilar national ethos'; III) different approach to Islam, their shared faith.[20]

Durand Line and the Emergency of the Doctrine of Strategic Depth

Pakistan's unarticulated aims have created problems for status quo on the Durand Line. Whether they stem from its desire for a flexible frontier or from its role in the resurgence of the Taliban and even in the Taliban's growing influence in Federally Administered Tribal Areas (FATA), Pakistan views its interests in maintaining a high level of influence within Afghanistan, eventually covering the Central Asian theatre. Whereas traditionally Pakistan has claimed the Durand Line as its international border, some leading Pakistan scholars maintain that a perceptible change in the thinking on the line seems to have occurred during General Zia's time.

In this regard, Farzana Shaikh, a Pakistani author and expert on Pakistan and South Asian Islam, has written about 'a shift in Pakistan–Afghan policy in exchange for guarantees involving a mutually acceptable resolution of its disputes with Afghanistan over the status of the Durand Line'[21] and arguments by some 'to maintain a porous border with Afghanistan rather than a press for recognition of the Durand Line'.[22] Ahmed Rashid, a Pakistani journalist and bestselling foreign policy author, maintains that

Pakistan did not use the many opportunities that came its way from 1988 up to 9/11 to obtain Afghan support on the Durand Line. To substantiate his argument, he quotes Sahabzada Yaqub Khan, Pakistan's foreign minister during the 1980s, that 'the Pakistan military deliberately never asked for Afghan recognition of the Durand Line.'[23]

The reason, according to Ahmed Rashid, is that Gen. Zia as President had worked passionately for the creation of an Islamic pro-Pakistan government in Afghanistan, which, in his scheme of things, was to be followed by Islamization of Central Asia.

> In military parlance, this was Pakistan's strategy to secure 'strategic depth' in relation to India. Zia's vision of a Pakistani-influenced region extending into Central Asia depended on an undefined border with Afghanistan, so that the army could justify any future interference in that country and beyond. A defined border would have entailed recognizing international law and obligations and the sovereignty of Afghanistan. As long as there was no recognized border, there was also no international law to break if Pakistani forces were to support surrogate Afghan regimes such as the Taliban.[24]

This may be Pakistan's preferred solution. But for obvious reasons, it has not been officially stated. At the same time, a timely word of caution may have been sounded by a Peshawar-based author, Dr Azmat Hayat Khan, in his book on the Durand Line, 'Pakistan would be advised to re-evaluate its past policy and approach to the question. Because over the years the Pashtunistan issue may evolve into a problem with totally new dimensions.'[25]

Afghanistan is conscious of the importance of Pakistan as well as its mischief potential. No government in Afghanistan will entirely agree with the Pakistani viewpoint in toto, but they realize they have to live with them, particularly in view of safe havens in Pakistan which assist militancy and militancy affecting stability in Afghanistan.

Pakistan's Objectives in Afghanistan

Pakistan's policy in Afghanistan, even in the post-9/11 phase, continued to be guided by its longstanding objectives.

The central objective was to reinstate Afghanistan's dependence on Pakistan with the Taliban as a partner in the government. That would, in Pakistan's assessment, enable them to achieve a number of strategic objectives, including (i) to be able to have their own say on the Pashtunistan issue/Durand Line (ii) negating Indian influence (iii) ensuring smooth trade links with Central Asia (to treat Central Asia as a part of their strategic depth) (iv) exploiting potential oil and gas reserves in Afghanistan (v) having ready availability of jihadi forces for use in Jammu and Kashmir, and (vi) above all, achieving strategic depth. Articulated in 1989 by then Chief of Army staff of Pakistan, Aslam Beg, it meant 'hiding Pakistan's military assets in Afghanistan beyond the current offensive capabilities of the Indian military'.[26] This is based on five assumptions: (i) in a crisis Pakistan would have the leisure of time (ii) Pakistan could transfer equipment to a place of their choosing (iii) logistical support would always be available (iv) places west of the Durand Line would remain safe from Indian attack and (v) Pakistan could maintain, dominate and sustain huge safe havens, hundreds of miles inside of Afghanistan. Rizwan Hussain had said Pakistan believed the post-Soviet Afghanistan would address its strategic inferiority.

No Connection between Afghan Issue and India–Pakistan Relations

The periodic attempt to link the Afghan issue with India–Pakistan relations is lacking in merit. There is no connection—it is an unfair attempt by those who wish to blame India for their own failures.

i) A study of Pakistan–Afghanistan relations since 1947 reveals these have almost always been thorny and full of problems except during the brief Taliban period. Even during that period, there were some differences on issues like the Durand Line. India–Pakistan relations have not impacted Pak–Afghan relations.

   India and Afghanistan had never exploited their excellent bilateral relations to harm Pakistan. This is clear from both the 1965 and 1971 wars. Afghanistan was noncommittal and had not supported India. Similarly, India had not supported Afghanistan on the Durand Line. Both India and Afghanistan have throughout been conscious of not allowing their bilateral relations to affect their relations with Pakistan.

ii) When Pakistan decided to redeploy over a 1,00,000 of its security forces from its eastern border to its western border with Afghanistan in 2010, India did nothing to take advantage of the situation.

iii) India or Indo–Pak relations were not responsible for the situation which prevailed in Afghanistan after the departure of the Soviet troops which took Afghanistan back to medieval times.

iv) Neither did India have any hand in bringing the Taliban to power in Afghanistan nor did it help Al-Qaeda and Osama Bin Laden in their activities in the region.

v) India had nothing to do with the U.S.–NATO intervention
   in Afghanistan. No extremist groups—Taliban, Haqqani,
   Lashkar-e-Taiba—are based in India or have Indian assistance.

vi) If the U.S. had to take action to kill Osama Bin Laden
   or use drone attacks in Afghanistan, it was because of the
   prevalent situation that had nothing to do with India or
   Indo–Pak relations.

India has always been a part of the solution and did not create any
problems in Afghanistan.

Taliban

As high commissioner in Pakistan, I recall how Benazir Bhutto's
interior minister, Naseerullah Babar, took pride in claiming credit
for the emergence of the Taliban in 1994. Sahabzada Yakub Khan,
ex-foreign minister of Pakistan, described the Taliban at the time
of their birth as 'militant reformists with sword in one hand and
Quran in the other'.[27] Even prior to this, the ISI of Pakistan had
used the US$10 billion obtained from the USA and Saudi Arabia in
subsidizing Mujahideen groups, particularly Hekmatyar. The first
battle between Hekmatyar and the Taliban was in mid-October
1994, at Spin Boldak on the Afghan–Pakistan border, when
the Taliban overran a garrison of Hekmatyar. Initially, Pakistan
helped both Hekmatyar and the Taliban, but gradually promoted
the rapid advance and takeover of Kabul by the Taliban.[28]

Subsequently, there was support for the Taliban to take
charge of Kabul from army corps headquarters in Peshawar.[29]
After General Musharraf came to power in 1999, he increased the
assistance. He said, 'This is our national interest . . . the Taliban
cannot be alienated by Pakistan . . . we have a national security
interest here.'[30]

Not only did Pakistan's support continue after 9/11, they also persuaded the U.S. to refrain from a military campaign against the Taliban.[31] Though they made an official U-turn, they continued to provide the Taliban with weapons and other requirements. The U.S. campaign was to be confined to Al-Qaeda and its affiliates.

The U.S. State Department, in a background analysis, 30 December 2009, stated,

> Although Pakistan senior officials had publicly disavowed support for these groups, some officials from Pakistan ISI, continued to maintain ties with a wide array of extremist organizations, in particular the Taliban . . . these extremist organizations continue to find refuge in Pakistan and . . . readily provide extremist organizations with recruits, funding and infrastructure for planning attacks.[32]

Pakistan's military and ISI maintained a tight control over the activities of the Taliban, even as the U.S. and others tried to independently reach out to them, especially the relatively moderate sections, after 2009, or when there were efforts to initiate direct talks between the Taliban and the Afghan government. It put down Taliban members who made efforts to act with some independence or differed with the ISI thinking.

A case in point is Mullah Abdul Ghani Baradar. He was most recently in the news as the main face of the negotiations between the Taliban in Doha and the Americans, which led to the final withdrawal of U.S. forces from Afghanistan in August 2021.

In mid-February 2010, the *New York Times* reported the arrest of Mullah Baradar, the number two of the Afghan Taliban leaders, by Pakistan security forces at an Islamic school near Karachi. The U.S. government responded to the news with pleasure, and there were also reports that this was a result of a joint operation variously described as a 'turning point in Pakistan's policy towards Taliban's "strategic recalibration"', etc. An interesting point made by Dexter Filkins, an American journalist, was that a member of the security forces confirmed, 'We picked up Baradar and others because they were trying to make a deal without us . . . We are not going to allow them to make a deal with Karzai and the Indians.'[33] It is interesting that after releasing Mullah Baradar from jail in Pakistan in 2010, Pakistan did not allow him to play a role for many years, because they did not want any direct negotiations between Afghanistan and the Taliban.

Appointment of Holbrooke

I had earlier explained the context and circumstances behind renewed U.S. diplomacy on Afghanistan and the appointment of Richard Holbrooke as the special envoy for Afghanistan and Pakistan (Af–Pak).

I had been visiting Washington as co-chair of the Indian side, for the Aspen Indo–US Track II dialogue. Joseph S. Nye Jr. (Harvard University Distinguished Service Professor, Emeritus and former Dean of Harvard's Kennedy School of Government) and Brent Scowcroft (former U.S. National Security Advisor) were the co-chairs on the U.S. side. The U.S. delegation had leading lights of the Democratic Party, who had held important cabinet posts under the Democratic presidencies. When Obama took over as President, I was asked in Washington what would be our reaction if a high-powered person was appointed to look after relations with India, Pakistan and Afghanistan. I said it would be a non-starter and not acceptable, and would be reverting to the old failed policy of dealing with India and Pakistan. Among those who raised the subject were former assistant secretary of state during the Clinton administration, Karl Inderfurth, former ambassador to India,

Frank Wisner, and some serving State Department officials. Later in the evening they asked if this was my personal opinion. I said that as co-chair of the Aspen dialogue, it could be personal but as special envoy of the prime minister, they should treat it as official. Before I left, I was told the matter had been settled and Holbrooke was likely to be designated as special envoy for Af–Pak. I had kept my colleagues, Tarun Das (Former Director General and chief mentor of Confederation of Indian Industry) and G. Parthasarthy (Former High Commissioner of India to Pakistan), as well as the embassy informed of my discussion. I thought Holbrooke would be unhappy with me for being deprived of the India portfolio. On the contrary, we had an excellent partnership.

Holbrooke made several visits to India. On one he brought Admiral Mike Mullen, chairman joint chiefs of staff, with him to Delhi, who had made over a dozen visits to Pakistan, seeking to develop a personal rapport with General Kayani and was considered partial to Pakistan. This was his first visit to India. Later, he was also remembered for his remarks made in Islamabad on Pakistan, when he said they have a 'long standing relationship' with the militant Haqqani group.

Holbrooke was not much liked either in the U.S. State Department or in South Block, Delhi. I found him good to work with, and on one of his visits I arranged a brief call by him on Prime Minister Manmohan Singh.

Towards the end of March 2009, the Dutch government held an international ministerial conference on Afghanistan. I represented India. Pakistan ISI chief, Shuja Pasha, was an active participant. At the conference, Holbrooke told me that a new group was being set up and he was hurriedly calling a few countries for a meeting in Munich on 1 April. He wanted me to join. I did so. The international contact group (ICG) was established in Munich on that date. Its nomenclature changed a couple of times till it started being called by this name. The Munich meeting was eventually attended by seventeen countries and international organizations. Later, its membership was around sixty. During the period 2009–14, twenty meetings were held in different world capitals. I represented India in all of them, accompanied by a representative of the MEA. Holbrooke and I started the practice of hosting each other, alternatively, for a lunch or dinner before each meeting. This proved helpful.

The functioning of the group was coordinated by the German envoy, who played an important role. India and Russia, in those days, worked closely and were a vital part of the set-up. Towards the closing stages, an informal 6+1 group was set up, which virtually took the decisions. India was a part of it, and at our insistence, Afghanistan was included, which is reflected in the +1 mentioned above. India's active role in the group is evident from the fact that the twentieth session of the ICG was held in New Delhi on 16 January 2014, attended by representatives of fifty-two countries and seven international organizations. Afghanistan was represented by senior ministers (interior, women affairs, chairman of Independent Election Commission (IEC) and deputy foreign minister), and the Afghan minister and I delivered the inaugural address. The external affairs minister, Salman Khurshid, delivered the keynote address. India's important role had been once again acknowledged.

In 2010, I accompanied External Affairs Minister S.M. Krishna to two conferences on Afghanistan—the London Conference in January 2010 and the Kabul Conference in July 2010. As part of the multiple international initiatives, there were also Afghan Compact (2006), Istanbul Regional Conference (2011) and thirteen meetings of the International Contact Group (ICG). In all of these, I represented India.

The only meeting to which India had not been invited was the Istanbul regional summit. The draft statement on the London conference welcomed the Istanbul statement. At the officials' meeting, India was represented by two able diplomats, Jayant Prasad, then ambassador in Kabul and Y.K. Sinha, then head of the Afghanistan desk in the MEA. They told me in the evening that the statement remained unchanged. Just before dinner I had a word with Holbrooke and gave him the background. I said my minister and I had come to London, not to welcome a statement that had not even been shared with us. It was not our intention to create problems but I had some action in mind which he may not like at the end of the day. He got worried and said, that as usual, he expected a solution from India. I suggested to him that the word 'welcome' could be changed by 'noted'. He was delighted and immediately rang his assistant who was involved with the negotiations. Later that night, at around 2 a.m., I observed a paper being thrust under my room door. This was the final draft, which mentioned that 'the conference participants noted the recent Istanbul Regional Summit on Friendship and Cooperation in the "Heart of Asia" and its statement.' The head of the Turkish delegation later told me, 'Without India we are only noted. With India we would have been welcomed.'

Interestingly, soon thereafter, India became an active part of the Istanbul process, participating in six of its confidence buiding measures (CBMs) and leading the trade, chamber and investment CBM. On 28 June 2012, India hosted the Delhi investment summit attended by 100 business delegations from Afghanistan, over 150 from India and around eighty from countries in the region and beyond.

The tenth anniversary of the Bonn Conference was observed with a ministerial conference attended by eighteen countries and fifteen international organizations. Germany was the host on both occasions in 2001 and 2011. Pakistan boycotted Bonn 2011, as a result of a major attack on its soldiers. The Chinese participated in Bonn 2011 at the foreign minister level. The role of both had been low-key in 2001. The atmosphere of the two meetings was different. The first was closed and the second a public event. The message of Bonn 2011 was that the international community was committed 'to remain strongly engaged in support of Afghanistan beyond 2014'. Of the 1000 delegates at the Bonn Conference 2011, there were only four who were present at the conference in 2001. They were Afghan Foreign Minister Zalmai Rassoul, Senior Minister (later President) Ashraf Ghani, Russian representative Zamir Kabulov and me.[34]

Visits to Washington

I visited Washington, D.C. from 28 July to 2 August 2010 for political, official and public interactions. This visit took place in the context of the ongoing review of the U.S. strategy in Afghanistan, ordered by President Obama, that was to be completed in December 2010. The review was going to shape the U.S. force posture and the political process in Afghanistan. A view was being projected that Pakistan's lack of cooperation stemmed from its paranoia about India. Pakistan was also using various pretexts for lack of action on prosecuting the perpetrators of the Mumbai terror attack.

I had an excellent set of meetings. In the government, I met National Security Adviser General Jim Jones, deputy Secretary of State Jim Steinberg, CIA Director Leon Panetta, Undersecretary of State William Burns, Undersecretary of Defence for Policy Michèle Flournoy and Richard Holbrooke. As Secretary of State Hillary Clinton was away for her daughter's wedding, I could not meet her.

In the Congress, virtually the entire leadership met me. These included Senator John Kerry, chairman, Senate foreign relations committee, Senator Richard Lugar, ranking member foreign relations committee, Senator Carl Levin, chairman, Senate armed services, Senator John McCain, ranking member, Senate armed services committee, Senator Joseph Lieberman, chairman homeland security and governmental affairs and member armed services committee, Senator Lindsey Graham, Senate armed services committee, Senator Christopher Bond, ranking member, Senate intelligence committee.

In the House, I met Steny Hoyer, House majority leader, Howard Berman, chairman foreign affairs committee, representative Chris Van Hollen, chairman of the Democratic congressional campaign committee, rep. Buck McKeon, ranking member, House armed services committee and Gary Ackerman, chairman of House foreign affairs subcommittee on the Middle East and South Asia.

In addition, I had meetings with senior journalists and think tanks, besides chairing a session of the liaison group of Special Representatives of Afghanistan and Pakistan (SRAPs) which was attended by thirty-five embassies.

I was accompanied in all my meetings with Minister Political Jawed Ashraf, who had arranged the appointments, and was to soon leave for Delhi as joint secretary (America) in the ministry. Deputy chief of mission (DCM) Arun Singh also attended some of the meetings.

Washington, D.C. was beset with doubts, if not downright pessimism, about the efficacy of military operations, the human and financial cost that it involved, and the prospects for its success. The U.S. was contemplating political reconciliation and the possibility of integration of Taliban fighters into the Afghan National Force. There was recognition that Pakistan was not cooperating fully with the U.S. but it was accompanied by a sense of helplessness to change its course, but also a rationalization that

Pakistan's projected concerns about India—the so-called Cold Start doctrine and raising new false claims about water and trade wars—was preventing it from fully supporting the U.S.

This view was expressed most clearly by Richard Holbrooke and James Steinberg. Others like Jim Jones, William Burns and Michèle Flournoy had a clear appreciation of the challenges from Pakistan and in Afghanistan. There was, however, appreciation for India's development assistance to Afghanistan. NSA Jones and William Burns were also focused on President Obama's visit to India that was to take place in November 2010 and did not want to have the Afghanistan and Pakistan issue cast a shadow on the visit.

The support for India and the appreciation of India's position was much stronger in the Congress, except perhaps from John Kerry who tried to equate India and Pakistan and sought to put the India–Pakistan competition as the source of the problem in Afghanistan. I had to remind him of the facts and tell him he was in a minority of one among all the members of Congress I had met (he was the last I met). He did, however, call me the following day on the phone, just before my departure, to express regret for his remarks and say that the U.S. valued India's contribution to Afghanistan.

My second visit to Washington was fixed from 5–8 December 2010. Ambassador Meera Shankar and deputy chief of mission, Arun Singh, arranged an excellent programme which included meetings with the new NSA Thomas Donilon, Admiral Michael Mullen, chairman joint chiefs of staff; Michèle Flournoy, William Burns, Howard Berman, Senator Joseph Lieberman, and representatives Ros-Lehtinen and Ed Royce. In addition, meetings had been arranged with think tanks, journalists and with the chief of the CIA, Panetta, at a lunch hosted by the ambassador. The embassy had sent me this programme prior

to my departure for Washington. There was no mention of a
meeting with Secretary Clinton. From the Delhi airport, I spoke
to Holbrooke and told him about this. His response was, 'Sati,
when would it be convenient for you to meet with Hillary?' I
told him to convey the secretary of state's availability to the
embassy so that the timings of the other meetings could be
worked around it.

CIA chief, Panetta, in his meeting referred to the ISI–R&AW
discussions. I told him we were favourably inclined and I would
convey his views to Delhi. However, the important aspect of the
lack of any action by Pakistan on the Mumbai attack remains
uppermost in our minds.

During my visit, there were six meetings with Richard
Holbrooke, three of which were at my hotel, Ritz Carlton. He
hosted a private dinner for me at his favourite French restaurant,
La Chaumiere, where he told me he would be inviting only me.
Later, when he decided to call his colleague, Vali Nasr, I suggested
he also call Yashwardhan Sinha, Head of the Pakistan–Afghanistan
desk, MEA, who had come with me. He did. We had a great
evening with delicious food and excellent conversation.

As it turned out, I happened to be the last foreign interlocutor
Holbrooke spoke to, for he passed away a few days later. He had,
however, recorded the gist of my conversation with Secretary
Clinton and him after the meeting, as it appeared later in his
biography.

Holbrooke kept on telling me that the purpose of his
discussions with me was of the utmost importance and known
only to five persons. He would share full details only after he
had met President Obama. Unfortunately, he could not. From
Holbrooke's biography published a decade later, it appears he had
received some messages from the Taliban and he perhaps wanted
India and Pakistan to work together with him in his negotiations.

I met Secretary Clinton first with our delegation and later alone with Holbrooke. Both she and he suggested the creation of a four-country (U.S., India, Pakistan and Afghanistan) negotiating process. When I told her it might give the impression of an India–Pakistan angle, she said the purpose was 'not to discuss bilateral India–Pakistan issues, but Afghanistan'. She further mentioned the aim would be to have 'a low-key meeting about Afghanistan, with Afghanistan present'. She added that Undersecretary Burns, Assistant Secretary of State for South Asia Robert Blake and Holbrooke had been tasked to take this further. Pakistan had not yet been approached and it was unclear if they would be willing. She concluded by saying that the U.S. was not keen to extend the format beyond this group, because 'if Russia was there, Afghanistan would not be candid and China will not give unbiased views'.

Quoting from Holbrooke's account of that meeting Packer wrote,

My Indian counterpart, S.K. Lambah, came here at my invitation to test a new idea that I had come up with, which would be to see if we could get the Indians and the Pakistanis to agree to talk to each other, but only about Afghanistan, not their bilateral issues. Frank Wisner had predicted this would fail, but we got it put together. Today Lambah went in to see Hillary Clinton. He did extremely well with her. At my suggestion she saw him alone for a while in her big ornate room, her legs occasionally tucked under her, which means she's feeling quite informal, after we threw everyone else out and it went down to she, S.K. Lambah and myself. She liked the idea very much.

Holbrooke had earlier told me that a political solution for Afghanistan was essential and that the U.S. was guided by a policy based on 'no surrender, no partition of Afghanistan and no power sharing with the Taliban while preventing Afghanistan from becoming a field for surrogate competition'.[35] He made some complimentary references to my role since 2001 and said that this proposal was being made following President Obama's visit to India and in recognition of India's global role, and that this was the first example of a collaboration they were seeking from us in an area of vital common interest. What is clear from the accounts of his inability to reach President Obama, though, is that it probably did not have authorization from President Obama. This proposal, he said, had not till that time been discussed with their embassy in Delhi as they wanted our response first.

I told him that Pakistan will not accept this proposal, but I would discuss it with Delhi and give our response. Parker wrote that Holbrooke understood my scepticism regarding the proposal, just as Pakistan's Ambassador Husain Haqqani did but 'Holbrooke's optimism had the smell of desperation.'[36]

> S.K. Lambah and I saw each other privately later in the day at his hotel. He was very enthusiastic. I'm going to have breakfast with Ambassador Haqqani in the morning, and then we're launching a very highly difficult process to see if we can get India and Pakistan to be willing to talk to each other if the talk is restricted just to Afghanistan. So that's the essence of it, and we will see what happens next. End of Tuesday, December 7.[37]
>
> After breakfast, Holbrooke met Lambah at his hotel. Lambah was just as sceptical as Haqqani. He was willing to take the idea back to Delhi, but he had little confidence that Pakistan would change, even after Holbrooke showed him Kayani's latest white paper. Pakistan had never had any desire to talk about Afghanistan with India—it regarded Afghanistan

as one of its dominions. Holbrooke's optimism had the smell of desperation.[38] . . . 'Bullshit,' Gelb said. 'They always tell the Americans they agree with us and they never deliver, and Kayani's not going to deliver on this.'[39]

After Holbrooke's death on 13 December 2010, Secretary Clinton spoke to me on the phone on 14 December, saying she was personally following up on our discussions. I had conveyed to the prime minister on my return that Kayani and Pakistan would not agree, but as a gesture of goodwill, and because it would put Pakistan on the defensive, we could convey our concurrence to the Americans. This was done through an aide-mémoire handed over by our ambassador in the USA to Undersecretary William Burns on 14 January 2011. In April 2011, Holbrooke's successor, Marc Grossman told me that they were still awaiting Pakistan's reply. As we had expected, it did not come.

Holbrooke's last diplomatic initiative to advance a settlement in Afghanistan indicates that he had not completely abandoned the view that the lack of progress in Afghanistan stemmed from an India–Pakistan competition. While that may be true, I also believe that he had begun to recognize that India mattered to the political class and people of Afghanistan, and had played a constructive role in Afghanistan. But he had not fully appreciated how strongly Pakistan wanted to retain an exclusive say and deny India any role in shaping the future political course in Afghanistan. This was entirely in keeping with Holbrooke's nature that he constantly explored and was willing to grasp even the slimmest chance to move forward in his mission.

It is an irony, and maybe a fulfilment of Holbrooke's wish, that his last hours were spent in the hands of an Indian-American doctor, Monica Mukherjee, and a Pakistan-American doctor, Dr Farzad Najam. They worked as a team, with surgery lasting twenty hours, but he did not recover. When he died, his fiercely loyal staff wept in the arms of Secretary Clinton, who broke the news. His funeral was at the Kennedy Centre, reflecting the esteem in which he was held in Washington, D.C.

* * *

The Region beyond Pakistan

Holbrooke's successor, Marc Grossman, was an astute and able diplomat. He had earlier served as the undersecretary of state for political affairs. Diplomatic initiatives in various formats kept representatives of various countries busy. But these were becoming increasingly peripheral to two important trends.

One, of course, was the internal debate within the United States, which increasingly veered towards seeking a way out of the war in Afghanistan. The idea of a temporary military surge, followed by drawdown by a notional timetable, seemed to signal to the Taliban and their backers in Pakistan that it would only be a matter of time before the U.S. and NATO forces started leaving Afghanistan. There was always tension between an increasingly weary and sceptical political establishment and the view in the U.S. military that the Taliban could still be defeated militarily or that a military presence was needed to guarantee Afghanistan's political transition, security and stability. The issue really was the terms of political settlement, the resilience of the political project and military capacity building in Afghanistan, the timing of departure and what would follow.

The debates for the presidential election in 2016 saw a growing consensus across the political divide on the need to leave Afghanistan. By the time the 2020 elections came, the issue was settled and it was only a question of the exact date of departure.

The second factor was that despite multiple formats for regional and global discussion on Afghanistan, the U.S. continued to rely heavily on Pakistan for military success and political breakthroughs with the Taliban. Eventually, the U.S. would conduct hasty negotiations directly with the Taliban in Doha, leaving its allies and regional countries in the dark. Perhaps, the UK might have been an exception, and one ally that the U.S. consulted most closely with, as I discovered during my own engagements with the U.S.

However, Afghanistan's history has also been critically influenced by a complex set of regional interests that should have been taken into account, not just those of Pakistan, in international efforts to reach a settlement in Afghanistan.

I have already spoken about our historical relations and contemporary interests, primarily the welfare of Afghan people, and concerns, including terrorism; and the absence of any effort on our part since Independence to use our relations with Afghanistan against Pakistan.

Iran is a key neighbour of Afghanistan and has vital stakes in the country. Afghanistan, within its current boundaries was intermittently ruled by Iran for over 2000 years. Iran at one time considered western Afghanistan, including Herat, a part of Iran. They had to relinquish the claim following their defeat by British forces in the Anglo–Persian War of 1856–57. Persian cultural traditions are widely followed in Afghanistan, and Nowruz, the Persian New Year, is celebrated throughout Afghanistan. Farsi is widely spoken in Afghanistan, where it is known as Dari. The Hazaras, who make up 10–20 per cent of the Afghan population, are predominantly Shias. Iran made a significant contribution to Afghan reconstruction after the fall of the Taliban, with a pledge of US$570 million in 2002 and an additional US$100 million in 2006.

The American presence in Afghanistan had brought its 'arch-enemy' to its doorstep. For Iran, the principal immediate objectives were the withdrawal of American and International Security Assistance Force (ISAF) military and intelligence forces from Afghanistan and the formation of a regime in Kabul that was friendly to Iran and not dominated by Pakistan or Pakistan's Taliban proxies. Though the Shia minority in Afghanistan had been on the receiving end of Sunni Taliban, Iran also wanted to use the Taliban, both to hasten a U.S. exit from Afghanistan and to counter what it believed was Western help to the Jundullah insurgency in western Iran, home to about 1.2 million Baluchis.

In the long run, it would want to ensure that any regime in Afghanistan would protect the interests of traditional allies such as Farsiwan Heratis, Shia Hazara and Tajiks; ensure that Afghanistan is not a base for Jundullah; prevent flow of drugs from Afghanistan; enable the return of 2–3 million Afghan refugees in Iran; and ensure that Iran could use its location to have a stake in Afghanistan's trade, transit and energy flows. Cross-border flow of river water is another issue of interest.

The Central Asian Republics have ethnic links with the Afghan population, and three of them—Turkmenistan, Tajikistan and Uzbekistan—are immediate neighbours. They have a high level of concern about the fate of their ethnic minorities living in Afghanistan as also the flow of narcotics, radicalism and terrorism from Afghanistan into Central Asia. Economic ties to South Asia through Afghanistan are of long-term interest to them.

The last of the immediate neighbours is China. In the course of the past twenty years, China has transformed itself into a global power. It has increasingly seen Afghanistan through the prism of geopolitics and its immediate security interests. The U.S. presence in Afghanistan and the fall of Al-Qaeda and the

Taliban reduced the risk of Afghanistan being used by Islamist insurgents to stage attacks in the restive Xinjiang region and elsewhere in China. But, U.S. military presence in its immediate neighbourhood also presented risks to a rising China increasingly in a contest with the U.S. China was willing to work with any regime in Kabul that was stable and able to take care of China's security interests and help China advance its regional and economic interests, from expanding the ambit of the Belt and Road Initiative to strengthening the role of the Shanghai Cooperation Organization to ensuring access to raw materials. Cautious it may have been in the early years, but it is increasingly willing to assume a more active profile in Afghanistan. It has a mutually beneficial relationship with its closest ally, Pakistan, in Afghanistan. However, China may well find itself dragged into a complex situation that it would find hard to manage, as others have found at a great cost.

Russia is not an immediate neighbour after the collapse of the Soviet Union. But, for the Russian strategists, Afghanistan was always a frontier. For Russia, the U.S. presence was useful for its concerns regarding terrorism and narcotics, but was undesirable geopolitically. As Russia–West relations worsened after Russian annexation of Crimea in 2014, Russian strategy in Afghanistan increasingly worked against U.S. interests and presence. In the long run, Russia will always have strong interests in Afghanistan and will not hesitate to play a role in securing those interests.

None of Afghanistan's neighbours, nor other regional powers, would be indifferent to the developments in Afghanistan. The U.S. presence introduced a degree of complexity, because it could have different implications for the short-term and long-term interests of the regional countries. That was equally true of Pakistan, the neighbour with the most influence and the one in which the U.S. invested the most.

A Possible Settlement? Neutrality of Afghanistan Guaranteed by Neighbours

Taking into account the competing interests of various powers and the role of Afghanistan in the strategic calculations of various countries, a proposal for neutrality of Afghanistan has been made from time to time, but it was not accepted by Afghanistan. However, suddenly in May 2021, Afghan President Ghani, in an interview to a German news channel, made the same proposal. Sometime around 2007, Chinmaya Gharekhan and Hamid Ansari had made this suggestion in an article in *The Hindu* without going into the details of the concept of neutrality.

I recall that at a meeting of India's National Security Council on Afghanistan held on 12 February 2010, I had suggested that we should make a proposal for neutrality of Afghanistan. I might mention here that this was also suggested to me by the Russian deputy foreign minister on the sidelines of the London Conference on Afghanistan.

I had suggested that among the measures to remain involved, we should make a proposal for neutrality of Afghanistan. The stabilization of Afghanistan, which is sine qua non for preventing it from becoming a source of terrorism threatening the region and the world, is predicated on the continued engagement and support of the international community. At a time of pessimism and equivocation, also manifest in some sections of the media, it was imperative to take measures to protect our interests in Afghanistan and ensure our continued involvement in important diplomatic engagements.

The broad outlines of a proposal I had suggested for neutrality of Afghanistan were:

1. To end outside interference.

2. To deny sanctuaries and support outside Afghanistan to terrorist groups (like Al-Qaeda, Taliban) operating in Afghanistan.

3. Take effective measures to redouble counter narcotic efforts (this will be particularly appreciated by the Russian and Central Asian Republics for whom drug trafficking from Afghanistan is posing a major problem).

4. Speedy augmentation, training and equipping of the Afghan national security forces—both the Afghan National Army and the police—to ensure the security of Afghanistan.

5. Strengthen and empower the Afghan state and accelerate building institutions and public goods (health, education, agriculture, etc.) through adequate resourcing with a sense of urgency. The economic development of Afghanistan to be given priority.

6. Mechanism/guarantees for the above, particularly (1–3) to ensure effective implementation. The guarantors can be the neighbours of Afghanistan, the Central Asian Republics, Iran and the U.S. Thereafter, the proposal can be formally made.

NSA Shivshankar Menon sent a letter to then Foreign Secretary Nirupama Rao two or three days later telling her that the prime minister had approved my proposal and the MEA should prepare a non-paper for discussions with different governments.

That idea never gathered traction and got little attention in discussions on options for a solution in Afghanistan, and it was surprising to see it being mentioned by President Ghani at a time when it was evident that the Taliban, with the help of Pakistan, were once again preparing to make a surge into Afghanistan as the deadline for U.S. withdrawal was nearing.

* * *

Conclusion

I began to write this chapter at a time when the wheel was coming to a full circle. Twenty years after invading Afghanistan, the U.S. and allied forces left the country in August 2021. The Taliban had marched into Kabul, without a semblance of resistance from the shell-shocked Afghan security forces, even before the U.S. personnel had fully evacuated the country. President Ashraf Ghani fled, even as the Taliban stood at the doorstep. The chaotic and tragic sequence of events that unfolded thereafter, as Afghans and foreign nationals tried to flee the country through a severely disrupted and poorly managed evacuation, will remain permanently etched in the memories of everyone in the world. Afghans were once again paying a huge price, as the world's largest powers watched helplessly as the Taliban began to assert power in the only way they had known.

A humanitarian crisis is unfolding in Afghanistan. Women and ethnic minorities face marginalization once again. The economy is teetering. The moderate factions of the Taliban seem to have lost power to the hard-line factions. Fears of narcotics smuggling and terrorism in the region have risen again. And, once again, the regional countries are weighing the consequences of the Taliban's return to power. Pakistan feels that it can once again exercise control over Kabul and achieve its cherished goal of strategic depth. China is a different power compared to in 2001. India, Russia, Iran and Central Asian countries will work on their own, and sometimes together, to safeguard their traditional interests. Perhaps, no one faces painful consequences more than the Afghans themselves.

The wheel had started turning after the Iraq War began and Afghanistan became a secondary U.S. concern. It accelerated with the Obama administration, which included the current

U.S. President as vice president, with a well-known antipathy to U.S. involvement in Afghanistan. President Trump made his intention to leave Afghanistan very clear and tried to hasten it before the 2020 election. President Biden completed the process with a firm resolve. No one could begrudge an American desire to leave after two decades of a war that seemed to go on without a clear objective but very evident cost. The questions will always remain: whether the terms of exit could have been better negotiated, could a system of checks and balances have been instituted, could a feasible political solution have been found, whether there was any way the Afghan National Army could have been supported, could effective pressure have been brought on Pakistan over the years to dismantle the sanctuaries and end its support to the continuous insurgency—indeed, could the end have been any different than it was?

The contours of political choices and the history of diplomacy over the past two decades suggest that it could have been. However, we are at the beginning of a new chapter. And, how this one will end remains to be seen.

9

A New Sustained Approach and a Near Solution

Dr Manmohan Singh became prime minister of India in May 2004 and remained in office for ten years, over two terms of the Parliament, from 2004 to 2014. Born in the village of Gah in present-day Pakistan, his parents migrated to Punjab, India, after Partition. He became a renowned economist, teaching in Punjab University, Cambridge and Delhi School of Economics. He had a long life in public service too, as finance secretary, the governor of the Reserve Bank of India and finance minister. As finance minister in Prime Minister Narasimha Rao's government, he was at the centre of the most consequential turns in independent India's economic policy with the launch of economic liberalization and market reforms in 1991. He was leader of the Congress party in the Rajya Sabha when he was elected, by the Congress-led United People's Alliance (UPA), as prime minister in 2004.

Although widely acknowledged as an outstanding economist, he always took a keen interest in global affairs. His tenure witnessed many achievements. This included the civil nuclear agreement with the United States leading to India-specific exemption from the Nuclear Suppliers Group, which overturned decades of civil nuclear isolation from the world without compromising India's military nuclear programme. It also led to the announcement by the U.S. and other key countries of their support for India's membership of the four international export control regimes. His term saw the emergence of broad-based support for India's permanent membership of a reformed UNSC, including by the U.S. During his tenure, there was also sustained engagement with and stability in relations with China, continuing partnership with Russia and deepening of India's engagement in what is today called the Indo-Pacific region with membership of the East Asia summit.

This period will also be remembered for mature handling of relations with Pakistan. Though Dr Manmohan Singh never managed to visit Pakistan during his tenure, there was active and frequent bilateral engagement. President Musharraf made an official visit to India in 2005, President Asif Zardari visited Delhi and Ajmer Sharif, Prime Minister Shaukat Aziz visited India twice (in November 2004 and in April 2007 to attend the SAARC summit) and Prime Minister Yousaf Raza Gillani visited Mohali at Dr Singh's invitation to watch the India–Pakistan cricket match. In addition, he met Musharraf in Havana and Gillani in Sharm el-Sheikh in Egypt and later in Thimphu in Bhutan.

Apart from these, other visits from Pakistan to India included those of Punjab Chief Minister Shehbaz Sharif, Foreign Minister Shah Mahmood Qureshi (he was in India on the fateful day of 26/11), Foreign Minister Hina Rabbani Khar and Adviser on Foreign Affairs Sartaj Aziz. There were various ministerial visits from India too, that included those of foreign ministers K. Natwar Singh, Pranab Mukherjee and S.M. Krishna.

Immediately after elections in Pakistan and the victory of Nawaz Sharif in May 2013, Dr Manmohan Singh sent me as his special envoy to Lahore to convey greetings ten days before Nawaz Sharif formally took over as prime minister of Pakistan. Later, the two prime ministers met in New York on the sidelines of the UNGA on 29 September 2013, which led to a meeting of DGMOs of the two countries at Wagah on 24 December 2013.

These engagements helped to ease tensions. India was able to secure peace along the Line of Control and the international border. Dr Singh also made travel and trade possible across the Line of Control and inaugurated the Amritsar–Nankana Sahib bus service.

The situation within Jammu and Kashmir remained relatively calm. Elections were held in Kashmir. The Amarnath Yatra was held peacefully every year without fail. The pilgrimage to Amarnath cave, one of the holiest for Hindus, takes place annually between July and August. At an altitude of 3900 metres, it is believed to be one of the abodes of Lord Shiva, where an icy lingam forms naturally. Because it involves a trek of one to two days from Baltal or three to five days from Pahalgam, the annual pilgrimage, which draws hundreds of thousands of devotees, is linked to the security situation in the state. Its uninterrupted conduct during the ten years was an important indicator of the environment in the state during his tenure. In this century, the only years it was not held were in 2000, 2002 and 2017 due to terrorist attacks, and more recently in 2020 and 2021 due to the Covid-19 pandemic.

However, his tenure also saw stone-pelting incidents in Kashmir in 2010 and the horrific terrorist attack in Mumbai on 26 November 2008, which was carried out by cadres of Lashkar-e-Taiba and planned, organized and executed from Pakistan, that played an evident official role in it.[1] The attack, which targeted some of Mumbai's iconic places, claimed 166 lives from India and several other countries. There was deep national shock, pain and anger in India. After a long period of relative quiet, tensions between India and Pakistan rose to a dangerous level. Much has been written about the 26/11 attack, accompanied by considerable debate, some with the benefit of hindsight, on whether India should have launched a military strike against Pakistan or, at the very least, against terrorist camps. Dr Singh and the government decided against that course of action because of the risks of a full-scale war with an uncertain impact on terrorism infrastructure in Pakistan. At that point of time, the decade-long U.S. war in Afghanistan, with the footprint in Pakistan, was an indicator. Instead, the focus was on orchestrating a global diplomatic effort against Pakistan. This resulted in strong global support for India along with the demand for Pakistan to bring the perpetrators to justice. Additional measures against Pakistan-based terrorist groups were taken by several countries. In the U.S., the congressional legislation on a five-year aid package for Pakistan contained several conditions regarding terrorist groups and infrastructure in Pakistan that were specifically directed at India.

An important feature of Dr Singh's tenure was the continuation of the back channel. Dr Singh's famous Amritsar speech on 24 March 2006, along with Musharraf's four-point formula, spelt out the broad contours for the back channel, enabling the finalization of a draft agreement between India and Pakistan on Jammu and Kashmir. This went in parallel with his internal initiatives on J & K.

Kashmir Initiative Taken by PM Manmohan Singh

Dr Manmohan Singh took a keen interest in developments in respect of J & K and made visits to Jammu and Srinagar on 25 February 2006, 24–25 May 2006 and 24 April 2007, for the three Kashmir round-table conferences. These were attended by representatives of all political parties, except the BJP, and representatives of different regions and organizations in J & K. In his opening remarks at the 2006 meeting, Manmohan Singh called the round table 'a dialogue of equals' that would achieve historical importance provided 'we are able to unleash a process by which we can arrive at a workable blueprint that can help create a new chapter in Kashmir's history. Not by compromising on one's ideals, but in a spirit of mutual tolerance, understanding and accommodation.'[2]

Earlier, PM Manmohan Singh had met with Hurriyat leaders in New Delhi on 5 September 2005, and had agreed to look at the list of people they wanted released from jail. The Hurriyat eventually did not send a list. He even met Sardar Qayyum Khan, ex-President of POK. On Qayyum Khan's first visit, he sent me to meet him. When he came a second time, his son, who was heading the POK government, told me on the telephone, that his father was getting old and would not live long, but was keen to meet the Indian prime minister. PM Manmohan Singh invited him for a breakfast meeting. Qayyum was elated.

As a result of the round-table conferences, four working groups were formed to take measures on specific subjects. These groups, headed by eminent people, included representatives of all political parties including the BJP and different segments of society. These working groups gave a comprehensive set of recommendations.

Working Group I on confidence-building measures across segments of society in the state, chaired by Mohammad Hamid Ansari (later vice president of India) recommended measures to improve the conditions of people affected by militancy; schemes to rehabilitate orphans and widows affected by militancy; issues related to relaxation of conditions for persons who had forsworn militancy; effective rehabilitation policies including employment for Kashmiri Pandit migrants; an approach considering issues relating to the return of Kashmiri youth from areas controlled by Pakistan; measures to protect and preserve the unique cultural and religious heritage of the state; problems faced by refugees; requirement of accelerated economic development of deprived communities like Gujjars, Bakarwals and Pahari-speaking people.

Working Group II chaired by former Foreign Secretary M.K. Rasgotra recommended measures to simplify procedures to facilitate travel across the Line of Control, increase goods traffic, expand people-to-people contact, including promotion of pilgrimage and group tourism; constitution of a joint consultative group or committee of ten members of each of the legislatures of both sides of LoC to exchange views on social, economic, cultural and trade-related matters; consultations on disaster and relief measures during calamities and epidemics as well as joint consultative groups for horticulture, tourism promotion and environmental protection; suggested new routes such as Kargil–Skardu, Jammu–Sialkot, Turtuk–Khaplu, Chhamb–Jourian to Mirpur (across Munawar Tawi), Gurez–Astoor–Gilgit, Tithwal–Chilhana (across Neelum Valley), and Jhangar (Nowshera)–Mirpur and Kotli (the route will bifurcate at the LoC).

Working Group III on economic developments of J & K chaired by Dr C. Rangarajan made detailed recommendations on investments; reforms in the power sector; communication, particularly in respect of rural roads and telecom; initiatives in the tourism sector; improving productivity in agriculture, horticulture, health, industrial development; education and employment; emphasis on regional development; and the setting up of a monitoring authority for implementation of the recommendations.

Working Group IV ensuring good governance chaired by N.C. Saxena recommended appointments of a chief information commissioner; introduction of e-governance in specified areas; simplification of rules and procedures; performance assessment by an independent committee once in three years of departments such as the police, municipalities and revenue which have more public dealings; new transfer policy stressing that officials are in place for at least three years; publication of a citizens' charter giving details of services provided; strengthening local self-government; zero tolerance for human rights violations; adequate security for all segments of society, particularly of minority communities.

* **

National Security Advisory Board (NSAB)

Shortly after Dr Manmohan Singh took over as prime minister in May 2004, I received a message stating I was being appointed convener of the NSAB. Since I had not responded, J.N. Dixit called me as soon as he took over as NSA, to say my response was awaited. I asked if he had instigated this appointment. He clarified he had not, and as proof of that mentioned that Hamid Ansari, who later became vice president, was being appointed a member, even though he was three years my senior, something that as a former colleague he would not have proposed. I gave my written concurrence.

The first meeting was held on 16 July 2004. I took the decision that the board should meet four times a month, on the first and third Thursday and Friday of the month. Over the next few months, we worked on papers on Manipur, declaratory hostage policy, India and the Muslim world, policy initiatives to enhance defence preparedness, economic security, Nepal, J & K, Indo–U.S. high-technology cooperation, illegal migration, national security review, human security review of the Official Secrets Act, area studies and impact of China on South Asia. In addition, we gave our comments on papers on India's relations with neighbouring countries.

This was an interesting experience that gave an insight into the workings of important foreign policy and security issues. My three successors as chair of NSAB were people with whom I had the privilege of working in different spheres. They were M.K. Rasgotra, former foreign secretary, Shankar Bajpai, former secretary in the ministry and ambassador to the United States and China, and Naresh Chandra, former governor and ambassador to the United States. Each, on account of their experience and knowledge, improved upon the functioning of the NSAB. Naresh Chandra was also chairman of the committee on national security, known outside as the Naresh Chandra committee, of which I was appointed co-chairman. It was this committee that originally recommended the creation of the post of chief of defence staff.

Appointment as Special Envoy

Unfortunately, within a year of assuming office as NSA, J.N. Dixit passed away. Dr Manmohan Singh appointed me as special envoy in the PMO to look after the back channel with Pakistan in 2005.

The Road to the Back Channel

This was, in a sense, a continuation of the back channel between Brajesh Mishra and his Pakistani counterpart, and of various earlier initiatives under different prime ministers, for a final settlement with Pakistan on Jammu and Kashmir. Each involved varying adjustments to the ceasefire line or, later, the Line of Control, and its conversion into the international border. PM Manmohan Singh wanted a solution that did not entail redrawing borders. Despite its public insistence on a UN resolution, Pakistan never actually believed in pursuing that option for the resolution of the Kashmir issue and preferred a negotiated settlement.

UN Resolution on Kashmir Did Not Suit Pakistan

It is evident that Pakistan, right from the start, had not favoured the proposal for ascertaining the will of the people of Kashmir through a plebiscite or referendum to determine the future of the state, unless the outcome of the process guaranteed it the state's accession. This was confirmed by the National Conference's Bakshi Ghulam Mohammad, who after holding discussions on the issue of a plebiscite with the Pakistani leadership, gave a statement to this effect to the *Dawn* of Karachi.[3] The record shows that whenever a plebiscite was offered to Pakistan, it rejected the proposal. In this regard, there are four known instances of Pakistan rejecting offers of a plebiscite in Kashmir. Very briefly, the narrative begins after the acceptance of the Instrument of Accession of the princely state of Kashmir in favour of India on 26 October 1947. Concurrently, the Indian Governor General Lord Mountbatten wrote to the maharaja of Kashmir: 'As soon as law and order have been restored in Kashmir and her soil cleared of the invaders the question of the State's accession should be settled by reference to the people.'[4]

It is important to note here that the process of acceptance of the Instrument of Accession and the writing of the afore referred letter were not one and the same; they were two distinct activities. In Mountbatten's own words:

> This decision to hold a plebiscite in no way invalidated the legality of the accession of Kashmir to India. The position then was that Kashmir was legally part of the Dominion of India and the voluntary, unilateral, decision to hold a plebiscite to confirm this was only intended to be held after the tribesmen had been withdrawn and peaceful conditions had been restored throughout Kashmir.[5]

Narendra Singh of Sarila cites instances of the British government's partisan attitude on the Kashmir issue as it immediately swung into motion to offset the advantage gained by India through the legal process. On 29 October 1947, the British Prime Minister Attlee wired Pakistan Prime Minister Liaquat Ali Khan advising that if an Indo–Pak agreement on Kashmir were not reached, then Pakistan should not pull back its irregular and regular troops.[6] Alongside, Major William Alexander Brown and Captain A.S. Matheson of the Gilgit Scouts began their operation on the night of 31 October 1947 and on 2 November 1947 raised the Pakistani flag at their headquarters, signalling accession of the erstwhile Gilgit Agency to Pakistan. Although Britain distanced itself from the actions of their own officers of the Indian Army, it bestowed on Major Brown the most exalted order of the British Empire. Further, Mountbatten was given a reprimand for the 'provocative mistake' in accepting the Instrument of Accession, conveyed through the British high commissioner.[7] Mountbatten, in the tradition of a true and loyal British naval officer, immediately fell in step by calling on Jinnah in Lahore the very next day on 1 November 1947, when he offered:

> It is the sincere desire of the Government of India that a plebiscite should be held in Kashmir at the earliest possible date and in the fairest possible way . . . They [Government of India] suggest that United Nations Organisation (UNO) might be asked to provide supervisors for this plebiscite, and they are prepared to agree that a joint Pakistan force should hold the ring while plebiscite is being held.[8]

In an All India Radio address the very next day on 2 November 1947, Nehru reiterated the offer of a plebiscite. He said on restoration of peace and establishment of law and order, India would be prepared to hold a referendum under international auspices like the United Nations.[9] It is another matter that Jinnah did not accept Mountbatten's offer of a plebiscite in Kashmir, which appeared highly favourable to Pakistan. Campbell Johnson recorded that when Mountbatten made an offer to Jinnah of a plebiscite in Kashmir under the auspices of the United Nations, he (Jinnah) is believed to have suggested a plebiscite to be conducted bilaterally instead of one under UN supervision, which Mountbatten rejected as going beyond his remit.

According to Alastair Lamb, a diplomatic historian and author, Jinnah did not wish to pursue the idea of a plebiscite because he was convinced Sheikh Abdullah, an Indian political leader, would determine its result.[10] Lamb also suggests that Jinnah was aware that the memory of the horrors of the Pakistani invasion of Kashmir was still fresh in the Kashmiri mind. In 1947, the overwhelming majority of Muslims of the Valley of Kashmir, where well over half of the people of the state resided, supported Sheikh Abdullah's National Conference that was aligned to Nehru's Congress. In contrast, the position of the Muslim Conference aligned to Jinnah's Muslim League was quite weak. It was known that the Muslim Conference's call for 'direct action' in Kashmir in 1946 had failed to take off, thereby demonstrating the absence of a communal feeling in the state. Jinnah also knew that whatever Abdullah's other ambitions might have been, he could not be counted on for support in the event of a plebiscite in Kashmir, for he was known to be totally against the idea of accession of Kashmir to Pakistan. By rejecting a plebiscite, Jinnah chose to decide the issue by force of arms.

The second offer of a plebiscite in Kashmir was made to Pakistan a few months later. The principles of it were set out by the UNCIP resolution of 5 January 1949. The commission's resolution of 13 August 1949, calling for a plebiscite in Kashmir after withdrawal of Pakistani invaders and other citizens from the territory of the state, was not accepted without a host of reservations by the then Pakistan foreign minister, through his reply of 19 August 1949, which was tantamount to a rejection. Surprisingly, the Pakistani side showed keenness on an alternative UNCIP formulation under which both sides would retain the territory of Kashmir under their control and, by inference, forgo the plebiscite option.

Two interrelated issues require highlighting here. First, it was not within UNCIP's terms of reference to consider the option of a plebiscite in Kashmir, as the framework of the resolution of the UN did not envisage such a procedure. Plebiscite would have been outside the scope of the UNSC resolution of 21 April 1948 (S/726) under which it had been set up. For it to consider the plebiscite under Chapter VI (that envisaged a conciliation procedure), the commission had to first obtain India's prior consent to explore that option. Second, while recognizing the sovereignty of India over Kashmir, the commission never recognized the legality of the presence of Pakistani troops in Kashmir. Accordingly, while the commission stipulated the condition of complete withdrawal of the Pakistani forces, it only asked India to withdraw a part of its forces, while permitting it, and even giving it special rights, to maintain internal order and take charge of the external defence of the state. For the same reason, the commission recognized India's right to be consulted while denying the same to Pakistan in drawing up the rules and regulations for the plebiscite, except in an advisory capacity.[11]

In May 1950, Owen Dixon, the UN mediator, made yet another offer of a plebiscite to Pakistan. To minimize bloodbaths and mass migrations, Dixon considered regional plebiscites. On this basis, he came to the conclusion that partition of Kashmir could possibly offer a reasonable solution. Accordingly, he suggested that Hindu-dominant areas could go to India, and Muslim-dominant areas to Pakistan, with a plebiscite to be conducted only in the Kashmir Valley. However, his plan was rejected by Pakistan, which did not wish to expose itself to the risk of a plebiscite in the Valley.[12]

The fourth and last time plebiscite was offered to Pakistan was in New Delhi on 20 August 1953 through a joint communiqué issued at the conclusion of the Nehru–Bogra talks, which was rejected by Bogra on 1 December 1953.[13]

Importing the Cold War in the Subcontinent

In its aftermath, the Indo–Pak war of 1947–48 created a tailor-made opportunity for others to fish in, to the detriment of the peoples of the two countries. Consequently, the Cold War was imported into the subcontinent in 1953–54 on Pakistan being offered military assistance on becoming an ally of the United States.

One consequence of the US–Pak mutual defence assistance agreement, signed in May 1954, was that it changed the whole context of the Kashmir issue. Since the proposals for a plebiscite advanced by the United Nations were contingent on demilitarization in Kashmir, the military pact effectively scuttled the plebiscite proposal. The second consequence was that these pacts brought about military parity, or even superiority, vis-à-vis India. Military assistance to Pakistan continued to increase after it became a member, first in September 1954, of the South East Asia Treaty Organization (SEATO), although, ironically, it did not even form a geographical part of that regional grouping, and subsequently of the Baghdad Pact, later renamed the Central Treaty Organization (CENTO).

In 1960, Pakistan gave up the idea of plebiscite. Ayub Khan and Foreign Minister Manzur Qadir began referring to methods other than plebiscite. In this regard, on 26 September 1960, Ayub said that any international agreement worth its name must be a compromise.[14] An opportunity presented itself immediately after the Sino–Indian conflict of October–November 1962, when Indo–Pak talks were held to explore ways and means for resolution of the Kashmir issue. At that time India was willing to cede some 1500 square miles of Kashmir territory under its control, in addition to what was already held by Pakistan. However, on the evening of the arrival of the Indian delegation under Swaran Singh, on 27 December 1962, the then minister of railways, on Radio Pakistan announced in a news bulletin the signing of an, in-principle, Sino–Pak boundary agreement. Earlier, during that very day, when Swaran Singh met Bhutto and Ayub, they had not considered it appropriate to inform him in advance of the intended announcement.

Through the Sino–Pak agreement of 2 March 1963, Pakistan agreed to cede to China the Shaksgam Valley of northern Kashmir. The agreement was violative of generally accepted international principles. However, Indo–Pak talks on Kashmir continued to take place under American inducement of military assistance. Before the proposal for the division of Kashmir could be placed in front of the Indian cabinet for the second time in succession on 19 April 1963, news came in of an Anglo-American division plan for Kashmir that had been shared only with the Pakistan side. This plan titled, 'KASHMIR—The Elements of a Settlement', envisaged recognition of the claim of both India and Pakistan to the Valley, with its inhabitants having the right to 'local self-governance', 'sovereignty' and free movement. Further, in violation of the Indo–Pak Indus Waters Treaty, Pakistan was to be given storage facilities in the Chenab basin. The Anglo-American plan went way beyond the scope of concessions that were being discussed by the two sides themselves.[15] This was the second time the Kashmir issue, that appeared ripe for resolution, could not be taken forward because of third-party intervention.

An opportunity did present itself for resolution of the Kashmir issue, in the aftermath of the Indo–Pak war of 1971, during the Simla meeting in 1972 between Indira Gandhi and Zulfikar Ali Bhutto. There were intense negotiations on a range of issues, which also included the question of permanent settlement of the Kashmir issue. As former diplomat Chandrashekhar Dasgupta points out in his recent book on the Bangladesh Liberation War, 'Mrs Gandhi was not ready to immediately convert the Line of Control in Jammu & Kashmir into a full-fledged international boundary, lest she should be accused of "surrendering" territory across the line. She envisaged this as the long-term solution, and wished to move in this direction.'[16] The negotiations reflected the complexity of the issue for both sides. Eventually, the two sides focused on the modalities for settling the issues. It was resolved to settle all differences by peaceful means, through bilateral negotiations or by any other peaceful means mutually agreed upon between the two sides. As a result, Pakistan accepted that Kashmir is a bilateral issue to be resolved accordingly.

* * *

The Chenab Formula

Ever since Independence in 1947, exchange of territories either took place, or was the purpose of discussions whenever there was a conflict or negotiations between India and Pakistan in respect of Jammu and Kashmir.

The Indo–Pak war on Kashmir (1947–48) resulted in the creation of POK, with Pakistan obtaining 85,792 sq. km of the territory (POK–13,297, Northern Areas–72,495). Later, Pakistan illegally ceded to China 5180 sq. km from this very territory. During the six rounds of the Sardar Swaran Singh–Bhutto talks (1962–63), India offered 1500 sq. miles to Pakistan for the new international boundary, but Bhutto rejected the offer demanding the entire Valley.

There was a very interesting conversation on this most generous offer made to Pakistan between Bhutto and Commonwealth secretary, MEA, Gundevia, best described in Gundevia's words:

> The Kashmir map was before us on the table, showing only the Cease-Fire Line. I told Bhutto that Sardar Swaran Singh had showed him exactly where he would like the new international boundary to run, with 1500 sq. miles more given away to Pakistan. How would he like this new line still further modified? Would he show us on the map what he actually wanted? Bhutto said, 'Of course, of course', and leaned over the table and pointed to the little town of Kathua on the Kashmir–Himachal border, drew a circle somewhere there with his forefinger and said, 'You can have this part of Kashmir. We want the rest.' 'Do you really want us to go home with this?' I asked. The discussion was going on in Urdu, Pakistan's official language, which we all spoke perfectly well. What do we tell our people? They will tell us that we went to Pakistan for three days, *'aur kachhua le ke aye!'*—we came back with a turtle! . . . Bhutto burst out laughing. We all laughed . . . it was approaching midnight . . . There was nothing left to talk about.[17]

During the 1965 war, India had captured two important posts—Haji Pir and Tithwal. In terms of Article 2 of the Tashkent Agreement, which envisaged that the two countries will withdraw all armed personnel to positions held prior to 5 August 1965, these posts were returned to Pakistan. Again, even after the Simla

Agreement on the international border, India had to return 1000 sq. km in the salient Sialkot–Shakargah area and 4700 sq. km in Sindh (Naya Chor). This followed from Article 4 (1), which stated that the forces of the two countries will be withdrawn to their respective sides of the international border.

During the R.K. Mishra–Niaz Naik back-channel negotiations, before and during the Kargil crisis in 1999, Pakistan and Indian commentators agreed that the Chenab formula was discussed. There have been many comments in the public domain on these discussions. G. Parthasarthy, who was high commissioner of India in Pakistan during the Kargil conflict, in his article in the book, *Diplomatic Divide*, stated that this would have resulted in adjustment in the Line of Control, eventually leading to it being moved to the Chenab River basin.

This narrative, prevailing since 1947, was changed by Dr Manmohan Singh who said there can be no change or redrawing of borders.

* * *

The Four-Point Formula

After having failed to resolve the Kashmir issue, either by military or non-military means and specially after the Kargil misadventure, Gen. Musharraf came out with a four-point formula on Kashmir.

Musharraf was aware of the history of Pakistan's reluctance to pursue the plebiscite route under the UNSC Resolution 47, notwithstanding the country's official public position on it. He had seen the non-viability of any formula that entailed fresh divisions or new boundaries being drawn. The lessons of the Kargil misadventure also showed him the futility of military intervention to wrest Kashmir from India, although it took some time after the end of the Kargil War and reported persuasion by his U.S. interlocutors to reach that sober conclusion.

Musharraf's new interest in settlement and peace may have been the result of the Kargil War, but it would also have had to do with the consolidation of his own position, in the dual role of a President and army chief, as also his ambitions for his legacy. And, with the failure in Kargil, the non-acceptance of the Chenab formula and lack of real interest in the UNSC resolution, Musharraf realized he had to approach the issue with a new perspective.

He understood that the framework could not harp on positions that would be unacceptable to India, but had to be something that would change the status quo in a positive way for Pakistan. The formula would also address the aspirations of the people of Kashmir, as the interest of the people of Kashmir had been the central pillar of, and projected justification for, Pakistan's Kashmir campaign at home and abroad.

Over the period of 2001–06, Musharraf articulated, with varying degrees of detail, what amounted to his four-point proposal. But, for him, the starting point was to narrow down the issue to the region of Jammu and Kashmir that needed a resolution—essentially the Kashmir Valley. His four points were (i) demilitarization together with the cessation of military activities, (ii) self-governance in the region, (iii) a joint mechanism involving representatives of India, Pakistan and Kashmir, for the purpose of overseeing self-governance and for issues that were beyond the scope of self-governance, and (iv) trade and movement of people between the two parts of Kashmir. The principles were, of course, to be applied equally on both sides.[18]

His formula clearly recognized that the stated positions of the two countries on the territory of Jammu and Kashmir were not acceptable to either side, and an approach was required that obviated the need for settlement of the territorial issue. His proposal on a joint mechanism would result in a 'status quo plus' outcome for Pakistan with a say in the affairs of all of Kashmir. At the same time, self-governance in Kashmir would appear to be a fulfilment of Pakistan's commitment to the people of Kashmir and bury the possibility of independence.

The Hurriyat leader Prof. Abdul Ghani Bhat described the four points as an effective roadmap to peace in Kashmir and explained them as 1) Self-governance; 2) Demilitarization; 3) The removal of irrelevant borders implying free movement of people and trade between India, Pakistan and the two Kashmirs; 4) Joint management forming a group to manage common interests and common issues like trade, tourism and river waters, etc.

As soon as the four-point formula was released in bits and pieces, we did an internal study and found it would be manageable to discuss Jammu and Kashmir with Pakistan on the basis of this formula along with Prime Minister Manmohan Singh's Amritsar speech.

As regards the regions, it was made abundantly clear that because of Pakistan's mishandling of the territorial issue since 1947 (creation of POK) and 1963 (illegal cession of territory to China), the area to be discussed was the entire state of the erstwhile state of J & K. Musharraf wanted to know if discussions could be limited to the problematic areas. His objective appeared to be to keep out the Northern Areas in the Pakistan side and Ladakh on the Indian side. Right from the beginning, it had been made clear to Pakistan that communal settlement was not acceptable.

The other element was disarmament. It was made clear to our Pakistani back-channel interlocutors that our forces had to deal with our China border as well. The important element of the four-point formula was demilitarization. Musharraf said he understood total disarmament could not take place in a day and suggested two stages. Pakistan would be willing to withdraw troops on the LoC as part of an overall settlement to deal with military confrontation between the two countries. He wanted Indian troops to be shifted from urban centres like Srinagar, Baramulla and Kupwara. This he justified as a part of the well-being and human rights of the Kashmiri people. Pakistan was told that there had to be an end to hostility, violence and terrorism. There could be withdrawal of Indian troops from selected urban areas if this was put into practice.

For the first time, Manmohan Singh came up with the idea of economic integration through soft borders. Borders, he said, could not be redrawn but progressively softened by encouraging trade and travel, the results of which were already apparent during the 2006–08 period when it started.

In any case, our own Kargil Review Committee had mentioned that the large-scale involvement of army encounter and insurgency operations was not in our interest. The removal of the Indian Army troops from internal security duties would also be in accordance with the report of the Kargil Review Committee.

Pakistan was aware that the reduction of army deployment in internal security duties in Jammu and Kashmir was already under way as part of the internal process. The group of ministers which had been formed after the Kargil War had noted that, 'The ultimate objective should be to entrust Internal Security [IS] and Counter Insurgency [CI] duties entirely to Central Para Military Forces and the Rashtriya Rifles, thus de-inducting the Army from these duties, wherever possible.'[19]

Another important point was self-governance for internal administration. What was agreed to was not in violation of both the Indian and Jammu and Kashmir Constitution.

As regards Pakistan's proposal of a joint mechanism, the answer was to be found in PM Manmohan Singh's Amritsar speech.

A brief history of the UN resolution and negotiations on various formulas by the two sides show that the narrative prevailing since 1947 was changed by Dr Manmohan Singh who said there can be no change or redrawing of borders.

Dr Manmohan Singh, in his speech in Amritsar on 24 March 2006, laid the basic guidelines of how he wanted Kashmir to be resolved and it is best to quote him:

> I am aware that General Musharraf has often stated that the normalization of relations between our two countries cannot move forward unless what he calls the core issue of Jammu & Kashmir is dealt with. In my view, it is a mistake to link normalization of other relations with finding a solution to Jammu & Kashmir. But we are not afraid of discussing Jammu & Kashmir or of finding pragmatic, practical solutions to resolve this issue as well . . . I have often said that borders cannot be redrawn but we can work towards making them irrelevant— towards making them just lines on a map. People on both sides of the LoC should be able to move more freely and trade with one another. I also envisage a situation where the two parts of Jammu & Kashmir can, with the active encouragement of the governments of India and Pakistan, work out cooperative, consultative mechanisms so as to maximize the gains of cooperation in solving problems of social and economic development of the region.[20]

Prime Minister Singh and President Musharraf approached the issue from different perspectives, but there was enough convergence to provide a substantive basis for dialogue and negotiation. Dr Singh was clear that there could be no settlement along communal lines, so he wanted to deal with the entire state of Jammu and Kashmir, not just the Kashmir Valley.

Beyond that, though, Dr Singh's own internal initiative on Jammu and Kashmir and the recommendations of the working groups contained elements that would also be consistent with the approach to negotiations with Pakistan. Reducing military presence in the state was an internal objective, but Dr Singh was clear that it also required an end to, or at least reduction in terrorism emanating from Pakistan. Similarly, the question of good governance and autonomy to Jammu and Kashmir within the constitutional framework of India, which had progressively eroded, was also being examined as part of a set of internal measures to advance peace in the state and address the concerns of the people. But, he did not go as far as proposing self-governance or joint sovereignty of the two countries.

Dr Singh proposed three ideas that would change the status quo, without redrawing the borders. At the same time, it would provide the people of Jammu and Kashmir, on both sides of the LoC, a deeper sense of control of their destiny, as also the benefits that arise from interaction, connection and collaboration. He advocated free movement of people, goods and ideas across the LoC. Second, he suggested that the two sides of Jammu and Kashmir could develop joint mechanisms of consultation and cooperation for common social and economic development. And, third, he suggested that the common resources of the whole area should be used for the benefit of the people of the whole of Jammu and Kashmir.

Thus, for all the differences in substance and nuances, there was sufficient basis to move forward with negotiations. Both also realized that by keeping out the territorial issue, they were leaving it to be addressed in the future. But they also felt that what they were embarking upon, if successful, could lead to a future of boundless potential for the two countries and for the relationship that was hard to foresee from the prism of the existing situation and the historical position and orthodox ideas on both sides.

Guidelines

Political leaders' statements set the direction and act like guidelines. This was precisely the signal that came out of Musharraf's four-point formula and Dr Singh's Amritsar speech, though neither would find any reference in the draft agreements later.

After intensive internal discussions, a set of informal guidelines was made on the basis of which negotiations with Pakistan and Jammu and Kashmir could be conducted. These included principles, prerequisites and outcomes in terms of possible arrangement in Jammu and Kashmir.

1) There cannot be any redrawing of borders.
2) No joint sovereignty.
3) LoC has to be respected like a normal border between the two countries.
4) People on both sides of LoC should be allowed to move freely from one side of LoC to another. This helps ethnic groups and divided families living on both sides.
5) Encourage meaningful trade across LoC.
6) To ensure trade flow, there has to be progressive removal of tariffs and non-tariff barriers in specified locally produced goods. The current trade across LoC is a zero duty and barter trade permitted for twenty-one categories of goods of Jammu and Kashmir origin only.
7) It is essential that based on experience of LoC trade, measures are taken to increase it, open more routes and take effective steps to discourage malpractices.
8) End of hostilities, violence and terrorism.

9) Progress on any discussion with Pakistan on Jammu and Kashmir was based on twin pillars—respecting the ceasefire on the LoC and disavowal by Pakistan of use of terrorism as state policy and allowing use of its territory by non-state actors. These remain essential prerequisites for now and the future.

10) Once this happens, military formation on both sides of LoC to be kept to the minimum, particularly in populated areas.

11) Important to ensure self-governance for internal management on both sides of LoC.

12) Respect for human rights on both sides of LoC.

13) Ensure that population on both sides is kept informed of progress made.

14) Based on Dr Singh's vision, articulated in his Amritsar speech, of a cooperative consultative mechanism for cooperation in solving problems of social and economic development of the region, joint consultative mechanisms could be explored for specified socio-economic issues like tourism, travel, health, education and culture.

Those guidelines formed the basis of negotiations and were fundamentally different from various solutions, including the Chenab formula, considered in the past.

When I paid my last call on Prime Minister Manmohan Singh as prime minister, at the time of the May 2014 elections to hand over my resignation as special envoy, he was as usual warm and graceful. He followed me to the door and questioned me as to why Musharraf agreed to negotiations on this set of guidelines. He understood my brief response as he had the background to the history of various initiatives, including Musharraf's own reported advocacy of the stillborn Chenab formula.

* * *

The Indian Team

I started my new assignment as special envoy towards the end of March 2005. Vikram Doraiswamy, then private secretary to the prime minister, later ambassador to Uzbekistan and high commissioner to Bangladesh, helped me adjust in the environment of the PMO. Jawed Ashraf, currently ambassador to France, whom I have known since his first posting to Germany when I was ambassador and have remained in close touch with since then, always provided vital inputs and advice at different stages that were of great help, including when he was political counsellor/minister in Washington, D.C. and head of the Americas division in MEA, and later as joint secretary in the PMO under Dr Manmohan Singh, a position he continued in under Prime Minister Narendra Modi.

Jaideep Sarkar, director in the PMO, was appointed to assist me in my new responsibilities as special envoy. Shortly thereafter, he was appointed private secretary to the PM. I requested the PM to allow Jaideep to continue working with me. When he asked the reason, I explained that he would be able to keep the PM informed of the progress of the back channel and all papers would be kept with him; it would facilitate my work, including fixing meetings with the PM and it would send a good signal outside, including in Pakistan, of the seriousness the PM attached to the back channel. He agreed. This proved beneficial. Jaideep Sarkar provided significant help and contributions in the formulation of the back-channel agreement. Later he was ambassador to Israel, Bhutan and South Africa. He was succeeded by another able officer, Vikram Misri, who was with me in the last six meetings of the back channel. His input and advice was equally valuable. Vikram Misri has since been ambassador to Spain, Myanmar and China and is currently deputy NSA.

On many subjects we had prepared a brief background/ talking points, to be used if necessary. We knew that Pakistan would not raise the UN resolution; however, a brief note was always kept handy to be used if the need arose. Pakistan raised the UN resolution in the initial stages, but as expected, did not do so in the substantive back-channel discussion.

* * *

Three Phases of Negotiations

I had three interlocutors from Pakistan in the back channel between 2005 and 2014. Each coincided with three distinct phases in back-channel negotiations, which corresponded with three different situations in Pakistan's internal politics that reflected the structure of the government in Islamabad and the state of civil–military relations.

The first phase took place during the tenure of President Musharraf, who was both President and chief of army till November 2007. He relinquished the charge of army chief and continued as President till August 2008. There was strong momentum until 2007, and almost the entire progress in negotiations was made while he held dual charge. As his internal problems increased, including the standoff with the judiciary, he was both distracted and unable to conclude the agreement.

General Kayani succeeded Pervez Musharraf as the eighth army chief in November 2007, a post he was to remain in till November 2013. The former ISI chief quickly consolidated power within the army structure. By September 2008, Asif Zardari became the President of Pakistan and remained in office till July 2013. The second phase, thus, coincided with Zardari as President and the powerful General Kayani as army chief. This period saw little engagement and no progress in negotiations. It was obviously also marred by the horrific 26/11 terrorist attack in Mumbai.

The third phase began with Nawaz Sharif winning the May 2013 election and returning to power. Elected with a strong mandate, he wielded considerable power. By July, Zardari had left office and in November, Kayani retired. Nawaz Sharif resumed back-channel negotiations and injected new momentum and urgency into the process. By the time there was progress in the back channel, attention in India turned to the 2014 general election, with the UPA battling a resurgent opposition Bharatiya Janata Party, which was seeing a surge in the popular vote.

The Pakistan Team

I had three different interlocutors for the three phases of negotiations.

Tariq Aziz

My first interlocutor was Tariq Aziz. In all, there were thirty-six meetings of the back channel from May 2003 to March 2014, of which the largest number was with Tariq Aziz. He met Brijesh Mishra on five occasions between May 2003 and March 2004. The most significant achievement was the joint statement issued by Vajpayee and Musharraf at the end of the SAARC summit on 5 January 2004. Thereafter, Tariq Aziz met J.N. Dixit on four occasions from June 2004 to December 2004. In these meetings, India–Pakistan relations were discussed in general, including the situation in J & K, but there was no discussion on any specific agreement, except opening of the LoC for travel and trade.

Tariq Aziz and I had eighteen meetings from April 2005 to August 2008, in different cities. It was during these meetings that a draft agreement on J & K in the back channel was negotiated, discussed and formalized.

It is interesting that much of the criticism regarding the agreement came from retired members of the foreign service in both countries. In Pakistan, Tariq Aziz was vehemently criticized. Quoting from Kasuri's (Ex foreign minister of Pakistan) book, 'Criticism was levelled against Tariq Aziz as a back-channel negotiator when senior Foreign Service Officers used to mutter, not always in low tones, at that time as to how can Tariq Aziz, an officer of Pakistan Taxation Service, hold his own against experienced Indian Foreign Service Officers such as Brijesh Mishra, J.N. Dixit and S.K. Lambah.'[21] Shamshad Ahmad, former foreign secretary of Pakistan, was blatantly expressive. 'Tariq Aziz or his boss had no idea what they were doing to their country'[22], referring in context to the back channel.

Based on my experience of dealing with Tariq Aziz in sixteen meetings spread over a hundred hours, I can say he negotiated diligently in his country's interest. It was possible to reach the agreement because of his deep knowledge and patience and his access to Musharraf and the army leadership. He had studied with Musharraf in Forman Christian College in Lahore. Musharraf, writing about him in his book, said, 'Tariq Aziz, who was my Principal Secretary after I became President, was later appointed Secretary to the National Security Council . . . He was senior to me and we were not that friendly, probably because he was a "good boy" reluctant to join me in mischief-making . . .'[23] He showed complete loyalty to me personally and to my agenda.'[24]

Tariq Aziz, a member of the Pakistan Revenue Service, had various other interests. An accomplished bridge player, he was longtime president of the Lahore race course.

Riaz Mohammad Khan

President Asif Zardari was keen to retain Tariq Aziz as the back-channel negotiator, but the latter requested to be released. Thereafter, Riaz Mohammad Khan, foreign secretary of Pakistan and ambassador to China, the European Union and Kazakhstan, was appointed in his place. Khan had an uneasy relationship with Zardari, and it is believed that his appointment was prompted by the new army chief, General Kayani. Since Kayani, as army chief, was distancing himself from the back-channel negotiations, there was no progress during the tenure of Riaz M. Khan. He had two meetings with me, one in 2009 and another in 2012, and at both he reiterated that the back channel had made remarkable progress, but that some work needed to be done. He did not indicate what the work was. Though the back-channel draft agreement had been finalized, I did not highlight this fact too much, as I was aware that the back-channel documents could be changed any time, till signed. Riaz Khan is respected by colleagues, including Indians, who have interacted with him in different postings. He was clearly constrained by the power equation between Rawalpindi and Islamabad, and the attitude of General Kayani. His hobbies include painting. His book on Central Asia is widely read.

Shahryar Khan

After Nawaz Sharif's convincing victory in May 2013, Dr Singh spoke to him early in the morning, even before the full results had been declared. Dr Singh asked him if India could do anything for him. Nawaz Sharif asked for electricity and gas supplies from India to overcome the crippling shortages in Pakistan. Dr Singh agreed to examine grid interconnection and power supply arrangements. I worked on this with Joint Secretary in PMO Jawed Ashraf. There was progress on the idea, but it appears to have been sabotaged from within the Pakistan establishment, as the dialogue went cold by July.

Nawaz Sharif was also keen to resume the back channel with renewed vigour. He appointed veteran diplomat Shahryar Khan as the back-channel negotiator to replace Riaz Mohammad Khan. I had known Shahryar since 1981, during my first tenure, when he was additional secretary in the Pakistan ministry of foreign affairs. He was foreign secretary almost throughout my tenure as high commissioner in Pakistan, and it was a pleasure dealing with a gentleman like him. Shahryar had no meeting with the army chief during the period he negotiated with me. During our back-channel negotiations, the Pakistan Army and ISI regarded him as a man from Bhopal, who was not a Punjabi, Pathan or Kashmiri, but an Urdu-speaking Muhajir.

Shahryar Khan also served as special representative of the UN secretary general to Rwanda and wrote the book, *Shallow Graves of Rwanda*. He was later chairman of the Pakistan Cricket Board. His recent book is on his mother, Princess Abida Sultan, of the royal family of Bhopal.

I had six meetings with him from July 2013 in New Delhi, Dubai and Muscat. For the first time since my last meeting with Tariq Aziz in 2008, Shahryar Khan brought with him the draft agreement negotiated in the back channel. There had been some mystery regarding its whereabouts in Pakistan, and whether it had been retained at all after Musharraf demitted office.

Tariq Aziz told me he had to take a difficult decision when Musharraf left, as he (Tariq Aziz), too, was contemplating leaving his responsibility. He sent copies of the draft agreement in sealed covers to both the army headquarters and the Pakistan foreign office following his resignation. This was a wise decision, because had he not sent a copy to the foreign office, under General Kayani it might have been lost. In fact, he feigned complete ignorance of any back-channel negotiations or the existence of a document, even though as DG/ISI, he had been, according to Musharraf, kept informed about the negotiations.

* * *

Pakistan Army's Support to Musharraf on Back-Channel Negotiations

As the back-channel negotiations were conducted quietly, there was at that time not much public discussion. Gen. Musharraf confirmed to me when I called on him in Islamabad on 2 March 2007, that the back channel had his approval.

Khurshid Mahmud Kasuri, who was foreign minister for a major part of the negotiations, has written in his book that the Pakistan Army supported the back-channel agreement. Here it may be mentioned that the shelf life of a corps commander is not more than eighteen months, and during the tenure they are normally supportive of the army chief. Kasuri writes, 'On the peace process with India, the Pakistan Army was completely on board during this period.'[25] He further writes:

> I have already pointed out that General Ashfaq Parvez Kayani, the Chief of Army Staff, who was then DG/ISI, attended all the meetings on the backchannel on Kashmir.[26]
>
> President Musharraf is on record stating on more than one occasion that he took his Corps Commanders into confidence over the peace process with India.[27]
>
> It is clear that the Pakistan Army had been on board on the solution of J & K that we were trying to achieve and continues along the same path even after our government's

tenure ended and President Musharraf was no longer in power.[28]

Lt General Hamid Javed as Chief of Staff to the President attended all meetings of the in-house committee dealing with the back channel and supported the ongoing peace process with India . . . Lt General Shafaatullah Shah [then Major General] sometimes attended meetings on the backchannel on Kashmir, as did Lt General Shagqaat Ahmed [then Major General] and Lt General Nadeem Taj [then Major General] as Military Secretaries to the President. Lt General Nadeem Taj later commanded the Gujranwala Corps. He also served as Director General Military Intelligence and Director General ISI. Lt General Shafqaat Ahmed commanded the Multan Corps and was President Musharraf's military secretary till I left office. I found them supportive of the peace process. This does not turn them into 'doves'; instead it shows that they are 'realists' who understand where Pakistan's core national interests lie.[29]

During the negotiations it was very clear to me that Tariq Aziz had the support of the army. On different occasions, he even told me about the discussion with then DG/ISI, General Kayani, who was also supportive at that time. However, on becoming chief of army staff, Kayani changed his stance.

* * *

General Ashfaq Parvez Kayani's Change of Attitude

We observed that General Ashfaq Parvez Kayani, after taking over as army chief, started distancing himself from the back-channel negotiations. I realized this first during my discussions with Tariq Aziz and later with former army chief General Jehangir Karamat and others. This also confirmed our assessment on General Kayani's role. We in India were aware that General Kayani was the first ISI chief to become army chief and be given an unprecedented three-year extension. During his watch, the Afghan Taliban recovered and regrouped in Quetta; Osama Bin Laden stayed in Abbottabad from 2005 onwards. The current Al-Qaeda chief, Ayman al-Zawahiri, is still there and so is Dawood Ibrahim, the master brain of the 1993 Bombay killings, and Lashkar-e-Taiba chief, Hafeez Sayeed and others had a free run. The planning began for Lashkar-e-Taiba's attack in Mumbai in November 2008. He was DG/ISI when David Coleman Headley began his reconnaissance trips to Mumbai to prepare for the 26/11 attack.

Interestingly, the British foreign office also made a similar assessment, as had been confirmed with the release of messages from the U.S. Embassy in London through WikiLeaks, which mentions they saw Kayani as an 'obstacle' to the deal on Kashmir.

A cable dated November 28, 2008 [180571: confidential/ noforn] from the U.S. Embassy in London showed that until a day before the 26/11 Mumbai bombings, the view in the British Foreign Office was that India and Pakistan were close to an agreement on Kashmir with a 'text' ready, but General Kayani was 'reluctant'. He was seen as the only 'remaining obstacle'. The view was based on British Foreign Secretary David Miliband's visit to Pakistan on November 25, 2008. A U.S. diplomat quotes Laura Hickey of the Pakistan Team of the Foreign and Commonwealth Office as saying that Mr. Miliband's assessment was there was a 'deal on paper' and both Prime Minister Manmohan Singh and Pakistan President Asif Ali Zardari were 'ready' to sign it. Hickey said Miliband concluded during his trip that it was time to get a deal done on Kashmir. Zardari and Singh were ready, and there was a text on paper. Miliband thought the remaining obstacle was Pakistani Chief of Army Staff General Kayani; he remained 'reluctant' and needed to be persuaded the cable said.[30]

Ms Hickey said Mr. Miliband had 'resolved to put energy behind an Indian–Pakistan deal on Kashmir'.

She thought the November 26, Mumbai bombings would likely strengthen his resolve. HMG [Her Majesty's Government] is nervous, however, that over-reaction on either government's part could result in a hardening of positions over military action in Kashmir, once again derailing any progress, the cable said.[31]

* * *

Support of the Pakistan Foreign Office for Back-Channel Negotiations

Kasuri has claimed that there was support for the back-channel negotiations by the Pakistan foreign office. He wrote:

No draft of a non-paper was ever sent to the Indians without it being vetted by myself and Foreign Secretary Riaz Muhammad Khan. Tariq Aziz, who interacted as the backchannel with Ambassador J.N. Dixit, and later, after the latter's death, with Ambassador S.K. Lambah would carry various drafts in the form of non-papers. The Committee presided over by President Musharraf, which met often on the backchannel on Kashmir, comprised, inter alia, the Foreign Minister, Foreign Secretary, Vice-Chief of Army Staff General Ahsan Saleem Hayat, General Ashfaq Parvez Kayani who was DG-ISI at that time, as well as Lt General Hamid Javed, Chief of Staff to the President, and, of course, Tariq Aziz, our backchannel negotiator. Ambassador Riaz Muhammad Khan and I always studied the draft and made our recommendations. After incorporating the results of our discussions at the meetings, we would send back to India our revised version of the draft non-papers through Tariq Aziz.[32]

I should mention that Pakistan foreign ministers, who had been shown the papers, publicly denied it. Kasuri had ceased to be the foreign minister when the crucial negotiations were completed.

* * *

Consultations in India on the Back-Channel Negotiations

During the crucial period of intensive negotiations between 2005 and 2007, my diary recalls I had sixty-eight meetings with Prime Minister Dr Manmohan Singh. These included visits with him to Jammu and Srinagar, where there was an opportunity to have discussions with a large number of people from J & K.

During my meetings with the prime minister, the strategy and details of the draft agreement were discussed. I was fortunate in getting clear-cut instructions, which were helpful in finalizing the draft agreement. A crucial meeting took place on 9 November 2006, in the PMO where Congress President Sonia Gandhi and External Affairs Minister Pranab Mukherjee were also present.

I was asked to give a brief background of the progress in the discussions up to that time. The Congress president asked some questions, including the impact of the agreement on the majority community in India. Pranab Mukherjee did most of the talking, saying he was convinced that if we were able to get the agreement signed, it would be welcomed by the majority community and others. After my briefing I withdrew from the room. Later, after the Congress president and the external affairs minister left, the prime minister called me again to his room and gave me the signal to go ahead with my work.

Pranab Mukherjee was kept fully informed of all developments under instructions of the prime minister. In 2005–06, when he was defence minister, I had briefed him at a meeting in his office on 3 August 2005, where the defence secretary and chief of army staff, too, were present. Later, I had a meeting with the DGMO on 5 August 2005. I had sixteen meetings with Pranab Mukherjee from October 2006 to December 2007 when he was external affairs minister. Before each of my talks with the Pakistani interlocutor, I would discuss the strategy with him and brief him later on what transpired during the meeting. Most of my meetings with him were after dinner at his residence, 13 Talkatora Road. The guidance provided by him was crucial. Jaideep Sarkar was also present at the meetings.

I had also kept the earlier External Affairs Minister K. Natwar Singh informed of the initial discussions from January 2005 to October 2005. I also had various sessions with NSA M.K. Narayanan, foreign secretaries Shyam Saran and Shivshankar Menon and Indian high commissioners to Pakistan during that period—Shivshankar Menon , Satyabrata Pal, Sharat Sabharwal and T.C.A. Raghavan during their visits to India.

Among the opposition leaders, I had meetings with former PM Vajpayee, leader of the Opposition in the Lok Sabha L.K. Advani and leader of the Opposition in the Rajya Sabha Jaswant Singh. My meeting with former PM Vajpayee was on 10 June 2006. Thereafter, on account of his health, I was in close touch with former NSA Brijesh Mishra, who gave some significant suggestions that were incorporated in the agreement, particularly in respect of the joint mechanism.

Brijesh Mishra kept former PM Vajpayee informed of developments. I observed that both Brijesh Mishra and, four decades earlier, Sardar Swaran Singh had a somewhat similar approach that an eventual settlement would have to give the LoC some characteristics of an international border.

In addition, we tried to keep leaders of J & K informed. Some meetings were held during visits to Jammu and Srinagar. I separately met Omar Abdullah, then president of the National Conference, and Farooq Abdullah in Delhi on 11 December 2006. I also met Mufti Mohammad Sayeed and Dr Karan Singh. I briefed Ghulam Nabi Azad, chief minister of J & K. Jaideep Sarkar was invariably present at all these meetings.

Legal Opinions

Based on my experience after opening our mission in Bangladesh that the Indo–Bangladesh agreement on transfer of territory could not be formalized for decades as it had to be referred for a judicial review, I felt that the back-channel agreement on Kashmir, which was being negotiated with Pakistan, should not be subjected to similar treatment. It was decided to get a legal opinion at the negotiation stage so that if any rectification was required, it could be done while the agreement was being negotiated.

After considering the different possibilities, PM Manmohan Singh approved we could consult Justice A.S. Anand, former Chief Justice of India and chairman of the Human Rights Commission at that time. He had also been Chief Justice of J & K High Court and author of a book on the J & K Constitution. His doctoral thesis was on accession of J & K to India. Jaideep Sarkar and I had five meetings with him from 4 March 2006 to 27 October 2006, and later, after his retirement, at his house in Noida on 25 March 2007. He was shown the draft under negotiation of the back-channel agreement. His opinion was sought on three points—whether the draft agreement violated 1) the Constitution of India, 2) the Constitution of J & K at that time and 3) the Parliament resolution on J & K. After detailed discussions, he confirmed that the back-channel agreement did not violate either the Constitution of India or J & K or the Parliament resolution. The PM was kept informed.

Subsequently, I discussed with the PM and got his approval to also consult the eminent lawyer Fali Nariman. Jaideep Sarkar and I had five sessions from 18 October 2006 to 27 March 2007. He, too, confirmed what Justice Anand had said and made some valuable suggestions, which were incorporated by us in the draft. Both the PM and the External Affairs Minister Pranab Mukherjee were regularly kept informed of these discussions. The opinion of the two legal luminaries helped us to formalize the draft agreement. Pranab Mukherjee, thereafter, told us that in view of the legal opinion we had received, he would ask the legal & treaties division of the ministry of external affairs to only look at it just before the agreement was signed.

* * *

Public Statement on the Back-Channel Agreement

Dr Manmohan Singh was not a candidate in the 2014 elections for the post of prime minister. I proposed to him that before relinquishing his office, some kind of public statement on the back-channel agreement with Pakistan should be made. He agreed.

Meanwhile, at my last meeting with the Pakistan interlocutor Shahryar Khan, he and I agreed that at an appropriate time, the broad contours of the understanding reached should be shared with the public.

Eventually, it was decided that I would speak at a seminar organized by the Kashmir University in Srinagar on 13 May 2014. The date was selected as polling in the general elections in India would be over and counting of votes would start a few days later. The draft speech was read by a few people. Views of MEA and our high commissioner in Islamabad, T.C.A. Raghavan, were also taken. Finally, my wife and I went to Srinagar. Enroute, along with Greesh Dhawan, a family friend, on a private visit we went to the Vaishno Devi shrine. In Srinagar, I met Governor N.N. Vohra, Chief Minister Omar Abdullah, PDP leader Mufti Mohammad Sayeed and other leaders.

My counterpart in the back channel in Pakistan was informed of our decision. High Commissioner Raghavan came from Islamabad, collected a copy of my speech and delivered it to him personally in Lahore on 12 May, a day before it was to be officially delivered in Srinagar. This had been discussed with Shahryar Khan at our last meeting. The Pakistan government did not comment on the speech. In the case of Pakistan, the details had already been divulged by former Foreign Minister Kasuri in his book.

Originally, the speech was to have been made at Sher-e-Kashmir Hall in Srinagar, but as elections had been held and counting had to commence, the Election Committee did not permit the function to be held there. The venue was changed to the Lalit Hotel, where I delivered the speech to a packed audience.

The programme was conducted by the Institute of Kashmir Studies, University of Kashmir. The Chief Minister Omar Abdullah presided over the session. After opening remarks by Professor Gull Wani and a welcome address by Professor Talat Ahmad, vice chancellor of the University of Kashmir, I spoke.

Speech in Srinagar, May 2014[33]

'A Possible Outline of a Solution'

Full text of the speech by PM's envoy in his 'personal capacity', which has come under attack for suggesting that 'any agreement must ensure that the Line of Control is like a border between any two normal states'.

In 1947 when India became free there was simultaneously the process of Partition and integration. The modern Indian state was forged from British India provinces and hundreds of princely states. At the same time, a separate sovereign nation of Pakistan was carved out of India. The Kashmir issue is a product of the circumstances at the time of the birth of India, and the untenable foundation—discredited nearly 25 years later by the creation of Bangladesh—of Pakistan's coming into existence in the name of religion. India's position on Jammu and Kashmir is legally, politically and historically correct.

Yet, it has remained one of our major post-independence problems, contributing to three wars between India and Pakistan, decades of cross-border terrorism and violence, and incalculable suffering for the ordinary people of Jammu and Kashmir. It has consumed enormous political, economic and diplomatic resources and remains to this day one of our national security preoccupations.

Therefore, successive Prime Ministers of India have made resolution of the Jammu and Kashmir issue a priority. Prime Minister Nehru's initiatives culminated in the inconclusive Swaran Singh–Bhutto Talks in the early 1960s. Indira Gandhi's efforts to seek a settlement through the Simla Agreement reflected recognition, even in the moment of decisive victory in the 1971 war, that a solution to the Kashmir issue was important for lasting peace and security. In a generational shift, Rajiv Gandhi tried to chart a new course with Benazir Bhutto.

As India reoriented its foreign policy in the post-Cold War world and economic reforms era, first Narasimha Rao, and later I.K. Gujral in pursuance of the Gujral Doctrine, made serious attempts to improve Indo–Pak relations. Atal Bihari Vajpayee's bold attempt to reset the relations in 1999 took place months after the nuclear tests by both the countries; his bus journey to Lahore highlighted the proximity between our two countries and the centrality of people to this relationship. Kargil did not dissuade him to engage its perpetrator in Agra, nor did the Parliament attack of December 2001 stop him from making another journey to Pakistan in January 2004, in search of peace and settlement. And, despite discouraging signals, he continued with the back-channel discussions on Kashmir.

Dr Manmohan Singh picked up the baton and turned it into one of his foreign policy priorities. His vision is rooted in India's security, economic development and global aspirations, and in the transformation of a region that is central to India's destiny. He has consistently advocated a solution that does not seek to redraw the border or amend the Constitution; but one that makes the boundary irrelevant, enables commerce, communication, contacts and development of the Kashmiri people on both sides and that ends the cycle of violence. In this regard, he appointed a Special Envoy to conduct back-channel discussions with Pakistan.

Efforts made by India and Pakistan to seek a solution to the Kashmir issue have gathered momentum this century. It has been conducted quietly and without the knowledge, prompting and involvement of any third party. The process has survived and sustained itself despite brutal and high-visibility assaults—from the Parliament attack to the embassy bombing in Kabul and to the Mumbai terror attack—and through political transitions in both countries. This progress was based on two pillars—respecting ceasefire along the Line of Control and a disavowal by Pakistan of the use of terrorism as a state policy allowing the use of its territory by non-state actors. These continue to be essential prerequisites.

I have had the privilege of working with six Prime Ministers of India on matters relating to Pakistan in the last thirty-five years. Each one of them had given priority to improving relations with Pakistan. At the highest level of the government, there has always been interest, readiness and resolve. This has helped us to move forward.

In view of past history, emotions, disagreements, violence, wars and failure of negotiations, it is not easy to specify the outlines of a solution. However, as the past six decades have clearly shown, the Kashmir issue cannot be settled by war, force or violence. A solution will also remain elusive if we keep harping on positions that have failed to resolve the problem in the past.

That is why we have to look for ideas that are practical, workable and acceptable. We can also learn some useful lessons from the Simla Agreement and Lahore Declaration.

Let me today venture to make some suggestions of a possible outline of a solution in my personal capacity.

After three wars and long periods of disagreements, it is essential that any agreement must ensure that the Line of Control is like a border between any two normal states. There can be no redrawal of borders;

Alongside, in accordance with the normal acceptable behaviour between nations, it is imperative that the people of J & K on either side of the Line of Control should be able to move freely from one side to the other. This is particularly essential as on both sides of the Line of Control live not only the same ethnic groups but also divided families;

The process of progressive removal of tariff and non-tariff barriers in specified locally produced goods already under way has to be expedited to ensure meaningful trade between the two sides of the LoC;

The essential prerequisite is that there has to be an end to Hostility, Violence and Terrorism;

Once this happens, it would be important that military forces on both sides of the LoC are kept to the minimum, particularly in populated areas;

It would be important to ensure self-governance for internal management in all areas on the same basis on both sides of the LoC;

There has to be respect for human rights on both sides of the LoC and efforts need to be made to reintegrate into society those sections who had been involved in violent militant activities; and

Prime Minister Manmohan Singh in his speech in Amritsar on 24 March 2006 has stated that he 'envisaged a situation where the two parts of Jammu and Kashmir can, with the active encouragement of the governments of India and Pakistan, work out a cooperative, consultative mechanism so as to maximize the gains of cooperation in solving problems of social and economic development of the region'.[34] It should be possible to do so to enable it to look into socio-economic issues like tourism, travel, pilgrimages to shrines, trade, health, education and culture.

A settlement will give the people of J & K an opportunity to seek a future defined by the bright light of hope, not darkened by the shadow of the gun. It will revive relationships and reunite families. The people on both sides will benefit from an integrated socio-economic development and the possibility of harnessing the enormous economic potential of the area, including its water resources. Connectivity within the region and the world will improve. Investments will increase, tourism will prosper, trade will grow, handicrafts will thrive, the services sector will flourish and the youth will have more opportunities. It will unleash the full potential of a talented people of unmatched beauty and great diversity.

It is true that the Kashmir problem has not stopped India from forging its destiny as a secular, pluralist democracy and one of the world's major economies and a military power. However, a solution to the Kashmir issue will substantially enhance India's security, strengthen the prospects for durable peace and stability in the region and enable India to focus more on the rapidly emerging long-term geopolitical challenges. It will relieve the burden that our security forces have to shoulder in terms of lives and resources. It could provide a boost to the Indian economy in a variety of ways, open a market with one of the world's largest population, restore our historical links to Central Asia and Eurasia and contribute to enhancing our energy security through improved connectivity with West Asia and Central Asia. Above all, it will herald a new era of peace and prosperity for the entire region.

For Pakistan, a solution will enable it to contribute to the welfare of the people of Jammu and Kashmir and to their progress and prosperity. It will relieve Pakistan from a debilitating military competition with a much larger neighbour that has drained its economy. It will hopefully strengthen its ability to turn the tide on terrorism and radical militancy. Pakistan could refocus its energy on the task of economic transformation. It could prosper from the enormous economic opportunities that come from cooperation with neighbours. As Asia seeks to integrate across its many fragmented parts, Pakistan, at peace with India, could become the bridge between South Asia and West and Central Asia; and, a hub for regional commerce, energy flows and intellectual and cultural exchanges. Needless to say, a stable Pakistan is also in India's interest. Experience shows instability anywhere is bad for neighbours.

These expected gains from a solution may not be automatic and will require sustained effort. But, if it opens the door to a new future for India and Pakistan, without compromising our security, integrity and constitutional framework, it is worth pursuing. The alternative is status quo of a festering problem and lingering tragedy that will keep us from realizing our potential.

Great powers do not wait passively for events to unfold, but seek to shape their environment in pursuit of their national interests. We are undergoing enormous transformation in a world witnessing change and transition on an unprecedented scale. It has opened vast opportunities for us to accelerate our economic development, strengthen our security and expand our influence. This is our moment to seize. A stable, peaceful, cooperative and connected neighbourhood is essential for us to realize our destiny. Solution of the Kashmir issue will help us on that path.[35]

* * *

There was an immediate political reaction in J & K and extensive media coverage in the national and Kashmir media. Hurriyat leader Syed Ali Shah Geelani criticized the speech, stating, 'No agreement is acceptable without participation of Kashmiris.'[36] Others, including Omar Abdullah, welcomed the speech.

Media reports were factual. In J & K, there were two editorials in *Greater Kashmir* and the Urdu newspaper, *Daily Aftab*. The two editorials from Srinagar reported the speech factually. The *Greater Kashmir* editorial expressed the hope that the process would be taken forward by the new Union government that was to soon be formed in Delhi. The *Daily Aftab* editorial, too, stressed the need for an early settlement to the lingering dispute of six decades with a positive approach. The national media also covered the speech extensively. The editorial in the *Indian Express* supported the suggestions.

* * *

The Draft Agreement and the Transition

By the end of the second term of the UPA government and of Dr Manmohan Singh's ten-year term, the draft agreement had been approved and was ready for signature. The draft was not made for a particular individual in office or a particular situation. It was meant to have an enduring value and be relevant for a long-term solution. However, this point was not publicly made because it is well known that any draft on the back channel, until signed, is not a settled agreement and can be modified or rejected.

Shahryar Khan, in fact, suggested a change during our last meeting. I explained that this was my last meeting with him on behalf of Prime Minister Manmohan Singh, who was not a candidate for the prime minister post in the next election. He would, therefore, get the response from the representative of the next prime minister of India.

The official file contained all details of discussions together with a note by Prime Minister Manmohan Singh that this could only be opened on the instructions of the next prime minister.

Prime Minister Narendra Modi

This book does not cover the period of Prime Minister Modi. However, before he assumed office, he asked me to meet him at Gujarat Bhawan. I met him on 25 May 2014. He was very gracious and keen to speak to me. Among those waiting outside were the Chief Minister of Andhra Pradesh Chandrababu Naidu, Foreign Secretary Sujata Singh and High Commissioner to Pakistan T.C.A. Raghavan. Apparently, the chief minister was in a hurry to meet the prime minister, as a few notes were sent in to the new prime minister. I asked the prime minister whether I should return later, but he said no and carried on with our meeting.

His main query was regarding the visit of Nawaz Sharif for the swearing-in ceremony. I told him it was a good and positive action taken. I added that as far as I could recall Nawaz Sharif had last visited to attend the funeral of Rajiv Gandhi, and, as a result, he was coming to India after almost two decades. Sometime later, Prime Minister Modi again asked to see me in his office. This time he asked for my assessment on India–Pakistan relations and I briefed him on the back channel.

There appeared to be an intent to continue the back-channel process. The file on the subject had been reviewed. I was even once told that no major change was required. A distinguished diplomat was being considered to be appointed as special envoy by Prime Minister Modi. I was asked to meet him. However, when I checked with the PMO, I was told there had been a change in thought and I would be informed regarding the briefing.

On 20 April 2017, a senior official of the PMO came to see me at my house. He said the prime minister wanted me to go to Pakistan to meet Prime Minister Nawaz Sharif. I reiterated that such meetings are more valuable if the envoy has the public confidence of the prime minister. However, on the 22nd I was told I would be given details of the points to be discussed and was asked to give my travel documents to enable me to travel to Pakistan. The same day, the senior official and I met Fali Nariman to refresh some points. The following day, I saw a news item that a leading Indian businessman, who was an emissary, had gone to meet PM Nawaz Sharif, in his personal plane. I rang the official, who appeared surprised at this development. I told him that under the circumstances, it would not be proper for two people to represent the prime minister for the same purpose. Clearly, the emissary had not coordinated his visit to Pakistan with the PMO. This was the last conversation I had on this subject.

Comments on the Back Channel

There was considerable speculation and reporting on the back channel in India, Pakistan and internationally, especially in the earlier years. I am quoting from a few of them here.

India

Former foreign secretary of India, M.K. Rasgotra wrote in his book:

> Secret talks made considerable headway during Dr Manmohan Singh's prime ministership, till Musharraf's position weakened within Pakistan and even as a document was virtually ready for signing, he told Prime Minister Manmohan Singh that he was not able to carry the negotiations forward to a conclusion . . .
>
> Secret negotiations actually had led to agreement on many aspects of the Kashmir issue and there was a document ready for signatures. It was agreed, for example, that there would be no independence (azadi) for Kashmir and no change in the

border (LoC), but there would be freedom of movement across it for Kashmiris of both sides. There was no reference to UN resolutions, and India had agreed to reduction of military troops in Kashmir subject to Pakistan ensuring the end of hostilities and terrorism (a vitally important condition). Finally, a joint mechanism of the two Kashmirs, for socio-economic subjects only, and autonomy for J & K, like all other Indian states, was also agreed on.

It was Pakistan, not India, that balked at proceeding to a positive conclusion of the negotiations. While President Musharraf was also the army chief, his deputy general, Ashfaq Parvez Kayani and the ISI were on board, but as soon as Musharraf shed his role as head of the Pakistani army, the new army chief, General Kayani, withdrew his support compelling Musharraf to abandon the agreement.[37]

Radha Kumar, who was one of the Kashmir interlocutors appointed by the Government of India in 2010, wrote:

> The Aziz–Lambah back channel was perhaps the most successful confidence-building exercise of all between the two governments.[38]

In his blurb on the jacket of Radha Kumar's book, former Foreign Minister of Pakistan Khurshid Mahmud Kasuri wrote:

> As someone who was intricately involved with the most productive peace process between the two countries since independence, I agree with Dr Radha Kumar's views that the Aziz–Lambah framework ('the back channel') was the only one to work out a settlement in detail. I have given all the details in my book and feel that when the conditions are ripe, Indians,

Pakistanis, and Kashmiris will not need to reinvent the wheel and could proceed from where we left off.[39]

Pakistan

Khurshid Mahmud Kasuri, former foreign minister of Pakistan, has written in some detail his perceptions of the back channel in his book, *Neither a Hawk nor a Dove*:

> Given the importance of the issue of Jammu and Kashmir in the foreign policy of Pakistan, it can be said without any fear of contradiction that one of the most sensitive negotiations during our tenure related to the backchannel negotiations on this issue.[40]
>
> Pakistan and India were on the verge of resolving some outstanding disputes, including Kashmir, before these efforts were stalled by the judicial crisis in Pakistan.[41]
>
> Although for the sake of historical accuracy the origins of the composite dialogue can be traced to 1997, it is a known fact that almost all the detailed and concrete work towards real progress was carried out between 2004 and 2007.[42]

Riaz Muhammad Khan, former Pakistan foreign secretary and back-channel interlocutor from 2010 to 2012, observed,

> . . . the last and the most sustained discussions were carried out through a backchannel [2005–06] under President Musharraf and Prime Minister Manmohan Singh. Importantly, the two sides tried to evolve a text for an interim agreement towards a settlement of the outstanding dispute. Considerable progress was achieved. Leaders of the All Party Hurriyat Conference

were generally consulted except for Syed Ali Geelani who had
ab initio rejected the process.[43]

Pakistani historian and commentator, Fakir Syed Aijazuddin
wrote:

> Most notably, Mr. Satinder K. Lambah (once India's High
> Commissioner to Pakistan and later Special Envoy of Prime
> Minister Manmohan Singh, 2005–14) and Mr. Tariq Aziz
> (General Pervez Musharraf's trusted Secretary of the National
> Security Council) burrowed unobtrusively for two years beneath
> a compacted overlay of misunderstandings, misadventures, and
> suspicions to achieve a resolution of the core issue of Jammu
> & Kashmir. Each spoke with singular authority, because each
> enjoyed the absolute confidence of his Principal.
>
> Such furtive negotiations, akin to the Kissinger–Zhou Enlai
> contacts in 1970–71 that led to US–China rapprochement,
> involved unsigned, unmarked proposals passing back and
> forth. Non-papers became parentless emissaries: fathered if
> they succeeded, orphaned if they didn't.
>
> In 2007, after two years of negotiations, Lambah and Aziz
> reached a solution deemed acceptable to all parties—India,
> Pakistan and the Gemini-twin Kashmiris. The final document
> would have been signed by Manmohan Singh and Musharraf,
> had the Pakistani lawyers' movement not weakened and then
> emasculated Musharraf. He asked the Indians for time, then
> an extension. The Indians waited, and finally gave up hope.
> Lambah and Aziz were recalled, nursing their chagrin in
> private. Imagine an equivalent—British and French engineers
> working on the Channel, reaching the point of breakthrough
> that would connect both countries permanently, and then
> suddenly being forced to withdraw.

In May 2014, ambassador Lambah, speaking guardedly in his 'personal capacity' at the University of Kashmir in Srinagar, provided tantalising details of how close Pakistan and India came to declaring peace. A 'possible outline' provided that the Line of Control would be 'like a border between normal states'. There would be 'no redrawal of borders'. The people of J & K 'would move freely from one side to another'. Tariffs on locally produced goods would be removed progressively. Self-governance on both sides of the LoC would be ensured. 'The essential prerequisite', however, 'was an end to hostility, violence and terrorism', after which 'military forces on both sides of the LoC would be kept to the minimum, particularly in populated areas'. The 'D' word—demilitarisation—found no mention anywhere in the final text'.[44]

International

There have been both international speculation on the back channel and mention of it in official memoirs. I will mention a few.

William J. Burns, a distinguished diplomat, a former undersecretary of state, then deputy secretary of state and, now director of the CIA, had extensive interactions with India in his two roles in the department of state. He wrote in his book:[45]

The Indians had no interest in opening up much with us about their relations with Pakistanis. Active back-channel talks between them had nearly brought about a breakthrough over Kashmir and other disputes in the spring of 2007, but the collapsing political position of Pakistan president Pervez Musharraf had brought them to an abrupt halt, and they had made no more than fitful progress since then. We were increasingly worried about the risks of nuclear confrontation, but the Indians were not much interested in talking about their perceptions or how to avoid escalation, let alone any American mediation role.[46]

In a fourteen-page article, he wrote that the two sides had 'come to semicolons' in their negotiations, which could not be signed as Musharraf had become politically weak. Giving details, he elaborated,

> For several years, special envoys from Pakistan and India had been holding talks in hotel rooms in Bangkok, Dubai and London. Musharraf and Manmohan Singh, the Prime Minister of India, had encouraged the negotiators to seek what some involved called a 'paradigm shift' in relations between the two nations. The two principal envoys—for Pakistan, a college classmate of Musharraf's named Tariq Aziz, and, for India, a Russia specialist named Satinder Lambah—were developing what diplomats refer to as a 'non-paper' on Kashmir, a text without names or signatures which can serve as a deniable but detailed basis for a deal.[47]
>
> Negotiators involved in the secret back channel regarded the effort as politically risky and exceptionally ambitious—a potential turning point in history, as one official put it, comparable to the peace forged between Germany and France after the Second World War. At issue, they believed, was not just a settlement in Kashmir itself but an end to their debilitating covert wars and, eventually, their paranoiac mutual suspicions. They hoped to develop a new regime of free trade and political cooperation in the region, from Central Asia to Bangladesh. On January 8, 2007, at the height of this optimistic interval, Manmohan Singh remarked

in public, 'I dream of a day, while retaining our respective national identities, one can have breakfast in Amritsar, lunch in Lahore, and dinner in Kabul.'[48]

At around the same time, Joby Warrick wrote in the *Washington Post*, 22 February 2009:

> India and Pakistan engaged in three years of secret, high-level talks that narrowly missed achieving a historic breakthrough in the countries' decades-old conflict over Kashmir.[49]

In the *Financial Times* of 29 May 2007, Farhan Bokhari and Jo Johnson commented,

> The outlines of a possible deal have started to filter into the public domain. It has five elements: no change in the territorial layout of Kashmir, currently divided into Pakistan and Indian areas; the creation of a 'soft border' across the LoC; greater autonomy and self-governance within both Indian and Pakistan-controlled parts of the state; across-LoC consultative mechanism; and, finally, the demilitarization of Kashmir at a pace determined by the decline in the cross-border terrorism.[50]

Conclusion

As I look back on nearly a decade of negotiations, especially the first phase, I can think of three ingredients for the success of back-channel negotiations.

1. Mutual trust and understanding between negotiators, as also the ability to understand the mind of the interlocutor.

2. Access of negotiators to, and complete confidence of, the top
    leadership, which enables quick responses, detailed homework
    and complete confidentiality.
3. Discussions are more open than in official channels as there is
    no written record of discussions.

Since Independence, there have been several initiatives and
moments of hope of a settlement between India and Pakistan. This
one, perhaps, came the closest. Several factors aligned themselves
to create the circumstances that were conducive to the process.
Dr Manmohan Singh's determination, wisdom and patience were
key drivers. The process drew strength from the fact that it built
upon the initiative that Dr Singh's predecessor, PM Vajpayee, had
launched. As it also happens, developments external to the process
can close the window of opportunity—at least temporarily.

We would never know—at least not now—what would have
followed the signing of the agreement and if it would have endured
over time. It is possible that it would have turned the course of
history for our two countries and the region. That possibility still
exists and the principles and the text of the draft agreement are
still there to be taken up whenever the two sides feel the need to
resume the process. Or, they can start afresh with new guidelines
and parameters, but with the same objective—to seek permanent
peace between two neighbours.

10

The Choice at the Crossroads and the Way Forward

The winding course of relations between India and Pakistan has seen wars, terrorist violence, sharp hostilities and diplomatic duels, but also moments of hope and periods of cooperation and amicable relationships. As I have sought to bring out in this book, successive Indian prime ministers and generations of leaders in India, and often in Pakistan, have sought to resolve disputes, reconcile differences and establish durable peace. For, beyond the rhetoric, there is an acute awareness that no country's destiny is immune from its relationships with neighbours.

Today, we are at a point where the prospects for dialogue, engagement and a broader peace process have never seemed so distant. Pakistan's sustained hostility, and the political, security, diplomatic and, above all, human and psychological costs it has imposed on India are hard to ignore. Here, too, India–Pakistan hostilities are deeply enmeshed in domestic politics and have become an instrument of political mobilization. We see each other principally through the prism of religion. The painful memories of Partition are being revived. The absence of contact and regular engagement is producing a new generation of youth in both countries unfamiliar with each other and with perceptions based on the media and social media. This can only harden positions and widen the gulf between the two countries. This would be a tragedy for two people that were once one and retain so much in common.

Peace and cooperation might seem elusive forever. But memories should not become perpetual shackles on shaping our future. The pain and loss we experience should not stop us from continually seeking a path to healing, however difficult and arduous it might seem. My life and my professional journey tell me that.

My Journey

My memories take me back to a moment in late August 1947. I had come away a few weeks earlier as a six-year-old with my grandfather to spend the summer vacation in the hills of Solan, when riots suddenly erupted all over undivided Punjab. With little prospect of returning to Peshawar, my hometown, my aunt sought admission for me in a school in Simla. Admission to this school was initially declined on the grounds that my aunt's address, with whom I was temporarily putting up then, could not be construed as being my address. It was perhaps then that the realization dawned upon me that I had become a displaced person within my own country without an address. This incident, I presume, might have played a defining role in shaping my attitude towards the need for peace and reconciliation between a divided people.

I have been in public service for close to half a century during which period I was fortunate enough to serve in various capacities and assignments in India and abroad. By a quirk of fate or mere coincidence, more than half of that service had to do with matters relating to Pakistan, either in a direct capacity or otherwise. In addition, I served in several other countries, which too had beginnings in turmoil and bloodshed. Most of these countries have come to terms with the emerging realities. They realize that unless there was a break from the past, prosperity would bypass them.

The first challenging assignment that came my way was to be a part of the advance guard tasked to open our embassy in the newly independent state of Bangladesh, immediately after it had gone through a bloody and brutal separation war with Pakistan, in early 1972. The popular sentiment of the time had driven ordinary men and women in Bangladesh to bay for the blood of those considered responsible for unleashing the reign of terror. However, it was the sagacity of leadership that held back a people hellbent on seeking justice on behalf of their compatriots who had fallen victim to terror. We too played a role in cooling the tempers. Today, Bangladesh—the poor and underdeveloped eastern wing—appears better off in most development indicators than its erstwhile better half western wing—Pakistan. In this success story, the central message emanating from it is that peace and reconciliation can pay dividends in the long run.

Years later, one could perceive and witness changes when I was ambassador to Hungary between 1986 and 1989. It will be recalled that the Soviets, on their part, had unleashed winds of change while they were embroiled in a bloody war in Afghanistan. In nearby Germany, a wall that had been a symbol of a divided people during the Cold War was pulled down. We were witnessing an era that the American political thinker Francis Fukuyama would describe as the *End of History*. Subsequently, as ambassador to unified Germany between 1995 and 1998, there was on display this inexorable spirit of reconciliation and rapprochement, which would weld and seamlessly put back together a divided country and its people.

As ambassador to Russia between 1998 and 2001, I saw how unrecognizable that country had become from the time I had previously served there, between 1965 and 1968, as a junior secretary.

The Intent, Purpose and Mechanics of Engagement

There are lessons learnt from the engagement process that could be recounted here. Engagement with Pakistan, or for that matter any other country, has an embedded combative element as both sides move towards obtaining greater advantage for their side. Even so, making a continuous effort is required to remind oneself that engagement is not a zero-sum game. For engagement to succeed, it is necessary and desirable that both sides keep the big picture in view of the advantages of a fair and mutually beneficial resolution and the likely impact such a resolution could have on people on both sides. Taking into account how the geopolitical imperatives of the region developed over time, the engagement process cannot be anything else but bilateral, so as to maximize mutually beneficial outcomes. In most contexts, it would appear advisable to draw up expectations from an engagement process in advance, which requires adequate planning, preparedness and a great deal of understanding of the other side's intent. As a fundamental change in attitude towards bilateral issues is unlikely to occur in the near future, expectations have to be accordingly pegged at a realistic level. At times, it may be prudent to send appropriate signals in regard to the expectations in order to sensitize the other side beforehand. Hence, there has to be much more focus on the preparation of the agenda, which should help in making engagement more directed and purposeful. It may also be important that the process of engagement is insulated from domestic and electoral compulsions so as to not interject into it unnecessary complications. It is almost an accepted norm of diplomacy that engagement should not be driven by personal preference; a rigorous analysis has therefore to precede the use of judgement and intuition in the decision-making process. There will be temptations to keep the engagement process at bay until there is restoration of regional stability. While responding appropriately to Pakistani covert operations targeted at India, the process of engagement need not be frozen.

Expectations at Independence

Three-quarters of a century has passed since the creation of Pakistan and the carving up of India on religious lines, in 1947. Despite Hindus and Muslims having fought shoulder to shoulder as one to get rid of the British yoke some ninety years earlier in 1857, in what has often been described as the first war of independence, the fault lines between the two somehow began to surface towards the end of World War I. This was the time when the struggle for freedom was picking up momentum. Although it may not be apt to place the blame entirely on the British for the creation of the fault lines, they, at the same time, cannot be absolved of their responsibility. As is widely recognized, the British took full advantage of these fault lines. This led to, perhaps, one of the most turbulent, brutal and bloody of partitions ever to take place in recorded history.

Even so, there was hope at Independence that with a bit of maturity, trust and goodwill on both sides, good sense would prevail, driving the two to resolve outstanding issues in a peaceful manner. However, that did not happen. While various explanations have been offered for the uneasy state of the relationship, there appears to be little common understanding on both sides of the divide as to the underlying causes or appreciation of the facts.

The purpose here is not to revisit these but to recount some of the major events that could possibly have had a bearing on this relationship and to explore the broad shape of possibilities that exist for the way forward.

Importing the Cold War into the Subcontinent

It has been argued that left to themselves, India and Pakistan could have resolved their differences, keeping in view bonds of a shared heritage, not all of which were bitter. However, in the aftermath of Partition, the Indo–Pak conflict of 1947–48 over Kashmir created a tailor-made opportunity for others to exploit to the detriment of the peoples on the two sides. As a consequence, the Cold War was imported into the subcontinent in 1953–54, with Pakistan being given military assistance on becoming a non-NATO ally of the United States. Nehru cautioned the Pakistan Prime Minister Mohammad Ali Bogra that such an alliance would have serious consequences for Indo–Pak relations, through his letter dated 10 November 1953: 'If such an [U.S.–Pak military] alliance takes place, Pakistan enters definitely into the region of Cold War. That means to us that the Cold War has come to the very frontiers of India . . . This is a matter of serious consequence to us, who have been trying to build an area of peace where there would be no war . . . All our problems will have to be seen in a new light.'[1]

Nehru wrote once again to Bogra on 9 December 1953:

> Our ways of approach to these international problems are different from those of the nations of Europe and America. But it is obvious that such an expansion of Pakistan's war resources, with the help of the United States of America, can only be looked upon as an unfriendly act in India and one that

is fraught with danger . . . Inevitably, it will affect the major questions that we are considering and, more especially, the Kashmir issue.[2]

One consequence of the U.S.–Pak Mutual Defence Assistance Agreement, signed in May 1954, was that it changed 'the whole context of the Kashmir issue'. Since the proposal for a plebiscite advanced by the United Nations was contingent on demilitarization in Kashmir, the military pact effectively scuttled the plebiscite proposal. The second was that overnight, a major transformation took place in Pakistan's military capability, enabling it to punch substantially above its weight. As a result, Pakistan's attitude on the Kashmir issue shifted visibly, which from then on became intransigent. Incidentally, at that time, the two prime ministers were engaged in serious negotiations on resolution of the Kashmir issue, but the altered atmospherics retarded progress. In the following years, military assistance to Pakistan continued to increase, with it becoming a member of SEATO in September 1954, although, ironically, it did not even form a geographical part of that regional grouping. A little later, it was made a member of the Baghdad Pact, later renamed CENTO.

As major powers realized Pakistan's extreme predilection and weakness, unfortunately, Kashmir came to be regarded as a sort of a quarry with which Pakistan's behaviour, responses and actions could be altered. Pakistan has separately acknowledged to the Soviets and the Chinese that the prime driver that made them join the U.S. military blocs was the Kashmir issue. Pakistan went to the extent of offering to switch sides if it were helped on the Kashmir issue. From the very beginning, Pakistan has chosen to align itself with one power or another in the hope that somehow, someday, it might be able to place itself in a position from where it could swing the balance on Kashmir in its favour.

Pakistan has had to face the increasing influence of China, which, too, has managed to place itself in a position from where it can play its cards deftly. Like the U.S.–Pak relationship, the Sino–Pak relationship has been carefully crafted around Pakistan's insecurities and ambitions bordering on unrealistic geopolitical aims, which lend themselves to easy exploitation. Legitimate questions are being asked about the motives of these parties. A mention has been made in this chapter of instances of third-party intervention, which led to the derailment of the resolution process on Kashmir. Both sides need to acknowledge and take cognizance of this ground reality.

With Pakistan playing the role of a facilitator in the Sino–U.S. rapprochement (1971), the dynamics of the Cold War began once again to change in its favour, which continued to adversely impact Indo–Pak relations. Soon thereafter, it would lead to Pakistan being declared a frontline state to manage the war on Soviet troops in Afghanistan on behalf of the U.S. CIA. This was no ordinary war, but a holy war, entailing the radicalization of large sections of society in Afghanistan and to a somewhat lesser degree in Pakistan, through the madrasa route. Perhaps, President Ziaul Haq did not flinch in sparing the army personnel from being sensitized to Sunni Islamic fundamentalism. The Australian journalist, writer and filmmaker John Pilger and others like him believe that the West has deployed religious extremism against its adversaries, from time to time. The uniqueness of the victory over the Soviets was that it was achieved with no loss of American life, although it is estimated that over 1 million Afghans, mostly civilians, and some Pakistanis perished during the decade of fighting in the 1980s.

The significance of the defeat of the Soviets at the hands of the U.S.–Pak-assisted Mujahideen is that it gave the Pakistani establishment under President Ziaul Haq a new sense of belief and confidence in itself that the feat in Afghanistan could be replicated, to begin with, in Kashmir. From then onwards, Pakistan quickly reshaped its geostrategic objectives for its grand design in the region. As a first step, through a covert action it created conditions resulting in the exodus of more or less the entire Hindu population from Kashmir in 1989–90. Significantly, Pakistani machinations took place in Kashmir at a time when India and Pakistan had been engaged in back-channel talks at the instance of Rajiv Gandhi during the second half of the 1980s.

An Attempt at Understanding the Mind of Pakistan

It is not the easiest of tasks to attempt a pen portrait of the mental makeup of Pakistan, from an Indian perspective. To begin with, it is a state carved out of a state in the belief it was different from the rest of the country and ought to have a separate existence. Religion, which formed an integral part of its being, could not prevent its breakup. From that time onwards, as Pakistan's insecurities increased, its willingness to serve the interests of major powers also increased proportionately. Its big chance came in 1979 when it was required to manage a holy war in Afghanistan. The actions and steps became possible because after Jinnah, the army in Pakistan has been in power either directly or indirectly, and decision-making of this nature requires absolute power. That this absolute power of the army has remained unchallenged all these years is clearly on account of Pakistan's weak polity. That is so because it has managed to keep itself insulated from most key socio-economic reforms, including land reforms.

As a natural corollary, religious parties and radical groups have been expanding their base and influence, mostly with the aid and advice of the army–ISI combine, which has been termed by Husain Haqqani, a former Pakistan ambassador to the U.S., as an 'unholy alliance'.[3] The religious and radical groups have never been inclined towards improved relations with India for religious and historical reasons. The influence of such parties and groups over the Army–ISI combine was bound to increase through the process of reverse osmosis.

When dealing with Pakistan, it has to be borne in mind that it is a very different country from the one it was before President Zia took over in 1977. The country and its people have been sufficiently radicalized. Like radicalized people elsewhere, Pakistanis tend to view differences through the prism of religious dogma. And, above all, Pakistan's actions and responses, more often than not, appear to stem from a running sore left behind by the wounds of separation from Bangladesh. Ever since, Pakistan has been baying for vengeance. A fundamental change in the attitude of the Pakistani Army–ISI combine towards India is not very likely. Consequently, expectations have to be kept at a realistic level and policies have to be structured to manage the relationship.

Currently, the key issue could be to ensure respect for a ceasefire along the Line of Control and the international border, and disavowal by Pakistan of the use of terrorism and use of its territory by non-state actors. In dealing with India, Pakistan is often not alone, for it has counted on support from the United States, Saudi Arabia and China. In particular, China has, by its all-encompassing engagement with Pakistan, manoeuvred itself into Kashmir through the agreement on the Sino–Pak boundary, west of the Karakoram Pass, entered into nearly fifty years ago; the subsequent building of the Karakoram Highway through this territory, and currently through the CPEC (China–Pakistan Economic Corridor).

It is not a mere coincidence that the army's march to power came to be formalized in 1954 after Pakistan became an ally of the United States. It is from this point onwards that the role of the Pakistani Army as a stakeholder in the governance of the country was firmly established and acknowledged, as mentioned in Chapter 1. Since then the army's power and influence have not waned but on the contrary increased by the day, with the nuclear and missile facilities coming solely under its control. In addition, the Pakistan Army guarantees the personal safety of the royal families of Saudi Arabia and Oman through the deployment of Pakistani regulars and irregulars. The army finds itself firmly established as the centre of power in Pakistan, for it has the capability to remotely control the political situation from behind the scenes. This makes it the number one political broker with a veto on issues of national importance. Countries that successfully transact business with Pakistan understand and acknowledge this reality. As Pakistan has come to have multiple centres of power, the position of its prime minister remains relatively weak and cannot be equated to that of the Indian prime minister. Therefore, it is both expedient and essential to keep the Pakistani Army on board while engaging with Pakistan.

Historically, India and Pakistan have been successful in concluding agreements, treaties et al., when the Pakistan Army has been very much in the picture. Starting in 1958–60, during the tenure of President Ayub Khan, boundary disputes relating to the borders of the states of Assam, Punjab, West Bengal and the then union territory of Tripura were resolved. Again, in 1961, when Ayub Khan was in power, the Indo–Pak Indus Water Treaty was signed. In June 1965, when Ayub was once again in power, the dispute relating to the Rann of Kutch was resolved.

In Chapter 3 it has been narrated that with President Zia's blessings, the intelligence chiefs of the two sides had finalized an agreement on the LoC and even exchanged maps in that regard, but on his sudden death, these papers did not surface in Pakistan. Even the back channel has succeeded when the Pakistan Army is either in power or in a position to have a say in the matter, as borne out by the broad understanding arrived at on managing the Kashmir issue.

It needs to be appreciated that the Pakistan Army has been successful in projecting itself as a proxy for the will of the people of that country, in the absence of robust democratic institutions. The situation seems to be suiting its benefactors as well, who know which channel has to be tapped and when. India finds itself in an awkward position because it has not yet grasped the art of fully tapping the army channel, and to that extent, is at a disadvantage. To be fair, the Pakistan Army has, on its part, shown a certain degree of reluctance in dealing directly with India when all along it has not shied away from doing business with others, whether it has been directly in power or indirectly. It is not clear why the Pakistan Army has reserved this reticence for dealing with the Indians. This has been interpreted in different ways, leading to speculation that the Pakistan Army would like to keep the Kashmir pot on the boil to reinforce its raison d'être as the power of last resort. The answer may perhaps lie in the fact that sufficient effort has not been put in by both sides to mutually engage each other. Efforts could be increased to reach out to the Pakistan Army as other major countries do.

Complementing Official Engagement Channels

Back-channel engagement is known to play a positive role in complementing efforts through official channels, especially when these may show signs of blockages. The back channel operates on the underlying assumption that an actual or potential conflict can be managed and even resolved by appealing to common human capabilities to respond in goodwill and reasonableness. Solutions derived away from public view or otherwise can be explored without the requirements of formal negotiation or bargaining for advantage. Accordingly, it can lead to improved communication and a better understanding of each other's point of view. It played a key role in arriving at a resolution, as in the case of the Sino–U.S. relations.

Nearer home, it came quite close to a resolution on managing the Kashmir issue during which period the added benefit was a relatively quiet Indo–Pak border. In addition, there is Track II diplomacy concerning non-governmental, informal and unofficial contacts and activities between private citizens or groups of individuals, sometimes called 'non-state actors'. Track II aims at improved communication and a better understanding of each other's point of view, especially when a secondary, unofficial venue is needed to explore new and challenging possibilities. Track II diplomacy attracted attention when the Neemrana dialogue was initiated under the auspices of the United States Information Service sometime in 1990. Internal and external funding led to its significant growth. Track II is reported to have played a part during the Kargil conflict and in the aftermath of the 2008 Mumbai terror attacks. With the freezing of official channels after the Pulwama attack in February 2019, it was expected that Track II would play a more supporting role. This channel of communication could be further strengthened, preferably without external support.

On Widening and Deepening the Engagement Process

Engagement has to be all-encompassing. Economic, commercial and technological content, which are known to act as force multipliers, have to be accordingly built into it. Gradually, economic and commercial dimensions have to pave the way for collaboration in scientific and technological areas. The ultimate steps are in working together in dual-purpose technologies, such as data analytics, artificial intelligence and robotics, especially those relating to defence and peaceful uses of nuclear and space technologies. The Australia, UK and U.S. partnership (AUKUS) is a case in point in which people with a common bloodline have eventually got together for retaining a competitive edge in technology.

India and Pakistan too have to plan for the long-term and could think in terms of coming together to form partnerships in several areas of mutual interest and concern. To begin with, some steps could be taken through the SAARC initiative. It will be recalled in Chapter 3 that Benazir Bhutto had considered it expedient to take the economic engagement process forward through the SAARC route. There is so much that the two sides, who possibly share a common bloodline, can achieve through meaningful partnerships.

The Way Forward

A purposeful engagement directed towards attainment of realistic outcomes appears to be an option with a reasonable chance of success, if handled with care on both sides. At the outset, it needs to be recognized that Pakistan continues to be vague about its expectations on the Kashmir issue. Plebiscite in Kashmir, which Pakistan now supports after having rejected it in the past on different occasions, no longer appears a viable option. Moreover, with the creation of Bangladesh, the Indian subcontinent got further subdivided, with the addition of a third country, with each of them containing a Muslim population more or less equal in size. This geopolitical change altered Pakistan's preeminent position of being regarded as the representative of the Muslim voice of the subcontinent. Pakistan also knows it. Moreover, Zulfikar Bhutto had made it amply clear on the floor of the Pakistan Assembly on 14 July 1972 that the UNSC resolutions had asked Pakistan to withdraw all its troops (from Kashmir), while India was asked to withdraw only the 'bulk' of its forces. He added, 'That was the day, that was the moment when you jeopardized the right of self-determination in Jammu & Kashmir.' In 1963, Pakistan went to the extent of unilaterally changing the boundaries of Kashmir in a questionable agreement with China, and, as a result, imported China into Indo–Pak differences. Much water has flowed since then making plebiscite irrelevant.

A mutually agreed template for an overall understanding on managing the Kashmir issue exists, the broad outlines of which have been given in Chapter 9. It could not be taken forward for want of implementation on the ground and remains an unfinished agenda of the negotiation process between the two sides. It can be taken forward with or without modifications as considered necessary. Alternatively, it is possible to explore other viable options, as possibilities for resolution are unlimited. Since the Pakistan Army is an accepted stakeholder in affairs relating to that country, it would appear prudent that they are taken on board. Likewise, it would be appropriate in India to keep the Opposition fully informed of the happenings. Such steps would not only help facilitate the engagement process but might also help increase the level of acceptability of a resolution, were any to be arrived at.

Engagement as an Accepted Essential Tool of Diplomacy

Global experience reveals that engagement is regarded as an accepted essential tool of diplomacy. Even overtly inimical countries resort to it. Straight after the Bandung Conference of 1955, the U.S. and the People's Republic of China (PRC) engaged each other through their ambassadors to Switzerland and subsequently through their ambassadors to Poland, covering a wide range of issues. It was in one of these exchanges between the ambassadors of the two sides in June 1962 that the U.S. Ambassador John Cabot informed his Chinese counterpart, Wang Ping-nan, that he had been 'authorized to state that the US Government had no intention of supporting any Government of the Republic of China/GRC [Taiwan] attack on the Mainland [PRC] under existing circumstances', and that the GRC [Taiwan] was 'committed not to attack without [U.S.] consent'. Wang was so puzzled by the U.S. assurance that he made Cabot repeat it three times.[4] The U.S. at that time recognized not the PRC but the government in Taiwan. Then, there are innumerable instances of how the U.S. and the Soviet Union engaged each other during the forty-five years of the Cold War. The engagement prevented any direct military confrontation between the two sides, except during the Cuban Missile Crisis when there was a standoff between the two sides. Coming to more recent times, this is what the former German Chancellor Angela Merkel had to say on engagement during her visit to Moscow in August 2020:

> I want to say that over the past sixteen years I have been to Russia sixteen times, which is to say, I was open to contacts. Talks between us have not always been easy. There has been a lot of debate and controversy around them including on the international stage, but I always sought compromises. I think there is no alternative, at least no reasonable one to dialogue and the exchange of opinion. This invariably requires a lot of work. Everything could have been a lot easier, but our dialogue should continue. I have no doubt about this . . . All these differences notwithstanding, we have always managed to keep the negotiating channel open. I hope I have managed to contribute to this. I will always say that a failure to maintain dialogue is a poor choice.

The balance of advantage lies in keeping the engagement process in motion. We need to intensify and sustain engagement with all our neighbours. It does not necessarily imply agreement. It may not lead to the desired response nor does it guarantee success. However, it helps to discover convergences and differences in a relationship. It helps to understand each other's intent. Absence of engagement is not an option. Today China and the U.S. seek ways and means to maintain channels of communication, even at times of strain, especially between their militaries. For all these differences they pursue sanctions against Iran; P5 + 1 countries have not abandoned the prospects of engagement with Iran. Engagement is a necessity.

Our critical engagements are with China and Pakistan, the two neighbours. Time and again in the past we have reached out to Pakistan for dialogue to reduce tensions, resolve outstanding issues, foster friendship and build cooperation. There have been periods of crisis, but also moments of hope. This sense of cynicism about dialogue with each other is understandable. Pakistan's polity is relatively not as robust, and its interest in peace at this stage is uncertain. We can defend ourselves against hostility but instability in the neighbourhood can have unanticipated consequences. Not engaging a neighbour with a strong antagonism towards India, a growing nuclear weapons arsenal and worsening stability, is not a wise choice.

This has become especially important in the context of a rapidly transforming global and regional order. We see that visibly in our immediate neighbourhood, and the broader Indo-Pacific region. The period of transition from the old to the new creates a phase of flux and uncertainties. This is a time when countries examine existing assumptions and foundations of their policies and make adjustments and sometimes bold changes in their strategies. It may lead to conflicts, as we see in Europe once again, or in the tense situation in East Asia, or an unimaginable rapprochement, as in the Gulf region, between Arab countries and Israel. This is also a time for us in South Asia to reimagine our region as one of peace and cooperation.

Notes

Chapter 1: Pakistan: Evolution of a Military State

1. The English translation of this interview is available in *Covert Magazine* (1 November 2009). Details also in *Communalism Combat* (January 2010) and M.J. Akbar's book *Tinder Box*.
2. Ibid.
3. Alan Campbell Johnson, *Mission with Mountbatten* 2nd ed. (London: Robert Hale Ltd, 1972), p. 87, quoted from *The Struggle for Pakistan*, Ayesha Jalal, p. 3.
4. Ayesha Jalal, *The Struggle for Pakistan* (Belknap Press, Harvard University Press, 2014), p. 3.
5. Altaf Gauhar, *Ayub Khan: Pakistan's First Military Ruler* (Oxford University Press, 1996), p. 340. This was Ayub Khan's farewell address to his ministers, and after this the author writes, 'The atmosphere was that of a funeral service. And as soon as the ritual finishes everyone left quietly without saying a word.'
6. Sirdar Shaukat Hyat Khan, *The Nation that Lost Its Soul* (Lahore: Jung Publishers, 1995), p. 313.
7. A.A.K. Niazi, *The Betrayal of East Pakistan* (Karachi: Oxford University Press, 1998).

8. 'Tikka Khan', https://en.wikipedia.org/wiki/Tikka_Khan (last accessed 31 October 2022).

9. Sirdar Shaukat Hyat Khan, *The Nation that Lost Its Soul*, p. 316.

10. Sirdar Shaukat Hyat Khan, foreword to *The Nation that Lost Its Soul.*

11. Siddiq Salik, *Witness to Surrender* (Karachi: Oxford University Press), p. 3.

12. Ibid., p. 7.

13. Ibid., p. 95.

14. Ibid., p. 290.

15. Ibid., p. 298.

16. Gul Hassan Khan, *Memoirs of Lt Gen. Gul Hassan Khan: The Last Commander-In-Chief of the Pakistan Army*, (Oxford University Press, 1993).

17. Sirdar Shaukat Hyat Khan, *The Nation that Lost Its Soul*, p. 316.

18. Siddiq Salik, *Witness to Surrender*, p. 77.

19. Ibid., p. 213.

20. Stephen P. Cohen, *The Pakistan Army* (California: University of California Press, 1984), p. 39.

21. Ibid. p. 86.

22. Ibid., p. 95.

23. Farzana Shaikh, *Making Sense of Pakistan* (London: Hurst & Company, 2009) pp. 154–56.

24. Ibid.

25. Ayesha Siddiqa, *Military Inc. Inside Pakistan's Military Economy* (England, Pluto Press, 2016).

26. Stephen P. Cohen, *The Pakistan Army*, p. 121.

27. Christina Lamb, *Waiting for Allah: Pakistan's Struggle for Democracy* (London: Hamish Hamilton, 1991), p. 170. The rise of the drug trade created a parallel economy and another power centre in Pakistan.

28. S.K. Datta and Rajeev Sharma. *Pakistan from Jinnah to Jehad*, (New Delhi: UBS Publishers' Distributors Ltd, 2003), p. 177.

29. *Daily Mashriq*, Peshawar, 14 January 2001. In the 1990s the official figure was between 3 to 5 million addicts. Of these, 2 million were heroin users in Pakistan. In 1995, Charles Cogan, a former CIA director of Afghan operations, admitted the CIA had indeed sacrificed the drug war to fight the Cold War. *Journal of Kashmir Studies*, Volume I, No. 1, 2006, Centre for Kashmir Studies, Srinagar.

30. Morrice James (Lord Saint Brides), *Pakistan Chronicle*, (London: Palgrave Macmillan, 1993), p. 220.

31. Stephen P. Cohen, *The Pakistan Army*, p. 115.

32. Shalini Chawla, *Pakistan's Military and Its Strategy* (New Delhi: KW Publishers 2009), p. 5.

33. Stephen P. Cohen *The Pakistan Army*, p. 165.

34. S.K. Datta and Rajeev Sharma, *Pakistan from Jinnah to Jehad*, pp. 109–10.

35. Ibid. The authors quote Lt General Faiz Ali Chishti's *Betrayals Of Another Kind: Islam, Democracy And The Army In Pakistan* (London: Asia Publishing House, 1989), pp. 90–91.

36. Nilima Lambah, *A Life across Three Continents—Recollections of a Diplomat's Wife* (Mumbai: Lotus, 2008), p. 38.

37. 'Pakistan: The Dangers Of Conventional Wisdom', ICG Asia Briefing Paper, 12 March 2002. See https://www.refworld.org/pdfid/3de777b64.pdf.

38. '1990 Election Was Rigged, Rules SC', *Dawn* (19 October 2012).

39. European Foundation for South Asian Studies (EFSAS), 'Did US Gratitude for Afghanistan and the ISI's Dire Need for Fresh Terrorist Faces in J&K Precipitate the Release of Omar Sheikh?' (3 April 2020).

40. Ahmed Rashid, *Pakistan on the Brink*, (London: Penguin Books, 2012), pp. 184–85.

41. Altaf Gauhar, *Ayub Khan: Pakistan's first Military Ruler* (Lahore: Sang-e-Meel Publications, 1998), p. 167.
42. Bruce Riedel, *Avoiding Armageddon: America, India, and Pakistan to the Brink and Back* (Washington, D.C.: Brookings Institution Press, 2013). Also, Bruce Riedel 'Soviet, Afghanistan, and Kashmir', *News International* (17 August 2021), https://www.thenews.com.pk/print/879147-soviet-afghanistan-and-kashmir (last accessed 2 November 2022).
43. Bob Woodward, *Obama's Wars* (New York: Simon and Schuster, 2010), p. 89.
44. Ahmed Rashid, 'Why Sectarianism Is Tearing Muslim Societies Apart', *Financial Times* (23 August 2013).
45. Wikipedia on Ramzi Yousef, https://en.wikipedia.org/wiki/Ramzi_Yousef (last accessed 3 November 2022).
46. Zahid Hussain, 'Pakistan Gets Yemeni Man Wanted in USS Cole Attack', *Wall Street Journal* (20 April 2011).
47. 'Terror Suspect in Bali Bombings Caught in Pakistan', NDTV (30 March 2011).
48. EFSAS, 'London Bridge Attack 2019: Three out of Four Terror Plots in the UK Have Roots in Pakistan' (7 January 2020).
49. 'ICE Deports Pakistani Man Investigated during the Failed Times Square Bombing', U.S. Immigration and Customs Enforcement, 21 May 2011, https://www.ice.gov/news/releases/ice-deports-pakistani-man-investigated-during-failed-times-square-bombing (last accessed 3 November 2022).
50. Wikipedia on Madrassas in Pakistan, https://en.wikipedia.org/wiki/Madrassas_in_Pakistan.
51. Salman Hussein, *Friday Times,* Lahore (24–20 December 2001): 5, quoted by S.K. Datta and Rajeev Sharma, *Pakistan from Jinnah to Jehad*, p. 216.

52. Gauhar, Altaf. *Ayub Khan: Pakistan's first Military Ruler*, p. 167.

53. Wikipedia, 'Inter-Services Intelligence Activities in Afghanistan', https://en.wikipedia.org/wiki/Inter-Services_Intelligence_activities_in_Afghanistan (last accessed 3 November 2022).

54. Aarish Ullah Khan, 'Terrorist Threat and the Policy Response in Pakistan', SIPRI (Stockholm International Peace Research Institute), Paper No. 11, September 2005.

55. 'Pakistan Home to 12 Foreign Terrorist Organizations', Congressional Research Service Report, Washington, 18 October 2021.

56. Akbar S. Ahmed in his lecture, 'Identity and Ethnicity', as mentioned in Ian Talbot's 'Pakistan—A Modern History', in S.K. Datta and Rajeev Sharma, *Pakistan from Jinnah to Jehad*, p. 274.

57. Lawrence Ziring, *Pakistan at the Crosscurrent of History*, (Manas Publications, 2009), p. 248.

58. Morrice James (Lord Saint Brides), *Pakistan Chronicle*.

59. Maria Abi-Abid and Zia-ur Rehman, 'Poor and Desperate Hindus Accept Islam to Get By', *New York Times* (4 August 2020); Census, *Dawn* (19 May 2021).

60. Farzana Shaikh, *Making Sense of Pakistan*, pp. 182–85.

61. A.S. Bhasin, *India and Pakistan: Neighbours at Odds* (New Delhi: Bloomsbury, 2018) p. 341.

62. Ahmed Rashid, *Pakistan on the Brink*, p. 47.

63. S.K. Datta and Rajeev Sharma, '*Pakistan from Jinnah to Jehad*', p. 55.

64. Larry Collins and Dominique Lapierre, *Freedom at Midnight* (New: Delhi: Vikas Publishing House), p. 221; S.K. Datta and Rajeev Sharma, *Pakistan from Jinnah to Jehad*.

65. Farzana Shaikh, *Making Sense of Pakistan* (Foundation Book, Cambridge University Press, 2009), p. 247.

66. Nilima Lambah, *A Life across Three Continents—Recollections of a Diplomat's Wife*, pp. 152–53.

67. S.K. Datta and Rajeev Sharma, preface to *Pakistan from Jinnah to Jehad*, p. viii.

68. S.K. Datta and Rajeev Sharma, *Pakistan from Jinnah to Jehad*, p. 74.

69. Naseem Ahmed, 'Military and Foreign Policy of Pakistan', *South Asian Survey 17:2* (2010): 313–30, Sage Publications.

70. Stephen P. Cohen, *The Idea of Pakistan* (Washington, D.C.: Brookings Institution Press, 2006), p. 61.

71. Umair Javed, *Dawn* (26 September 2016).

72. Stephen P. Cohen, *The Pakistan Army*, (Oxford: Oxford University Press, 1998), p. 170.

73. Ibid., p. 105.; Stephen P. Cohen, 'Pakistan: Army, Society, and Security'. *Asian Affairs*, vol. 10, no. 2, 1983, http://www.jstor.org/stable/30172969.

74. *Daily Times*, 28 July 2008, and *News International*, 28 July 2008, where there is an article by Hamid Mir on how the decision was reversed so soon.

75. Sharat Sabharwal, *India's Pakistan Conundrum: Managing a Complex Relationship* (India: Routledge, Taylor & Francis Group, 2022), chapter 12.

76. Stephen P. Cohen, *The Pakistan Army*, p. 173.

77. Vinod Sharma, *Hindustan Times* digital platform, 7 May 2021.

Chapter 2: Bangladesh to Siachen: Military Wins and Peace Offers

1. Sisir Gupta, 'Kashmir: A Study of India–Pakistan Relations', https://archive.org/stream/in.ernet.dli.2015.113993/2015.113993, last accessed 6 November 2022.

2. Ibid.

3. Ibid.

4. Jawaharlal Nehru, *Selected Works*, Vol. 36, https://archive. org/stream/HindSwaraj-Nehru-SW2-36/nehru.sw2.vol.s36_ djvu.txt, last accessed 6 November 2022.

5. B.K. Nehru, *Nice Guys Finish Second* (Viking Books, 1997), pp. 426–27.

6. Pravin Sawhney, 'Step Forward, or Backward' (28 August 2014) *Daily Pioneer*, https://www.dailypioneer.com/2014/ columnists/step-forward-or-backward.html, last accessed 6 November 2022.

7. Reference statement in Lok Sabha, 16 December 1971.

8. Statement in Parliament, 17 December 1971.
   The Years of Endeavour: Selected Speeches of Indira Gandhi, August 1969-August 1972, Volume 2 (Publications Division, Ministry of Information and Broadcasting, Government of India, 1975).

9. Interview with *Time* correspondent William Steward, 3 January 1972.

10. Indira Gandhi speech, 10 January 1972.

11. Joint Declaration issued at the end of the visit of the Prime Minister of India Mrs. Indira Gandhi to Bangladesh, Dacca, 19 March 1972, https://www.hcidhaka.gov.in/pdf/bi_doc/ 5.doc

12. O.P. Khanna (ed.), *The Competition Master*, Vol 21, no, 8, https://archive.org/stream/in.ernet.dli.2015.110329/2015. 110329.The-Competition-Master-Vol21no8-12mar-july1980_djvu.txt

13. Indo–French Declaration, 27 January 1980. https://mealib. nic.in/?2508?000.

14. Statement in Rajya Sabha, 4 May 1981.

15. Maharaja Krishna Rasgotra, *A Life in Diplomacy* (India: Penguin Books, 2016), p. 324.

16. Zulfikar A Khan, 'Geopolitics of the Siachen Glacier', *Asian Defence Journal*, November (1985): 44–50.
17. Nilima Lambah *A Life across Three Continents. Recollections of Diplomat's Wife*, p. 53.
18. 'Zia Says Talks with Gandhi Helpful', *Washington Post*, 5 November 1984. https://www.washingtonpost.com/archive/politics/1984/11/05/zia-says-talks-with-gandhi-helpful/1cb65232-d768-49d3-a997-ecd7bc2cc4c5/

Chapter 3: A Fresh Start Cut Short

1. 'Charter of the South Asian Association for Regional Cooperation', https://training.itcilo.org/actrav_cdrom1/english/global/blokit/saarcc.htm, last accessed 8 November 2022.
2. Rahimullah Yousufzai, 'Gandhi Visits Peshawar to Honour Khan', UPI, 20 January 1988, https://www.upi.com/Archives/1988/01/20/Gandhi-visits-Peshawar-to-honor-Khan/5738569653200/, last accessed 8 November 2022.
3. Lok Sabha Proceeding, 20 April 1988.
4. A.S. Bhasin, *India and Pakistan: Neighbours at Odds*, p. 317.
5. A.K. Verma, 'When Humid Gul Offered Peace', *The Hindu*, 28 August 2015.

Chapter 4: Deft Handling Amidst Surging Challenges

1. Ramamohan Rao, 'Narasimha Rao Won India Economic Freedom in 1991, Says Sanjaya Baru', ANI, 6 October 2016, https://aninews.in/news/national/politics/narasimha-rao-won-india-economic-freedom-in-1991-says-sanjaya-baru/?amp=1, last accessed 12 November 2022.
2. Transcript of Parliament, Link: https://parliamentofindia.nic.in/ls/lsdeb/ls10/ses1/0218099107.htm, last accessed 12 November 2022.

3. F.S. Aijazuddin, 'The Dialect of Death', *Dawn*, June 2020.
4. M.G. Chitkara, *Benazir: A Profile* (New Delhi: APH Publishing Corporation, 1996), p. 44.
5. Robert G. Wirsing, *India, Pakistan and the Kashmir Dispute* (London: Macmillan, 1994); Irfan Waheed Usmani, *Bleeding Wound: Analyzing Pakistan's Kashmir Policy (1989–95)*, GC University, Lahore, Pakistan, https://www.academia. edu/385653/BLEEDING_WOUND_ANALYZING_ PAKISTAN_S_KASHMIR_POLICY.
6. Irfan Waheed Usmani, *Bleeding Wound: Analyzing Pakistan's Kashmir Policy (1989–95)*.
7. 'Who Is Syed Salahuddin and Why Is He Designated as a "Global Terrorist"?', *The Hindu*, 27 June 2017.
8. Victoria Schofield's interview with Azam Inquilabi, Islamabad 25 March 1994, cited in Schofield, Kashmir at Crossroads, p. 155.
9. *The Historian*, vol 7, no.1, Department of History, GC University, Lahore, Pakistan, https://www.scribd.com/ document/44946222/The-Historian-2009-1
10. Irfan Waheed Usmani, *Bleeding Wound: Analyzing Pakistan's Kashmir Policy*.
11. 'In New White House Contest, Kashmir as Old Debate Is Back', *Kashmir Observer*, 23 October 2020, https:// kashmirobserver.net/2020/10/23/in-new-white-house-contest-kashmir-as-old-debate-is-back/, last accessed 12 November 2022.
12. Nilima Lambah, *A Life across Three Continents: Recollections of a Diplomat's Wife*.
13. G. Jayachandra Reddy, *Dynamics of India and China Relations: Implications for New World Order* (China: UGC Centre for Southeast Asian & Pacific Studies, Sri Venkateswara

University, 2016), p. 227, https://moam.info/india-and-china-relations_5c982a2c097c477c1b8b4658.html.

14. Ershad Mahmud, 'Post-Cold War US Kashmir Policy', p. 90.

15. Farzana Shakoor, Farzana Shakoor, 'Kashmir issue and US global objectives', *Pakistan Horizon*, July 1994, https://www.jstor.org/stable/41393488.

16. Irfan Waheed Usmani, *Bleeding Wound: Analyzing Pakistan's Kashmir Policy*.

17. Ibid.

18. Ibid.

19. Nilima Lambah, *A Life across Three Continents: Recollections of a Diplomat's Wife*.

20. V.R. Raghavan, *Siachen: Conflict Without End* (India: Viking, 2002), Chapter 2.

21. Josy Joseph, 'Siachen Tragedy Could Trigger Demilitarisation', *The Hindu*, 7 February 2016, https://www.thehindu.com/news/national/Siachen-tragedy-could-trigger-demilitarisation/article14066045.ece?homepage=true, last accessed 12 November 2022.

22. V.R. Raghavan, *Siachen: Conflict Without End*, pp. 150–51.

23. Vinay Sitapati, *Half Lion: How P.V. Narasimha Rao Transformed India* (India: Penguin Random House, 2016).

24. My South Block Years, UBSPD, New Delhi ,1996, as quoted by Lt Gen. Raghavan in *Siachen: Conflict Without End*.

25. Peter Lyon, *Conflict between India and Pakistan*, https://vdoc.pub/documents/conflict-between-india-and-pakistan-an-encyclopedia-36n6r353gjog, last accessed 12 November 2022.

26. Editorial: 'Where is the moral high ground?', *Frontier Post*, 9 December 1992.

27. 'Pakistan reacts to Babri Masjid incident', *Friday Times*, p. 2 factfile, 10 December 1992.

28. PDA, 'NDA call rallies tomorrow', *Dawn*, p. 10 (10 December 2001).
29. Nilima Lambah, *A Life across Three Continents*, p. 125.
30. 'Shameful Incidents', *Dawn*, 13 December 1992.
31. Interview of Aakar Patel with Karan Thapar on the Wire Website, 30 December 2020, https://thewire.in/communalism/watch-karan-thapar-aakar-patel-hindutva-hindu-rashta-narendra-modi-anti-muslim.
32. Statements Made by Leaders on Muslims and Pakistan
    Union Minister Giriraj Singh: 'India paying price for not sending Muslims to Pakistan.' 'When our forefathers were fighting for Independence from British rule, Jinnah was pushing for the creation of an Islamic state.' 'Our forefathers, however, committed a mistake. Had they ensured that all our Muslim brothers were sent to Pakistan and Hindus brought here, the need for such a move [CAA] would not have arisen. This did not happen and we have paid a heavy price for it' (*Economic Times*, 21 February 2020, https://economictimes. indiatimes.com/news/politics-and-nation/india-paying-price-for-not-sending-muslims-to-pakistan-giriraj-singh/articleshow/74240863.cms.)
    Minister of State for Finance Anurag Thakur: '*Desh ke gaddaron ko, goli maaro saalon ko.*' (Scroll.In, 27 January 2020, https://scroll.in/video/951289/watch-anurag-thakur-minister-of-state-for-finance-lead-goli-maaro-saalon-ko-slogans-at-rally.)
    Karnataka BJP leader Renukacharya: 'There are few traitors who sit in a masjid and write fatwas. They collect weapons inside the mosque instead of praying. Is this why you want a Masjid. I will resort to such politics in my taluk where the money allotted for Muslims can be used for Hindus. I will put you [Muslims] in your place and show what politics is.' (*India*

Today, 21 January 2020, https://www.indiatoday.in/india/
story/karnataka-bjp-leader-renukacharya-targets-muslims-
caa-rally-remarks-1638686-2020-01-21.)

Suresh Tiwari, legislator from Deoria town in northern UP:
'Do not buy from Muslims.' 'Keep one thing in mind. I am
telling everyone openly. There is no need to buy vegetables from
"miyans" [Muslims].' (*Indian Express,* 29 April 2020, https://
indianexpress.com/article/india/coronavirus-no-one-should-
buy-vegetables-from-muslims-up-bjp-mla-6382120/.)

Yogi Adityanath, UP chief minister: 'In the name of dharna
and demonstration, if you raise slogans of azadi that were
once raised in Kashmir, it will come under sedition and the
government will take the harshest action.' (*The Hindu,* 29
January 2021, https://www.thehindu.com/news/national/
other-states/raising-azadi-slogans-amounts-to-sedition-says-
adityanath/article30627851.ece.)

BJP spokesperson G.V.L. Narasimha Rao: 'Congress party
conspiring with Pakistan to take revenge for its 2014 electoral
loss.' (*The Print,* 29 January 2021, https://theprint.in/
opinion/global-print/why-bjp-leaders-are-going-to-pakistan-
to-fight-2019-lok-sabha-polls/178503/.)

Gujarat BJP chief Jitu Vaghani to senior Congress leader
and MP from Gujarat Madhusudan Mistry: 'Go and live in
Pakistan.' (*The Print,* 16 January 2021, https://theprint.in/
opinion/global-print/why-bjp-leaders-are-going-to-pakistan-
to-fight-2019-lok-sabha-polls/178503/.)

Assam finance minister and BJP leader, Himanta Biswa Sarma:
'It was imperative to pass the Citizenship Bill [which gives
Indian citizenship to all non-Muslims who have taken refuge in
India from Afghanistan, Pakistan and Bangladesh], otherwise
Assam will go to the Jinnahs.' 'But Congress stand with
Pakistan. They know if Rafale comes to India then it [Pakistan]

cannot defeat India in air warfare. Therefore they are saying that India does not need Rafale.' (*The Print*, 16 January 2021, https://theprint.in/opinion/global-print/why-bjp-leaders-are-going-to-pakistan-to-fight-2019-lok-sabha-polls/178503/.) BJP deputy chief minister of Jammu and Kashmir, Kavinder Gupta: 'Shah Faesal, the 2010 IAS topper who quit the service last week to join politics may have got money from Pakistan.' (*The Print*, 16 January 2021, https://theprint.in/opinion/global-print/why-bjp-leaders-are-going-to-pakistan-to-fight-2019-lok-sabha-polls/178503/.)

33. The newspaper, *Pioneer*, in a report on 17 March 1993, under the heading 'Paying the Price' mentioned that the Indian High Commission had given prior notification to the Government of India.

34. *The Hindu*, 12 January 2021. External Affairs Minister points to delay in designating terrorist individuals, entities https://www.thehindu.com/news/national/mumbai-blasts-perpetrators-enjoying-5-star-hospitality-under-state-protection-says-jaishankar/article33560722.ece

35. A.S. Bhasin, *India and Pakistan: Neighbours at Odds*.

36. V.P. Dutt, *India's Foreign Policy in a Changing World* (India: Vikas Publishing House, https://archive.org/stream/in.ernet. dli.2015.131152/2015.131152.India-Foreign-Policy-In-A-Changing-World_djvu.txt, accessed 12 November 2022.

37. Joseph F. Pilat and Robert E. Pendley, *1995: A New Beginning for the NPT?* (Boston: Springer Science and Business Media, 2012), p. 109.

38. *Daily Excelsior*, 1 March 2014. A brilliant piece of shrewd statesmanship

39. A.S. Bhasin, *India and Pakistan: Neighbours at Odds*.

40. Manjeev Singh Puri, 'Why India needs to be on the 'rights' side of the United Nations', Dailyo, 26 May 2020.

41. Baqir Sajjad Syed, March 13 2020. Dawn Newspaper. Sustained efforts urged for settlement of Kashmir dispute

42. Sharat Sabharwal, *Law and Conflict Resolution in Kashmir* (India: Routledge, 2022), chapter 4, no. 6.

43. Suman Dubey, 'No war pact between Indian and Pakistan pushed out reach as Indian leaders spar', *India Today*, 11 October 2013.

44. S.K. Lambah, *The Unfortunate History of Gilgit-Baltistan since 1947*, New Delhi, Indian Council of World Affairs, 2018, https://www.icwa.in/showfile.php?lang=1&level=1&ls_id=2762&lid=1871, last accessed 13 November 2022.

45. Khurshid Mahmud Kasuri, *Neither a Hawk nor a Dove: An Insider's Account of Pakistan's Foreign Policy* (India: Penguin, 2015).

46. Pakistan Nuclear Chronology, NTI, https://media.nti.org/pdfs/pakistan_nuclear.pdf, accessed 13 November 2022.

47. https://www.nytimes.com/1993/07/25/world/pakistani-quoted-as-citing-nuclear-test-in-87.html

48. Khurshid Mahmud Kasuri, *Neither a Hawk nor a Dove: An Insider's Account of Pakistan's Foreign Policy*, pp. 90, 339–41.

49. Vinay Sitapati, 'Narasimha Rao, Not Vajpayee, Was the PM Who Set India on a Nuclear Explosion Path', Scroll.in, 1 July 2016, https://scroll.in/article/810874/narasimha-rao-not-vajpayee-was-the-pm-who-set-india-on-a-nuclear-explosion-path, last accessed 13 November 2022.

50. Vinay Sitapati, *Half Lion: How P.V. Narasimha Rao Transformed India*, pp. 279 and 292.

51. MEA Library. https://mealib.nic.in/?pdf2571?000

52. 'India's former prime minister Mr. Narasimha Rao's Statement: 50th Anniversary of the U.N.', 24 October 1995, https://pminewyork.gov.in/pdf/uploadpdf/43538lms46.pdf, last accessed 13 November 2022.

Chapter 5: Professional Engagement, Personal Interactions

1. Hashmat Ullah Khan, Dr Jamal Shah and Fida-ur Rahman, 'Ziaul Haq and the Rise of Religious Extremism in Pakistan', *Biannual Research Journal Grassroots*, Vol. 56, No. 1 (2020): 111–27.
2. See https://en.wikipedia.org/wiki/Insurgency_in_Punjab.
3. Nilima Lambah, *A Life across Three Continents*, p. 156.
4. Eqbal Ahmad, 'Farewell to an Adversary', *Dawn*, 18 July 1995.
5. S.K. Lambah, 'Pakistan's Sadequain and Ahmad Faraz favoured closer ties with India', *Indian Express*, 26 August 2020.
6. Ibid.

Chapter 6: Firm Hand in a Soft Glove

1. I.K. Gujral, *Matters of Discretion: An Autobiography* (India: Hay House Publishers, 2011), p. 283.
2. Shekhar Gupta, 'What I.K. Gujral gave Indian politics?' *Hindustan Times*, 4 December 2019.
3. I.K. Gujral, handwritten diary. Courtesy Deeksha Gujral, granddaughter of I.K. Gujral.
4. For full details of the incident, see Hamid Mir, 'Story of Two Khans', 31 January 2016, *Prothom Alo*.
5. I.K. Gujral, *Matters of Discretion: An Autobiography*, p. 283.
6. I.K. Gujral, handwritten diary.
7. Ibid.
8. I.K. Gujral, *Matters of Discretion*, p. 412.
9. Ibid., p. 415.
10. Ibid., p. 416.
11. I.K. Gujral speech, Chatham House, London, September 1996.
12. I.K. Gujral, *Matters of Discretion*, p. 406.

Chapter 7: The Persistent Statesman with a Vision of Peace

1. Satinder K. Lambah, 'Always a Peacemaker', *The Hindu*, 20 August 2018.
2. Ibid.
3. Ibid.
4. Nasim Zehra, *From Kargil to the Coup: Events That Shook Pakistan* (Lahore: Sang-e-Meel Publications, 2018), p. 62.
5. Satinder K. Lambah, 'Always a Peacemaker', *The Hindu*, 20 August 2018.
6. Conversation between Lt Gen. Aziz and Musharraf intercepted by RAW in 99, https://defence.pk/pdf/threads/conversation-between-lt-gen-aziz-and-musahraff-intercepted-by-raw-in-99.177390/, last accessed 17 November 2022.
7. https://www.scribd.com/document/385809158/From-Kargil-to-Coup-Events-That-Shook-Pakistan-Nasim-Zehra1
8. Pamela Constable, 'Domestic pressures imperil Kashmir peace deal', *Washington Post*, 6 July 1999.
9. 'Naik Divulges Details of Talks with Vajpayee', *The News*, 15 May 2003; https://www.rediff.com/news/2003/may/31arvind.htm
10. Y.D. Gundevia, *Outside the Archives* (Hyderabad: Sangam Books, 1984), pp. 287–88.
11. Ibid., pp. 288–91.
12. Ibid., pp. 292–93.
13. Syed Talat Hussain, 'Desperately Seeking Solutions, *Newsline*, June 2003, https://newslinemagazine.com/magazine/desperately-seeking-solutions/, last accessed 17 November 2022.
14. 'Kuldip Nayar and His Bus Ride with Atal Bihari Vajpayee', *Deccan Herald*, 27 August 2018, https://www.deccanherald.

com/specials/bus-diplomacy-689624.html, last accessed 17
November 2022.
https://www.deccanherald.com/specials/bus-
diplomacy-689624.html

15. 'Vajpayee's Thoughts on "Kashmir Problem", from
Kumarakom, December 30, 2000', *The Dispatch,* 16 August
2022, https://www.thedispatch.in/vajpayees-thoughts-on-
kashmir-problem-from-kumarakom-december-30-2000/,
last accessed 17 November 2022.

16. Ibid.

17. *Financial Express,* 18 August 2001.

18. *Financial Express,* 18 August 2001.

19. Dr. Nazir Hussain, 'The Role of Media in India-
Pakistan relations: A Reflection on Agra Summit',
https://www.researchgate.net/profile/Nazir-Hussain-7/
publication/340173900_THE_ROLE_OF_MEDIA_IN_
INDIA-PAKISTAN_RELATIONS_A_REFLECTION_
ON_AGRA_SUMMIT/links/5e7c531792851caef49d9d39/
THE-ROLE-OF-MEDIA-IN-INDIA-PAKISTAN-
RELATIONS-A-REFLECTION-ON-AGRA-SUMMIT

20. Ibid.

21. 'Any Framework Must Include Cross-Border Terrorism',
Outlook, 3 February 2022, https://www.outlookindia.com/
website/story/any-framework-must-include-cross-border-
terrorism/212639

22. Dr. Nazir Hussain, 'The Role of Media in India-Pakistan
relations: A Reflection on Agra Summit'.

23. Ibid.

24. Ibid.

25. Ajai Raj Sharma, *Biting the Bullet: Memoirs of a Police Officer*
(India: Rupa Publications, 2020).

26. Jaswant Singh, *A Call to Honour* (India: Rupa Publications, 2006), p. 266.

27. L.K. Advani, *My Country My Life* (India: Rupa Publications, 2008), p. 696.

28. Karan Thapar, 'The Untold Advani Story', *Hindustan Times*, 29 March 2008.

29. Brig. Gurmeet Kanwal, 'Lost Opportunities in Operation Parakram', *Indian Defence Review*, 13 December 2011, http://www.indiandefencereview.com/spotlights/lost-opportunities-in-operation-parakram/, accessed 18 November 2022.

30. India–Pakistan Joint Press Statement, Islamabad, 6 January 2004, https://www.mea.gov.in/Speeches-Statements.htm?dtl/2973/IndiaPakistan_Joint_Press_Statement_Islamabad, accessed 18 November 2022.

31. Sudheendra Kulkarni, 'Atal Bihari Vajpayee created a peace template for the subcontinent', *The Hindu*, 17 August 2018.

32. Raza Rumi, The Quint, 'Vajpayee Was a Bridge Between Our Countries: A Pakistani's Elegy', 17 August 2018.

Chapter 8: From Nowhere to Centre Stage

1. Ayesha Jalal, *The Struggle for Pakistan* (Harvard: Belknap, 2014), pp. 326–27.

2. Announcement in the Rajya Sabha, 21 November 2001, http://164.100.47.5/newsynopsis1/englishsessionno/194/21112001.htm, accessed 21 November 2022.

3. Matt Waldman, 'The Sun Is the Sky: The Relationship between Pakistan's ISI and Afghan Insurgents', Carr Centre for Human Rights Policy, Kennedy School of Government, Harvard University, 2010.

4. James Dobbins, *After the Taliban: Nation-Building in Afghanistan*, (Washington, D.C.: Potomac Books, Inc., 2008), p. 75.

5. Bonn Conference, https://ihl-databases.icrc.org/ihl-nat/ a24d1cf3344e99934125673e00508142/4ef7a08878a00fe5c 12571140032e471/$FILE/BONN%20AGREEMENT.pdf, accessed 21 November 2022.

6. James Dobbins, *After the Taliban: Nation-Building in Afghanistan*, p. 95.

7. Ibid., p. 72.

8. Ibid., p. 166.

9. Husain Haqqani, *Magnificent Delusions: Pakistan, the State and an Epic History of Misunderstanding* (New York: Public Affairs, 2013), p. 229, https://sanipanhwar.com/ Magnificent%20Delusions_%20Pakistan,%20the%20 United%20States,%20and%20an%20Epic%20History%20 of%20Misunderstanding.pdf, last accessed 21 November 2022.

10. Husain Haqqani, *Magnificent Delusions: Pakistan, the State and an Epic History of Misunderstanding* (New York: Public Affairs, 2013), p. 204.

11. Ibid., p. 253.

12. Ibid., p. 241.

13. Ibid., p. 264.

14. Ibid., p. 276.

15. Ibid., p. 215.

16. Ibid., p. 293.

17. Husain Haqqani, 'Pakistan's Man in Washington', *Politico*, 17 November 2013, https://www.politico.com/magazine/ story/2013/11/pakistans-man-in-washington-099871/, last accessed 21 November 2022.

18. Husain Haqqani, *Magnificent Delusions*, p. 282.

19. Rifaat Hussain, 'Pakistan's Relations with Afghanistan: Continuity and Change', *Strategic Studies*, Vol. 22, No. 4 (2002): 43–75, https://www.jstor.org/stable/45242325, last accessed 21 November 2022.

20. Ibid.

21. Farzana Shaikh, *Making Sense of Pakistan* (Columbia: Columbia University Press, 2009), p. 208.

22. Ibid., p. 208.

23. Satinder Kumar Lambah, 'The Durand Line', *Indian Foreign Affairs Journal*, Vol. 7, No. 1 (2012): 42–60, http://www.jstor.org/stable/45341803, last accessed 21 November 2022.

24. Ahmed Rashid, *Descent into Chaos* (New York: Viking, 2008).

25. Azmat Hayat Khan, *The Durand Line: Its Geo-strategic Importance* (Afghanistan: Area Study Centre, University of Peshawar, 2000), p. 243.

26. Savita Pande, 'Pakistan's Afghanistan Relations: A "Strategic" Shift?' https://archive.claws.in/images/journals_doc/50230827_SavitaPande.pdf

27. Kamal Matinuddin, foreword in *The Taliban Phenomenon: Afghanistan 1994–1997* (USA: Oxford University Press, 1999).

28. Adrian Hanni and Lukas Hedi, 'Pakistani Godfather: The Inter-Services Intelligence and the Afghan Taliban 1994–2010', *Small War Journal* (2013).

29. Ahmed Rashid, *Descent into Chaos*, pp. 29 and 52.

30. 'Quoting Musharraf's Press Conference of 25 May 2000', *The Nation*, 13 July 2000; https://www.cato.org/commentary/pakistan-us-troubled-marriage-convenience

31. 'The Pakistani Godfather: The Inter-Services Intelligence and the Afghan Taliban 1994-2010', *Small Wars Journal*, 4 February 2013, https://smallwarsjournal.com/jrnl/art/the-

pakistani-godfather-the-inter-services-intelligence-and-the-afghan-taliban-1994-2010

32. PTI, 'China Blocked UN Sanctions on 3 Pak-based Terrorists: WikiLeaks', *Deccan Herald*, 5 December 2010, https://www.deccanherald.com/content/118346/china-blocked-un-sanctions-3.html, accessed 21 November 2022.

33. Dexter Filkins 'Pakistanis Tell of Motive in Taliban Leader's Arrest', *The New York Times*, 22 August 2010, https://www.nytimes.com/2010/08/23/world/asia/23taliban.html, last accessed 21 November 2022.

34. S.K. Lambah 'Grave yards of Empires, Crucible of Coalitions,' *Outlook*, 26 December 2011.

35. George Packer, *Our Man: Richard Holbrooke and the End of the American Century* (USA: Knopf Publishing House, 2019).

36. Ibid., pp. 541–47.

37. Ibid., p. 540.

38. Ibid., pp. 541–42.

39. Ibid., p. 542.

Chapter 9: A New Sustained Approach and a Near Solution

1. Prem Mahadevan, 'A Decade on from the 2008 Mumbai Attack: Reviewing the Question of State-Sponsorship', *ICCT Journal* (27 June 2019), https://icct.nl/publication/a-decade-on-from-the-2008-mumbai-attack-reviewing-the-question-of-state-sponsorship/, accessed 25 November 2022.

2. Manmohan Singh, 'This Is a Dialogue of Equals', *Outlook*, 3 February 2022, https://www.outlookindia.com/website/story/this-is-a-dialogue-of-equals/230315, accessed 25 November 2022.

3. B.L. Sharma, *The Kashmir Story* (New Delhi: Asia Publishing House, 1967), p. 129; National Conference's Ghulam

Mohammed Sadiq, who too held discussions with the Pakistani leadership reconfirmed the same issue; S.C.O.R., Nos 1–15, pp. 213–14, as cited in Sharma, op. cit., p. 129.

4. Government of India, White Paper on Jammu and Kashmir, March 1948, as cited in Narendra Singh Sarila, *The Shadow of the Great Game: The Untold Story of India's Partition* (New Delhi: HarperCollins Publishers India, 2005), pp. 354 & 364.

5. Mountbatten's aide-mémoire to his chief of staff Lord Ismay, MBI/G25, BA, University of Southampton, as cited in Sarila, op. cit., pp. 354 and 364.

6. File L/P&S/136/1845-46, Attlee to Liaquat Ali Khan, 29 October 1947, OIC, British Library, as cited in Sarila, op. cit. pp. 356 and 364.

7. File L/P&S/136/1845-46 OIC, British Library, as cited in Sarila, op. cit. pp. 355 and 364.

8. Sardar Patel's Correspondence, Vol. X, p. 81, Nehru Memorial Library and Museum, New Delhi.

9. Nehru's address reported in the *Hindustan Times*, 3 November 1947, as cited in Sharma, op. cit., pp. 129–30.

10. Alastair Lamb, *Crisis in Kashmir* (London: Routledge and Kegan Paul, 1966), p. 50, as cited in Sharma, op. cit., p. 135.

11. Sharma, op. cit., pp. 132–33.

12. Lamb, op. cit., pp. 172–75.

13. Lamb, op. cit., pp. 225–27.

14. Deshmukh Pranwa, *'How Pakistan avoided Plebiscite'*. Link: http://www.hvk.org/2002/0202/29.html

15. Y.D. Gundevia, *Outside the Archives*, pp. 265, 288–92. Gundevia was a member of the Indian delegation for the Indo–Pak talks of 1962–63.

16. Chandrashekhar Dasgupta, *India and the Bangladesh Liberation War* (Juggernaut, 2021), p. 236.

17. Y.D. Gundevia, *Outside the Archives*, p. 280.
18. Pervez Musharraf, *In the Line of Fire* (London: Simon & Schuster, 2006, consulted reprint edition, London Pocket Books, 2008), pp. 302–03.
19. Ministry of Defence, Twenty-Second Report, 2006–07, http://164.100.47.193/lsscommittee/Defence/14_Defence_22.pdf, accessed 26 November 2022.
20. Dr Manmohan Singh in his speech in Amritsar on 24 March 2006.
21. Khurshid Mahmud Kasuri, *Neither a Hawk nor a Dove: An Insider's Account of Pakistan's Foreign Policy*, p. 354.
22. Ahmad Shamshad, 'Kashmir at backchannel', Editorial. Link: http://editorialsamarth.blogspot.com/2010/05/editorial-050510.html
23. Pervez Musharraf, *In the Line of Fire*, p. 32.
24. Ibid., pp. 166–67.
25. Khurshid Mahmud Kasuri, *Neither a Hawk nor a Dove: An Insider's Account of Pakistan's Foreign Policy*, p. 320.
26. Khurshid Mahmud Kasuri, *Neither a Hawk nor a Dove: An Insider's Account of Pakistan's Foreign Policy*, p. 472.
27. Khurshid Mahmud Kasuri, op. cit., p. 472.
28. Khurshid Mahmud Kasuri, op. cit., p. 328.
29. Khurshid Mahmud Kasuri, op. cit., p. 439.
30. Hasan Suroor, 'How the U.K. Saw Kayani &1squo; Obstacle" to Deal on Kashmir', *The Hindu*, updated 17 November 2021, https://www.thehindu.com/news/the-india-cables/How-the-U.K.-saw-Kayani-as-lsquoobstacle-to-deal-on-Kashmir/article14669545.ece, last accessed 26 November 2022.
31. Ibid.
32. Khurshid Mahmud Kasuri, *Neither a Hawk nor a Dove*, pp. 805–06.

33. S.K. Lambah, Speech in Srinagar, 'A Possible Outline of a Solution', *Outlook*, 14 May 2014.

34. Prime Minister Manmohan Singh in his speech in Amritsar on 24 March 2006.

35. 'Discussion between India and Pakistan on Jammu and Kashmir—A Historical Perspective', organized by the Institute of Kashmir Studies, University of Kashmir, Srinagar, 13 May 2014.

36. *Rising Kashmir*, 15 May 2014.

37. Maharajakrishna Rasgotra, *A Life In Diplomacy*, pp. 380–81.

38. Radha Kumar, *Paradise at War: A Political History of Kashmir* (India: Aleph Book Company, 2018), p. 241.

39. Radha Kumar, op. cit.

40. Khurshid Mahmud Kasuri, *Neither a Hawk nor a Dove*, p. 805.

41. Ibid., p. 116-117.

42. Khurshid Mahmud Kasuri, op. cit., p. 264.

43. Riaz Mohammad Khan, 'Can Pakistan India Ties Be Normal?', *Dawn*, 14 August 2017.

44. F.S. Aijazuddin, 'Secret Tunnels'. *Dawn*, 22 October 2015, https://www.dawn.com/news/1214710, last accessed 26 November 2022.

45. William J. Burns, *The Back Channel: A Memoir of American Diplomacy and the Case for Its Renewal* (New York: Random House, 2019).

46. Ibid., p. 263.

47. Steve Coll, 'The Back Channel', *New Yorker*, 22 February 2009, https://www.newyorker.com/magazine/2009/03/02/the-back-channel, accessed 26 November 2022.

48. Ibid.

49. Joby Warrick, 'India and Pakistan came close to deal over Kashmir', *The Irish Times*, 23 February 2009, https://www.irishtimes.com/news/india-and-pakistan-came-close-to-deal-over-kashmir-1.707318

50. Richard Bonney, Tahir Malik, Tridivesh Singh Maini (eds), *Warriors after War: Indian and Pakistani Retired Military Leaders Reflect on Relations between the Two Countries, Past, Present and Future* (Germany: Peter Lang AG, Internationaler Verlag der Wissensc, 2011), https://notesonliberty.files.wordpress.com/2021/01/warriorsafter-war-ebook-1.pdf

Chapter 10: The Choice at the Crossroads and the Way Forward

1. Nehru's letter dated 10 November 1953 to Bogra, as quoted in Sarvepalli Gopal, *Jawaharlal Nehru: A Biography*, Vol. 2 (London: Jonathan Cape, 1979, consulted reprint edition, New Delhi, Oxford, 1979), pp. 184–85.
2. Lamb, op. cit., pp. 228, 244.
3. 'Pakistan Army and Terrorism; An Unholy Alliance', European Foundation for South Asian Studies (EFSAS), 2017, https://www.efsas.org/publications/study-papers/pakistan-army-and-terrorism;-an-unholy-alliance/, accessed 27 November 2022. And Jeffery Goldberg, 'The ISI campaign against Husain Haqqani', *The Atlantic*, 22 November 2011, https://www.theatlantic.com/international/archive/2011/11/the-isi-campaign-against-husain-haqqani/248895/, last accessed 27 November 2022.
4. Ambassador John Cabot's telegram from Warsaw to the Department of State, 23 June 1962, in *Foreign Relations of the United States [FRUS], 1961–63, Vol. XXII, Northeast Asia*, Document 131.

Appendix*

Farewell to an adversary

By Eqbal Ahmad

(*Dawn* July 18, 1995)

Pakistan and India present a rare paradox in international relations. The complementary enemies are locked in an embrace both affectionate and antagonistic. There is anxiety and animosity in this relationship and also attraction, petty-minded harassments no less than grace and generosity, the paradox encompasses a complex and long history that began in India's middle ages and underwent a mutation midway into the twentieth century.

There were reminders of this phenomenon in Islamabad recently, all associated with the departure of Satinder Kumar Lambah, India's high commissioner in Pakistan, his wife Nilima and son Vikram who gathered warmth in this country and gained confidence in friendships. I am among those who experienced the institutionalized and apparently illogical expressions of animosity and distrust which characterize Pakistan-India relations. They insult intelligence, dishonour our traditions of civility, violate

---

* This article has been reproduced verbatim, without any editorial intervention.

citizens liberty, and symbolize the predominance of the irrational in the South Asian cold war.

A few weeks ago an Indian diplomat visited me. After the destruction of Charar Sharif I had written critically of the Indian government's conduct and its prime minister's attempt to find a scapegoat in Pakistan. During the conversation over tea, the visitor did not mention my article. So I understood that his was a courtesy call, acknowledging my criticism without agreeing with it. He also conveyed an invitation from Ambassador Lambah. When I saw him off I noticed that another car followed his.

A day later, I returned home from an errand to find my cook quite edgy. Men from an Intelligence agency had questioned him. Another Intelligence agent came the next morning asking for the "Hindus who live in this house". The portly and courteous man said he was from "the Special Branch". I told him what he wanted to know. Who was I? Why did an Indian diplomat visit here? Then I asked why he thought Hindus were residing here. 'The signboard on the gate, Sir', he said sheepishly, "It was reported that a Hindu family lives here and I was asked to report details".I should have fallen off the chair laughing but felt sad instead and sorry for the visitor. The owners of the house I rent have given it a name, inscribed in imitation marble: Dilaram. Servants in the neighbourhood know that a Doctor Sahib lives here. Whence the search for the whereabouts of Dr Ram!

Outside the Lambah's residence a few days later, a bunch of plain-clothed men were milling around taking the licence plate numbers of incoming cars, a practice not followed at other diplomatic residences in Islamabad. Among the guests inside were high officials both present and former of the Pakistan government and some well-known politicians. I wondered if the official cars were also noted and whether their owners would be followed or questioned. After dinner, Ambassador Lambah and his deputy stepped out to see me off, waited for the little Suzuki to collect me, and waved goodbye. This sight may have aroused extra suspicion, or perhaps the lowly Suzuki invited contempt. A carload of intelligence agents followed it - now close on tail, headlights blinding my driver, now to the front with the emergency blinkers circling. My driver became so nervous that I feared he would hit a pole or drive into a ditch. So I told him to stop, asked our pursuers what they wanted, and advised them to come over to my house if they wished to know more. Thankfully, they went away.

A couple of more visits which a servant handled. I have instructed him to treat these visitors with courtesy, offer refreshment, and answer questions honestly. At around 2 p.m. on July 13, a messenger from the Indian High Commission delivered an envelope containing visa forms and a copy of an Indo-Pakistan confidence-building agreement of which the text was published in the Press while I was abroad. A man arrived soon thereafter demanding to see me. He wanted to look at the papers which had just been delivered. He said he was from the Inter-Services Intelligence. The meek and sickly looking fellow wore no race of military bearing. So I asked to see his badge which he reluctantly flashed, long enough for me to note that he had lied: he was from the bureau of intelligence. I asked him to request his superior to call me.

May a citizen's suggestion be heard by relevant officials? It is normal practice in democracies for security agents to show their identity cards before they can ask questions. Agents here too should be required to do the same. Otherwise citizens shall remain unprotected from criminals and extortionists impersonating as security agents. The requirement to show their identity card shall also discourage authorised agents from violating the law. There are far too many of both variety around these days. It will be nice to hear from an official saying "Yes, we have heard you and we are doing something about it".

Other friends have told similar stories of being investigated. The practice of noting licence plate numbers, and of interrogation by Pakistan's intelligence operatives outside the Indian High Commission is particularly intimidating to the hundreds of citizens who apply for Indian visas. This is not proper intelligence gathering, nor a practice respectful of citizens' rights, nor does it enhance our reputation for forbearance and civility. In addition, it must cost thousands of wasted man-hours, much in taxpayers' money, and a lot in the diversion of security personnel from the proper tasks of ensuring public security. So why does the Pakistan government indulge in this wasteful activity?

"Quid pro quo!" says an official of the foreign office as though some law requires a mutual exchange of idiocy between India and Pakistan. My suspicion is that at work here is neither logic, nor national security but Parkinson's law: it was done at some point in a modest way, then bureaucratic momentum took over, "This is not an intelligence gathering operation," says a retired official who should know. "We merely want to discourage people from close contact with Indian diplomats." Dr. Parkinson would have been happy to hear this rationalization, and also the score. The Lambahs departed with a mind-boggling count of receptions and dinners. Few diplomats in Islamabad's memory had such a hearty send-off.

For four weeks they were on the social circuit. They were mostly non. official events though official grace was not lacking either. The Prime Minister and the leader of the opposition invited the Indians to private luncheons. Sati Lambah described the former as "memorably gracious" and the latter as "touchingly warm". His voice choked occasionally and eyes glistened with emotion as he spoke of how friends said goodbye. A feminist and social worker of modest income hosted a luncheon for some forty persons. A former Supreme Court judge sent a 'beautiful gift' in gratitude of a well-cultivated friendship.

Sati and Nilima are among those millions who symbolize the many unities which were overwhelmed by the partition of 1947 and the unexpected animosity which followed. He was born in Peshawar, a grandson of Rai Bahadur Ram Nath Lambah, President of Peshawar Municipal Corporation and founder member of Peshawar Electricity Company. His maternal grandfather Rai Bahadur Dina Nath Kakar, was a prominent philanthropist and Director of the Premier Sugar Mills of Mardan since its establishment. Among Lambah's old family friends are General Habibullah, the Saifullahs and Aslam Khattak. "The best gift I ever received was from one of them - a group photograph which had in it both my grandparents." He tells stories of chance meetings with family friends and says he found visits to Peshawar "warm, overwhelming, painful'. Nilima's family was from Lahore where the Mela Ram Road and also Lal Kothi were named after her great grandfather. The Lahore Flying Club was founded by an uncle. Old friends abound.

The collective memories of lives lived and friendships formed over centuries do cross the boundaries and overcome the discontinuities which history has imposed and national policies have perpetuated. We negotiate such polarities in our lives in differing ways. Often, I found Sati separating his official from his personal life. "The High Commissioner of India does not agree with you", he might say, "but as a friend Sati Lambah respects your views and honours your integrity." Occasionally, the private and the public person came together. Sati recalled Dr Mubashir Hasan who could not come to a dinner hosted by lawyer Raza Kazim and wrote instead: "It is sad to see you leave . . . The people and governments of India and Pakistan should feel indebted to you for the services you so ably rendered . . . by playing a key role in keeping the temperature . . . between the two countries within threshold limits. During your period has been laid the foundations of people-to-people contact between India and Pakistan. This is a beginning that holds great promise. One day the governments will have to respect their wishes . . ." As he heard this, I thought I saw a gleam in both eyes, Sati Lambah's and the Indian High Commissioner's.

(Courtesy: Estate of Eqbal Ahmad)

Acknowledgements

Mr Jawed Ashraf
Mr Ramu Damodaran
Mr James Edwin
Mr Naresh Gujral
Mr Sunil Khatri
Mr Rahul Kulshreshth
Mr Ramesh Mulye
Mr Ronen Sen
Mr Ashok Shrinagesh
Mr Natwar Singh

Index